Please return/renew this item by the last date shown
on this label, or on your self-service receipt.

To renew this item, visit **www.librarieswest.org.uk**
or contact your library.

Your Borrower number and PIN are required.

LibrariesWest

death of her brother from lung cancer seven years ago. She palpably
evokes the milieu of their London childhood and takes us through all the
twists and turns of a sibling relationship as the years pass. "The Man Who
Didn't Go to Newcastle" documents a terminal illness but it restores a
life. Elegantly written with great tact and without shying away from hard
truths, it is not so much a memoir of mourning as a love poem.'

Jonathan Wilson

4 1 0166821 0

THE MAN WHO DIDN'T GO
to
NEWCASTLE

ALISON CLINK

Matador
9 Priory Business Park
Kibworth Beauchamp
Leicestershire LE8 0RX, UK
Tel: (+44) 116 279 2299
Fax: (+44) 116 279 2277
Email: books@troubador.co.uk
Web: www.troubador.co.uk/matador

ISBN 978 1784622 350

British Library Cataloguing in Publication Data.
A catalogue record for this book is available from the British Library.

Printed and bound in the UK by TJ International, Padstow, Cornwall
Typeset in Aldine by Troubador Publishing Ltd

Matador is an imprint of Troubador Publishing Ltd

This book is dedicated to the memory of my brother
Adrian Nigel Tilbrook

Let me die a youngman's death
not a clean and inbetween
the sheets holywater death
not a famous-last-words
peaceful out of breath death

When I'm 73
and in constant good tumour
may I be mown down at dawn
by a bright red sports car
on my way home
from an allnight party

Or when I'm 91
with silver hair
and sitting in a barber's chair
may rival gangsters
with hamfisted tommyguns burst in
and give me a short back and insides

Or when I'm 104
and banned from the Cavern
may my mistress
catching me in bed with her daughter
and fearing for her son
cut me up into little pieces
and throw away every piece but one

Let me die a youngman's death
not a free from sin tiptoe in
candle wax and waning death
not a curtains drawn by angels borne
'what a nice way to go' death

Roger McGough

THE LIST

Saturday 10th March 2008

I've spent a lot of time over the past couple of weeks preparing for this event. I've phoned people, sent emails, written letters, left voicemails, cleaned the house, bought fresh flowers, had my hair cut, even treated myself to a new skirt. But now today has come and there's nothing else to do to take my mind off what is really happening. My brother's ashes are to be laid to rest in our local village churchyard.

In films funerals always take place against a backdrop of drizzle, an obvious symbolic device. Weather reflects mood, mood is gloomy, weather gloomy too. Rain is like tears. Today it's raining.

During the two minute car journey to the church I tell my twin daughters, Emily and Fran, I'm afraid I might start to cry.

'You're allowed to,' Emily replies. Yes, I know, but for some reason I feel the need to prepare myself for the possibility.

When we arrive I see everyone I've invited standing on the gravel path leading to the Great Elm village church, all looking somehow odd, as if they're in the wrong place. Like when Mum and Dad turned up at school for parents' meetings. The right people in the wrong setting. A kind of dream where people you know well unexpectedly appear out of context.

Dan, the vicar, arrives late, and bizarrely seems to be changing his clothes in the back of his people carrier. He strides up the path, his surplice flapping in the wind, smiling his toothy grin – reassuringly eccentric.

He unexpectedly unlocks the church door and ushers us all in out of the rain. The service was to have been outside, but I'm glad Dan is prepared to amend the plans in order to spare us from a soaking for a few minutes' prayer before the burial takes place. I love this church and Dan points out to his captive audience some of its unique features: the little doors at the ends of the pews, the ancient stained glass windows, the minstrels' gallery. He loves it too. I hope all the friends and relations are impressed.

Dan is clearly impressed by them. He obviously had no idea there would be so many of us for this interment of the ashes. He appears genuinely surprised by the number of people who've turned up. After all, this is a low-key service, not a true funeral as such. We did the funeral in Putney last September, seventeen days after Adrian died. This is a chance for everyone to get together in the place where my brother will stay, along the road from our house, in the graveyard of St Mary's Church in Great Elm.

Dan probably realises now why I took so long to come back to him with a day when everyone could be in the same place at the same time. I've been aware of his frustration at the number of phone calls I've made changing the date, and I sense an acknowledgement of the difficulty of the task I've undertaken. He asks where everyone is from and I reel off the list of places, feeling proud that people have come from so far. Norwich, London, Bristol, Devon, Taunton, Farnham, Basingstoke, Southend on Sea.

'And Great Elm,' my eldest son, Jack, jokes.

My brother wrote many instructions for his ending, most on odd bits of paper. I presumed he wanted his ashes scattered after the funeral in Putney Vale Cemetery. Only at the last minute did I come across a loose sheet saying 'Ashes to be buried at Great Elm Churchyard. Next to Mum.' I'm eternally grateful I discovered that piece of paper in time, yet I was also struck by its poignancy. Next to Mum. The instructions were so curt. So matter-of-fact. So decisively unemotional. So heartbreakingly sad. Only two-and-a-half years ago Adrian stood with me and the other men in my family in this same graveyard, with the same vicar, probably clutching the same prayer book for the burial of our mother's ashes. But how different that day was. How hot, lit with the brilliant sunshine of mid-June, and too hot to stand in the shadeless churchyard for any longer than was necessary. Today we shiver and huddle together under umbrellas, again missing the shelter of trees. Also missing my younger son, Ed, who is in Thailand.

Standing to my left is our old friend, Martin Phillips, who collected Adrian's ashes from the funeral directors in Putney. Disappointingly, the urn he's been given is made of green plastic, more like a garden compost pot than the polished wood miniature coffin I'd irrationally imagined. Irrationally, since I knew we hadn't been offered, or indeed paid for, such a thing.

Martin appeals to me for guidance when his moment arrives. Should he open the pot and truly 'scatter' or should he just place it in the hole? I indicate somehow that he should put the whole thing in, as it seems the best option to avoid farce. What if he pours and a gust of wind gets in the way? What if he pours and a last clump of ash refuses to budge from the inside of the pot? The comic possibilities seem many.

'Just put it in,' I hear myself say. I'm slightly perturbed. I am so bluntly telling Martin what to do. One of my big brother's friends. I'm still the same child I was all those years ago.

My husband, Peter, takes our garden spade he brought with him and shovels the earth back into place. Adrian was important to him too and now he seems strong and the right person to make the final gesture of closure.

I've held myself together well till now. In the event, rather than dwell on the emotional aspect of what's going on, I've managed to focus my mind on the pedantic. Counting heads, has everyone found the churchyard? Are the girls warm enough? Why aren't the boots I'm wearing waterproof? As we all huddle so close, will the spokes of my umbrella poke someone in the eye? Have we got enough beer, food, soft drinks at home? Did I remember to buy straws? Do we have twenty-five decent dinner plates?

I look around at the people standing with me and suddenly I see the list. The list Adrian made last summer – all the names of the people I should invite to his funeral written in his tiny handwriting. The list that I refused to read until I needed to. The list I watched him write as he sat skeletal in his baggy checked shirt, his chinos tied tightly with a belt to hold them up, and his Panama hat protecting his bald patch from the sun. A glass of white wine on the table by his writing pad and his Daily Mirror open on the racing page. The list that seemed so painful last August. So shocking. How could he care, how could he *bear* to work out who would come to mourn him?

Yet seven months later the instructions have been carried out. They're all here. Most have travelled long distances. Some of them couldn't make the funeral in September, but none of them has let him down today. I imagine his pleasure at seeing them all together. What might he have said? 'Oh, thanks, Ali.'

These are the ones who meant so much to him. The core people. The 'A' listers. The inner circle of friends he loved and thought about – even in the face of death. All present. Welsh Phil who went on a pub-crawl with him every Saturday night. Carol and Carole, Bryony, Phil Gullifer with his family, Den and Chris from Warwick, John Commerford, Mart and Lindsay, Mac and Minnie, all from our home town, even Clive Mason, who I'd never met before the funeral and had been Adrian's boss when he'd worked at British Telecom. All the names on his list have magically been brought to life. The list is finally and unbearably transformed into real people standing in a semi-circle with me now around the hole containing my dear brother's ashes.

In the end it's the memory of Adrian's list that makes me cry.

LONDON

Thursday 21st June 2007 (the longest day)

The phone in my study rings mid-morning. It's my brother, Adrian, with his new husky voice. I brace myself. It's usually me who rings him.

'Ali?' he croaks. 'The doctor's just been on the ward and I'm afraid it's bad news.'

I squeeze my fingernails into my palm. The fraction of a second while I wait for Adrian to go on seems long, yet somehow short.

'They think I've got lung cancer,' he says.

The remainder of the phone call is a blur. After Adrian has rung off I summon enough courage to ring one of my London friends, Jeannette, who is already in the know about my brother's health problems. I must cross the first hurdle of repeating the C word aloud.

'Adrian said they think he's got lung cancer,' I explain, amazed at my self-control. Maybe this is not going to be as difficult as I'd imagined. Providing Jeannette is not too nice, or overly sympathetic. Too much kindness might break me.

'Let me know if there's anything I can do,' she says. Perfect.

I carry on the rest of my day as a different person. I've just gone through one of those life-changing moments that come along from time to time. Like the morning I opened the letter telling me my 'A' level results were high enough to get me into university, or when I came round from the anaesthetic and Peter told me the premature twins I'd just given birth to by caesarean section were healthy girls. Today, however, there is nothing comforting about this tilt to the axis of my life. Just the bleak reality that my brother, my only sibling, may be about to die.

As it's June I'm working on the Frome Festival Short Story Competition. I return to what I was doing – writing a critique for a poorly constructed story and trying to think of something positive to say – but my mind soon strays again to my brother and his life-changing news.

Adrian was always someone who peaked too soon. At the age of eighteen he was tall, dark and handsome. He'd inherited my parents' dark curly hair (where did my mousy straight crop come from?), was slim, and strode around in clothes others wouldn't have had the bottle to wear. Green or maroon desert boots he'd dyed with Lady Esquire shoe dye, skin tight jeans with just the right amount of flare at the ankle, and a tight fitting chamois leather jacket he'd persuaded Mum to make for him. To me he was a celebrity in his own circle of friends. Intriguing, brilliant, special. Despite some of the things that have happened to him over the past couple of years, he remains one of the lights of my life. I have a space in my heart reserved for Adrian which could never be filled by anyone else.

I pause from my work and lean my elbows on my desk. On the windowsill, amongst several family photographs, is a black and white snapshot of Adrian and me sitting on a low wall outside the flat we lived in in Mitcham when we were little. On the back of the photo, in my mother's stylish longhand are the words 'Mitcham Oct 54'. She hasn't added our names, though she probably had to restrain herself. Even for Mum, who was always the zealous labelling type, the identities of her kids went without saying. In the photo I am two and Adrian is three. We're both smiling, dressed identically in berets, scarves and double-breasted herringbone overcoats, with long socks and bare legs. I guess this was a last photo shoot before we left our rented Mitcham flat and moved to the new post-war leafy suburban estate in Coney Hall near West Wickham in Kent where my father had bought, for one hundred pounds, a semi-detached house which looked out onto fields.

Dad was keen to escape the woman with the yellow teeth and grey beret who lived in the flat downstairs in Mitcham, and complained about the noise we made. Or did she have grey teeth and a yellow beret? Whichever, berets seemed to be bizarrely *de rigueur* in the South London of the mid-fifties.

In the photo, Adrian and I sit side by side with chubby cherubic smiles directed at whoever was taking the shot, squinting into the autumn sunshine, our two little black beret-clad shadows reflected against the wall behind us.

Post Mitcham we were brought up in the semi-detached suburbia our parents' generation aspired to, but which was so scathingly depicted in the pop songs of ours. "Semi-detached suburban Mr James," "Matthew and Son," "Little Boxes"... I think both Adrian and I decided early on that our individual futures would lie as far away from the Mr Jameses, the Matthew and Sons, and their little boxes as possible.

With only eighteen months between us, in those days we were sometimes mistaken for twins. Nowadays we are very different. Our lives are polarised. Adrian lives in London and I'm in rural Somerset. He lives alone in a two bedroom flat in Putney, has a degree in Pure and Applied Maths, and is a statistician. I studied English at university. I'm a writer, a teacher and a mother of four children. I've been married to Peter for twenty-six years. Adrian is single. When holidaying he tends to travel alone. I travel *en famille*. Our lives have ended up as opposite as South and North Pole. We are chalk and cheese, Town Mouse and Country Mouse. Every day I walk our dog in the woods opposite my house. Every day Adrian walks the pavements of Southfields to the pub. Twice.

I persuaded him to accompany me on a dog walk when he was visiting one Christmas. His unease was tangible. He turned back before we were halfway down the track leading to Vallis Woods.

Nevertheless, in other ways Adrian and I are similar. Sometimes if we're in a room full of people he's the only person who will understand a particular remark I make, or get a joke. Sometimes I'm the only person who will get a remark he has made, or a joke. In pub quizzes we share the same random trove of useless information. What was the first single by the Rolling Stones? *Come On.* Who wrote *The Dice Man*? Luke Rhinehart. Which actor starred in the Stephen Poliakoff TV drama *Caught on A Train*? Michael Kitchen. We both know all this stuff. And also, although I am only 55 and he is 56, Adrian is the only person left on the planet I've known since birth. He's the only person who has known me since day one. Dad died thirteen years ago and Mum died in 2005. There's only the two of us left. I find people who've known us all our lives to be deeply reassuring. Even if we have partners and children, our partners (in most cases) have only known us as adults, and our children see us as ancient has-beens who were brought up scratching pictures on cave walls.

I phone the hospital and, as Adrian's next of kin, manage to arrange for a doctor to ring me back. In the world of the NHS, next of kin is an important status. Adrian has never married, has no children and, as far as I know, hasn't ever lived with a woman. So that makes me his next of kin – which is turning out to be useful now as the key to getting anyone at St George's Hospital, Tooting to talk to me about what is happening to him.

In fact I know quite a bit of what has been happening. I've been phoning him on a regular basis for some weeks, ever since February when he told me he'd been suffering from breathlessness and pains in his back. On reflection, I've been worried about him for a couple of years. But my worry only turned into real concern a few weeks ago when I opened a text from him while I was out with Billy, our West Highland White terrier.

Am in St Georges – Rodney Smith Ward. Ring me. A.

I rang him immediately. Billy carried on sniffing the bracken and snuffling amongst the reeds of the river bank whilst I endeavoured to find out why on earth my brother was in hospital.

Adrian answered straight away and explained what had happened. He'd been washing up the night before and had cut his hand on a broken wine glass. Was he perhaps drunk? Duh – the clue's in the wine glass. The cut was deep into the skin that separates the thumb from the first finger and was bleeding profusely. The following morning he woke up to find the blood had seeped through the thickness of the towel he'd wrapped around his hand. His bed sheets were soaked. Rather than drive (these city folk seem to do anything rather than get behind the wheel of a car), he took two different buses to get to St George's Hospital. When he alighted from the second bus, he collapsed on the pavement outside the main gates, but they still sent an ambulance to pick him up and take him into A & E.

The cut hand led to the collapse, the collapse led to the hospital admission, and the hospital admission led to an analysis of the collapse. This instigated a series of tests, and now those tests are leading to something more sinister. A simple cut on the hand has brought my brother to a quite horrible place.

After lunch, while I'm working in my study, Doctor Felicity Harding, registrar at St George's, rings.

'Mrs Clink, we *suspect* lung cancer and cancer of the kidney.' Her voice is gentle, unassuming. Calm. 'But nothing at this stage is conclusive. Nothing is proven. We will have a more accurate diagnosis soon.'

I shiver and reach for my cardigan on the back of my chair, draping it over one shoulder.

'What will happen to my brother?'

'There are a number of options depending on the type of cancer, if indeed this prognosis should prove correct. Chemotherapy is a possibility, as is radiotherapy. However, for a more aggressive small-cell growth, treatment is not always offered, and if the cancer has spread then...'

I make notes as she speaks, jotting down key words on the back of the short story I've been critiquing: *nothing proven, chemo? radiother, small-cell, spread...* I feel my heart banging inside my chest.

'Thanks for phoning. For letting me know.' My reply is scant, my voice thin.

After this has sunk in I ring Adrian.

'They said they should have the results of a biopsy they've done on my lung tomorrow. Do you think you could come up to London tomorrow, Ali?'

'Tomorrow? Let me think what I'm doing. Yes I'm sure I can. I might have to rearrange a few things. The girls will be at school. Margaret can have the dog. The men can get a takeaway. Yes. I'll find out the train times.'

'Thanks, Ali. I really appreciate that. I'll see you tomorrow.'

My brother has done this before – three years ago when he was waiting for a heart bypass. Then he'd rung me and said the same thing.

'I'd like you to come up.' He said this as if it was me, and me alone, he wanted, although later I realised I was only one of a list of women he called on in moments of anguish.

I heeded the call and rushed up to the big city and found him in one of the green-walled wards in the older part of St George's, fully dressed, sitting on a bed with a DIY will laid out on the blanket.

'I need a witness,' he said, indicating the document. 'I need someone to sign this will for me.'

In the hospital ward of pre-op heart patients, Adrian was bright and chatty. More so than normal, in fact – waving jauntily at his fellow patients as they shuffled along in dressing gowns, with pale faces and uncombed hair.

He called over to a diminutive male nurse who looked to be from somewhere in the Far East, Malaysia perhaps – a part of the world Adrian visited during his travelling days – and explained he wanted him to witness the signing of his will. The nurse seemed more than willing to help.

'Wit – ness? Do you un – der – stand?' Adrian flapped the will in the air. 'I – would – like – you – to – sign – this!' he said. The nurse smiled and produced one of the many pens in his uniform pocket.

'Ah! Sign! Yes, yes! I sign!'

My brother has a knack of *asking* people to do things for him, which somehow seems to make people *want* to do things for him. How does that work? The nurse was so keen to help he was almost jumping up and down on the spot. 'I sign. But you no die,' he added.

All three of us laughed, relief bouncing round the hospital bed. No, Adrian wasn't going to die. Hundreds of people, thousands, had heart bypasses. And they didn't die. The nurse put his signature to Adrian's will. An illegible scribble next to the word 'Witness'. Just in case.

Friday 22nd June 2007

St George's, Tooting is the hospital I'm travelling to today. Of course, Adrian didn't die when he had the heart bypass and now I'm on my way to see him once more, but this time to ascertain from the doctors whether their suspicions from the scans and X-rays are borne out by the biopsy they did yesterday on his lung.

As yet no definite conclusions have been drawn, but in my heart I feel the news I'm heading towards on the 8.05am First Great Western Westbury to Paddington will be the worst I've ever heard. My brother might not be around for much longer.

People who've known us since the West Wickham days often refer to us as 'close'. But aren't all siblings? I've only ever had the one, so I can't imagine any different relationship. As children, we were inseparable. Being brought up in the fifties, our mother didn't send us to nursery – pre schooling was much less the norm then – so I missed Adrian when he went to school. I was desperate to start school myself and soon after my fifth birthday I joined Class Twelve at Wickham Common County Primary. By this time Adrian had gone up to Class Ten. What happened to Class Eleven I'm not sure. I guess it was the stream for the less able, those poor little ones who'd already been picked out as being destined to fail the Eleven Plus and spend their teenage years in secondary modern schools. Adrian would certainly not have been in that group of pupils.

Before I started school myself, I'd watched Adrian learn to write with my mother's help in an exercise book at home, and had been for an interview with the headmaster who asked me to write my name on a piece of paper and to add two and two together. But when I was taken to Class Twelve, otherwise known as The Babies' Class, and left by my mother to fend for myself, I felt as if my life had ended. My yearning to be at school hadn't been properly thought through. I cried when my mother said she 'had to go now' (Adrian had managed the separation from home to school without a tear) and tightened my little fists around the hem of her dress. At four o'clock when she collected me I couldn't believe I'd have to go through the whole traumatic experience again the next day.

As the days passed gradually I settled into the routine, and discovered the excitement of the slide, the sand pit and – my absolute favourite – the 'sweet shop' where small stones wrapped in old sweet wrappers were kept in a jar for sale, ready to be eagerly bought with cardboard coins. Clearly there were no health and safety issues in Wickham Common circa 1957.

The sun shone most days (or so it seemed) but Adrian was a hard act to follow. It was clear he excelled in everything. Sums, writing, sports, history, geography – all these things came easily to him, and he was popular amongst his peers.

I remember being proud of him from an early age. I felt blessed to be one of the few kids in my class who had an older sibling in the school, but at the first playtime when we met, as arranged, by the water fountain, Adrian introduced me to one of his friends.

'Ali, this is Smegglesworth,' he said indicating an older, more sophisticated looking boy – at least nine years old and definitely not from our road.

'Hello, Smegglesworth!' I whispered coyly.

'You can't call me that. Only Adrian can call me Smegglesworth,' Smegglesworth said, pushing past me to drink from the fountain. 'And you're not allowed to drink from this fountain either. You have to use the babies' fountain.'

I slunk off to the smaller fountain on the other side of the playground, still unsure what I was supposed to call him. Since then I've never been good at being introduced to new people.

However, I soon made my own friends, although I was always aware of Adrian in the class above at playtimes, lunchtimes or when he was sent to our class with a message from his teacher. Adrian was always chosen for message carrying, even though he wasn't the tidiest member of his class.

'Doesn't your brother *ever* have his shirt tucked in properly?' Mr Woollard (Class Three) once asked me as Adrian left the room with the answer to a message. Mr Woollard was a curly-haired gentleman whose brogue shoes curled up at the toes.

'Hardly ever,' I answered, immediately realising what a pathetic retort this was. Adrian would have come up with something far wittier.

One of the fads at our school was bead swapping. To take part in bead swapping you needed a tin, some beads and the correct way of running your fingers through them. Mum gave me an old tin (which originally contained blackcurrant throat pastilles) and a few beads from old necklaces. During playtime we sat with our tins and, with the correct finger movement, examined other girls' beads until we came to a mutually acceptable swap. After the first day at school with my tin, Adrian asked if he could also have a tin for beads. Mum, being a fair and kind parent, said she'd find him one, though I felt intrinsically uncomfortable on his behalf. Boys didn't have beads. It was only the girls who bead-swapped. Even at such a young age I could see Adrian occasionally got things wrong. His enthusiasm sometimes blinded him to the mores of the social status quo. Anxiously I watched him produce his bead tin the following morning at break time. A couple of the quieter boys joined him to look at his beads but there was some playful laughter amongst some of the more confident boys, with Smegglesworth at their helm. That night he gave his tin back to Mum.

I followed Adrian from class to class, also designated to the academic stream, until the ultimate – Class One – which was taught by a frightening gentleman, Mr Nielson. Mr Nielson seemed old despite his dark (probably dyed) hair. He produced all the school plays, conducted the choir, sweated a lot and spoke with a posh accent. Mr Nielson had a cupboard full of plimsolls (slippers), which he used to whack boys' backsides, and a drawer full of rulers for smacking girls' legs. He constantly taunted the most poised of the girls in my class by telling them they were conceited. I had no idea what conceited meant and although I could tell he wasn't flattering them I longed to be categorised with the same label. On reflection I suspect he gained satisfaction from abusing both sexes. If he was around now he'd probably be locked up.

Mr Nielson adored my brother, so I joined Class One already feeling a shadowy second best. I'd heard my father read Adrian's report. For English Mr Nielson said Adrian had so many ideas that sometimes his thoughts outstripped his pen. I wondered if my thoughts would ever outstrip my pen, and feared they might not. I'd also heard Dad tell Adrian he could be anything he wanted to be. He'd passed the Eleven Plus to grammar school. He could go to Oxford or Cambridge. He could be Prime Minister. Although only ten, I realised Dad was being over-ambitious on Adrian's behalf. But all the same I admired his sense of the infinite possibilities of life. Not that this ambitious streak had governed his own life. Dad sold brake linings for a living, although he sometimes mentioned a place at the London School of Economics which he'd had to sacrifice because of the war.

The Westbury train arrives on time at Paddington mainline where I disembark and scurry along the platform towards the steps leading to the Underground. As someone who left London in the eighties, returning to the smoke is a culture shock. London is home to a myriad of different nationalities who buzz around the platform in a cosmopolitan mix of fashions and races. Whenever I visit I feel excited by the atmosphere which is so different to Frome where I've lived for the past twenty-two years.

From Paddington I take the tube to Tooting Broadway and reach Tooting High Street on the last lap of my journey. I stop off in Blackshaw Road to buy a *Daily Mirror* for Adrian (Ascot is on, so he'll want it for the horse racing) and a sandwich for myself in a Sainsbury's the size of an airport terminal. I queue at the checkout with all the London folk, but I feel a bit lost. Most people around me seem joyless, ground down by inner city life. No apple-cheeked Somerset types here. Outside the shop, people gather in groups for a communal smoke-in, flicking their cigs away before pushing off through the glass doors with their trolleys. Don't these people realise what they are doing to their bodies? Don't they value their hearts, the tissue inside their lungs?

Adrian was a fifty-a-day man until he had the heart bypass. A couple of times when walking to East Putney tube he'd suffered debilitating chest pains and was in St George's for tests on his heart when the doctor refused to let him leave the building – even though Adrian had private health insurance via his job as a statistician for BUPA, and would, given the choice, have plumped for The Wellington. He shot to the top of the list for an emergency triple bypass and remembers going out onto a balcony at St George's for what he knew would be his last ever cigarette. Like a final kiss with a lover.

Adrian began smoking at the age of twelve. On our annual holidays to Christchurch, near Bournemouth, where our grandparents lived, he often disappeared along the esplanade returning, I guess, several fags later for his Mivvi or 99. When I think back to those childhood years, the weeks we spent in Bournemouth – and there were many – shine like a burning sun reflected across the surface of the southern English sea. On holidays the barriers of puberty and growing up were mostly put aside. Adrian and I played in the sea and on the sand for hours. There were a couple of years when our grandparents had colour television and we didn't. I would have been happy filling my bucket and swishing about on my rubber ring in the sea, but Adrian insisted we all packed up our stuff and went back to Grandma's in time to watch *Popeye* or *Huckleberry Hound*. That was the year we discovered Huckleberry Hound had been blue all along.

Whilst holidaying in Bournemouth, Adrian made friends with a girl called Sue who came from Essex and whose family rented a beach hut on our favourite stretch of beach in Branksome Chine. Sue was a blue-eyed, dark-haired beauty. She was petite, fourteen years old, and had a younger brother called Tim. When we went to see *Thunderball* at the Bournemouth Odeon, Sue and Tim tagged along. On reflection, it was probably Adrian's idea to take Sue, and Tim and I were invited as decoys to fool the parents. I was just thirteen and Adrian was fourteen. I didn't *get* James Bond, although I revelled in the excitement of the big screen, the Bond theme music and the Martini adverts. The cinema was huge and before the film had been on for more than about half an hour I realised I was bursting for the loo. But, sandwiched between Adrian and Tim, I was too shy to get up and squeeze past Tim, in order to get to the Ladies. *Thunderball* was an extremely long and uncomfortable film.

When we left, whilst waiting for Sue and Tim's parents to pick them up, Adrian snogged the face off Sue and then swore me to secrecy.

'Don't tell Mummy,' he warned as he fed his threepenny bit into the phone to arrange for our parents to collect us. I wasn't sure why not, and was a little miffed he'd presume I'd tell her anyway. He obviously saw me as a grass. Still, I probably would have told her the minute we'd got into the car.

I wasn't sure where I stood with Tim, especially as we were only thrust together because of our respective siblings' mutual lust. Tim was brown-haired and more ordinary looking than his striking sister, but I liked him well enough. Later that August when Adrian was away camping with the Scouts, I found a letter in his room from Sue. One line jumped out at me. *'Tell Ali Tim thought she was as beautiful as ever.'* I was shocked and a little put out since I hadn't heard about this before. Tim thought me not only beautiful, but *beautiful as ever* implying previous favourable references to my looks in years gone by.

I could hardly reproach Adrian for not passing on this piece of flattery since I knew I shouldn't have read the letter in the first place, but I'd never heard myself referred to as beautiful before.

I arrive at St George's at half-eleven and recall some of the layout following my visit here three years ago. Once inside, I sprint up a back staircase following signs to Rodney Smith Ward and pass several groups of young doctors coming down, but see no one else walking up. I reach Rodney Smith Ward with my heart dangerously close to explosion. What am I trying to prove? That I am healthy when so many other people in the building are not? I have to pause to get my breath back.

Unlike the Victorian ward Adrian was in last time, this is a new part of the hospital and the main doors of the ward lead to a corridor with smaller rooms off it. I ask a nurse where I can find Adrian Tilbrook, and, having located his room, search for my brother in the six beds containing six equally poorly-looking, elderly men.

An auxiliary with a hairdo worthy of any member of the Jimi Hendrix Experience is tending to one of these souls. She pulls the sheet up to his neck as if she can't think of anything better to do. If this is the standard of care, I fear for my brother. I catch her eye and smile. She smiles back, a shining happy smile. Her name badge shows she's called Lena.

'Just poke him,' Lena suggests once we've worked out which of the six corpse-like figures is Mr Tilbrook.

Adrian is asleep, snoring and with tubes sticking into his nose the way patients have in *Casualty*. I don't like to wake him – I never like waking anyone – so I ignore Lena's advice and begin tidying his bedside table, which is cluttered with plastic cups and half-opened bags of sweets. With nothing left to organise I sit down in the chair next to his bed and wait. He's still sleeping. I tuck into my Sainsbury's grape, Brie and something else sandwich and try to compose myself.

I quite like hospitals – the self-containedness and the sense (however unfounded) of being looked after. But I'm shocked by the sight of my brother. He's unrecognisable. He seems to have transmorphed into an old man. A thin old man asleep in a hospital bed with tubes stuck up his nose.

As I chomp my way through my sandwich, I try to remember the last time I saw him. He certainly missed Christmas with us last year. In fact the last time I did see him was a few months ago when I came to the London Book Fair. He walked down the road from his flat to meet me at East Putney station. He seemed breathless, yet still offered to carry my bag for me, which was very heavy. *Did I let him carry it?* I wonder guiltily. I can't remember now. Maybe I let him carry it a little way.

Eventually Lena comes over and wakes him up.

'Oh, Ali!' he croaks when he realises I'm here.

I'm so glad I came.

Adrian is wearing a cotton garment like a hairdresser's cape (which is undone at the back), and what appear to be disposable paper pants. I ask him if he wants me to bring him some pyjamas but he says no.

A young doctor with an Oxbridge accent arrives at the bedside and pulls the curtains around us. I take a deep breath and stab my fingernails into the palm of my hand again. So this is it – the reason I've travelled a hundred-and-fifty miles on three different trains halfway across the country. To support my brother while he's told the results of the biopsy on his lung.

However, the doctor has no fresh news. Contrary to the information I was given yesterday, the results of the biopsy haven't come through. The doctor just repeats what I already know, and yet somehow makes everything sound perfectly fine.

'There are lesions on the kidney and lung,' he explains. 'But we won't have any concrete diagnosis until we get the test results.'

For *lesions* I guess we are supposed to read *tumours*, although I don't find the courage to ask.

'Is there anything else you'd like to know?' the doctor says.

'No, no. I'm fine with that,' Adrian replies.

I maintain the unhappy expression I've worn since he began talking.

'I'm sorry you've come all this way without hearing the results,' the doctor says to me. 'We will know soon. If it is cancer, and if the cancer has spread, then there is no treatment. And I do suspect it may have spread…'

At last he's used the C word. He shakes my hand, opens up the curtains and takes his leave. I feel confused.

Once we are alone again, Adrian perks up.

'I'm very stoical about all this.' He pounds a fist on his chest. 'I'm not afraid of cancer in the way some other people practically fall over just at the mention of the word.'

This might sound like bravado, but he shows no sign of breaking down. I almost sense he finds what's happening to him rather interesting. Is he enjoying the attention his situation is generating? For how long has he needed some attention? He then pulls the tubes out of his nose as if they are nothing. What are they for anyway? Suddenly I feel protected and relieved that this isn't turning out to be the 'so many months to live' scenario I'd been dreading. I finish off my sandwich and drink my juice. Lena returns with lunch. Adrian picks unenthusiastically at a congealed brown glob with the unlikely description of 'beef stew'.

When he's finished eating he relates the saga of his illness to me from the first symptoms of breathlessness, to his final collapse on the street last week which brought him into St George's. But I've heard this before. Surely it's the same story he told me on the phone when I was out with the dog the other day. I let him carry on however, in the misguided belief that this is leading to some new revelation.

It isn't, though. The story remains the same...the washing up, the wine glass, the deep cut, which incidentally is still bandaged – he holds up his hand for me to inspect, telling me the doctors are considering an operation on the base of his thumb – the towel he used as a bandage, the blood seeping through said towel, the decision to take the bus to St George's...

As I listen to this story again, two things strike me about Adrian's life. Firstly, he is alone. He has no one at home or nearby to worry about him, or to take him to Casualty in the middle of the night. Although his friends are very important to him, and vice versa, none of them are close at hand. Secondly, he and most other Londoners I know tend to rely on public transport to get around. So, although he has a car downstairs in his garage, and numerous taxi cab numbers pinned to his notice board, Adrian takes the bus to Tooting. Two buses, in fact.

He pokes half-heartedly at his chocolate pudding topped with beige custard, and sighs.

'I don't think I'll ever get out of this place,' he says with a sudden downturn of mood.

'Don't be so pessimistic!' I reply, even though in my heart I fear he might be right. There is a chance he might not get out of this hospital alive.

But we have to be optimistic. We have to look to the future. And in view of his living conditions – up lots of stairs in a flat where he lives *alone* – we discuss the options for when he comes out of hospital. He might be able to rent a more accessible flat in London, or he could move to Frome into the flat we jointly own there but is currently let to tenants. Or one of his ex-girlfriends might move in for a while to help him...

After Lena has cleared away his lunch dishes, Adrian manages to haul himself out of bed and totter to the nearest toilet with the aid of a walking stick. When he comes back he eases himself down onto the bed.

'I've decided on one thing,' he says. 'Before I get out of here I'm going to walk to the other toilet at the end of the corridor without a stick.' Adrian is breathless. His legs are so thin, and pale. Little more than sticks themselves with white sports socks on the ends. I see now just how much weight he's lost. But I admire him for this ambition. So very much. I'm touched by his determination to achieve something despite his predicament.

We sit together for a few hours then I tell him I'll have to get going.

'Are you meeting Jeannette or anyone?' he asks.

His question reminds me I'm usually on a tight schedule, trying to fit in visits to all my London friends.

'No, I'm not.' I'm relieved I can honestly say I'm here only to see him today. There's something in his expression which makes me realise, just this once, I must devote myself to him.

'There's a couple of things I'd like you to do for me, Ali, if you don't mind. Can you go to the flat and get my paying-in book? It's in the spare bedroom in the filing cabinet. I need to sort out my finances. I don't suppose you could lend me a couple of grand?'

'Yes, of course,' I say. At this moment I feel so sorry for him, I'd do anything I could to help. Eventually we find the flat keys in his locker and I kiss him goodbye.

Friday 22nd June 2007 – afternoon

From St George's I walk back towards Tooting savouring my freedom, at the same time feeling guilty that I can leave, whilst my brother is so hopelessly incarcerated. I arrive at Tooting Broadway and notice a Primark store nearby. My body involuntarily diverts towards its automatic doors.

Five T-shirts, three skirts, a belt, three make-up bags and two overnight cases later I leave Primark a new woman. It's amazing what parting with thirty-two-pounds-fifty can do for the morale.

I approach the entrance of Tooting Broadway Underground station, the one made famous by the eighties' sitcom, *Citizen Smith*. Wolfie Smith, power to the people and all that... I chundle down the creaky escalator laden with my Primark bags and feel a little wobbly at the thought of entering the bowels of the earth in such an unnatural way. In Somerset the closest I get to the bowels of the earth is looking down badgers' setts. But gradually I feel myself slipping into the whole London thing. I spent most of the first half of my life in the capital, so it's just a matter of easing my way back into the loop.

I get off the Underground at East Putney intent on finding the short cut Adrian takes from the tube to his flat. I cross over West Hill and turn the corner, relieved to see Leylands sprawling before me. The block is purpose built, tidily kept and with a large lawn at the back. Adrian has always been proud of his flat, or '*the flat*', as Mum always called it. I don't think she ever went there, or to any of the other flats he lived in, but Mum regularly asked me the same question about my brother.

'How do you think Adrian is managing in *the flat*?' The way the question was put showed she clearly doubted he *was* managing.

'The same as anyone else manages,' I'd reply, irked by her obsessive concern for my (at that time) healthy, wealthy and firmly unattached brother.

'But he's on his *own*. I do wish he'd get married or something. And I do worry about him. I mean what will happen when he gets old or is ill? Who will look after him? I won't be around. He'll have no one to look after him. All alone in *the flat*.'

'But none of those is a good enough reason to get married,' I pointed out, particularly as sometimes my brother's do-as-you-please lifestyle seemed positively enviable to me as I spent night after night clearing up after my four children, cooking and changing nappies.

Some people think Adrian is gay. But if a man is unmarried or lives alone does that make him gay? Certainly not in his case.

For the first few years of my life I believed *I'd* marry Adrian, until Mum dropped the bombshell one afternoon while my best friend, Barbara Barker, was round for tea.

'When I'm married to Adrian,' I mused over my sliced split tin and homemade blackcurrant jam, 'I'm going to have a big house with a swing in the garden and...'

'...you can't marry Adrian, darling,' Mum cut in calmly as she removed the tea cosy from the tarnished silver teapot she'd had as a wedding present and poured herself another cup. 'Nobody can marry their brother.'

I was desolate. My brother, who I'd naturally presumed would one day become my husband, was suddenly off limits.

'Will *I* be able to marry Adrian as thoon ath I'm a big lady, Auntie Betty?' Barbara lisped, her chin resting on our second best, blue and pink checked tablecloth.

Open-mouthed I waited for my mother's response.

'Yes, Barbara. You could marry Adrian. If he asked you. It's just that Ali can't marry Adrian because he's her brother and no one can marry their brother or sister. Or any relation for that matter.'

'Why not, Auntie Betty?'

'Because…they might have funny babies,' Mum replied, popping the tea cosy back over the pot. 'My bridesmaid, Elsie, married her cousin and two of her babies were funny.'

I fought back tears, grappling with a vision of a pram full of funny babies. My world had been shot through in an instant. Not only had I lost my future husband in the time it took my mother to stir a spoon and a half of Tate and Lyle into her teacup, but I was faced with the prospect of having to conjure up a substitute groom. The thought of marrying someone other than Adrian was appalling. I'd have to spend my life with someone I didn't even know. My parents clearly knew each other well, as did the parents of my friends.

'You could marry Michael Thomath,' Barbara suggested in a small, slightly smug voice.

Michael Thomas – the cleverest boy in my class. I appealed to my mother. Would *this* at least be possible?

'Yes, of course you could marry Michael Thomas. You could marry anyone – when you're old enough. Just not Adrian.'

I felt mildly consoled. Well, I was only six.

During our primary school years in the frugal lower-middle-class housing estate in Coney Hall, West Wickham, Kent, England, The World, The Universe, Adrian and I were forced together to create our own entertainment, only occasionally joining forces with Barbara, who lived three doors away and came in handy to make up the numbers. We were doctors and nurses, mothers and fathers, Cowboys and Indians – although Adrian always got to be the cowboy. Barbara, being younger than us and therefore inferior in status, took on the supporting roles of patient, baby or horse.

With the double leather holsters Mum made us for Christmas fastened round our waists Adrian and I would hide behind the bushes in our front garden and frighten passers-by, shooting caps into the air. Not that there were many passers-by. We lived at the top of a very long road and the only people who came past our house were those trekking the extra few steps to the last six houses at the top.

We had a corner plot, hidden at the side by the privet hedge Mum hacked at every summer with a blunt pair of garden shears. The pavement which started out as a dirt track was laid with paving slabs when I was five. At the same time the gas lamps, which were lit every night by a man who rode up on a bike, were replaced by modern electric lights.

On the other side of the road, fields stretched to the horizon. Dad, who was brought up in Clapham, loved the semi-rural setting of our house which looked out onto the open countryside.

'We're so lucky to look out on the open countryside,' he'd say as we sat in our front room eating our poached eggs on toast. 'Green belt. What a view!' he'd proclaim, surveying the tree lined field from the panorama of the modern windows he'd made and installed himself. For years I wondered what he meant, imagining a belt like the one I wore with my Brownie uniform, but green.

What Dad didn't have, he made. When something didn't work, he fixed it. And if he didn't own the tools he needed, he borrowed them from Barbara Barker's dad.

Not one to chuck money about, Dad's philosophy was that if one man could do something, then so could he. We lived in a house with no shed and so he built one himself. He designed it, laid the foundations and cemented every brick. Adrian and I watched the shed grow inch by inch. I remember the excitement when it was finished. The smell of freshly sawn wood mixed with a drier smell of concrete and brick. I also remember the key to the shed which was black, and longer than any of our other keys. Dad was a great one for keys and locking things up. Security was an important part of his life. But building and making things was too.

For a salesman who sold brake linings and claimed never to have earned more than six thousand pounds in any one year of his entire life, building sheds – and anything else he wanted – was perhaps a necessity. Certainly he'd go to any lengths not to hand over his money to tradesmen. My father, who had no training in carpentry, also made fitted wardrobes in all our bedrooms. Years later when we moved he replicated them all in the next house. He added a porch onto both houses he owned, built a garage, dug a fishpond and constructed mantelpieces.

He was a prolific reader, but Dad didn't like to own books. He visited the library once a month and took out the maximum four books which he kept under his bed. The books were always non-fiction. He dismissed novels as a waste of time. Most of what he read related to Adolf Hitler, Joseph Stalin or biographies and autobiographies of the weirdly famous.

He loved music, and one of my earliest memories is of Dad cranking up the gramophone he'd made from a piece of wood, an old plate, a screwdriver for a handle and an on/off switch that started life as a teaspoon. He had ten 78rpm records kept in brown paper sleeves. A few of these were cracked, but he still managed to play them around the cracks. The ones I remember were: "The Flight of the Bumblebee"; "The Peanut Vendor" by Stan Kenton; "Oh, Island In The Sun" by Harry Belafonte; a strange talking recording of a man making a sound like a train gathering speed; and "Woodman, Spare That Tree" by an American called Phil Harris. This last record was also spoken rather than sung and was basically a plea from a man to a woodman who'd come to fell a tree near his house. The man begs the woodman not to cut the tree down because he climbs it to get away from his wife and it's his only place of refuge. I had to ask Dad to explain this as I couldn't grasp why a man would want to climb a tree to get away from his wife. Secretly I worried that my husband, if I ever had one (which seemed doubtful in view of my mother's recent revelation about my

25

brother), might head for the nearest tree. The "Woodman" record was Dad's favourite. He didn't just sit back and listen to his 78s, he joined in, sang (or spoke) along and flailed his arms while we soaked up his enjoyment.

When Dad's shed was half built he took a test tube from Adrian's chemistry set and a sheet of paper from Mum's Basildon Bond writing pad. He told us to write a message for the future. We wrote our names, ages, the names of our cat (Bengy) and our fish (Sammy) and the date, 3rd November 1960. He rolled the paper up and slid it into the test tube. The tube was then ceremoniously cemented into the gap between two of the bricks on the left hand side just under the window frame.

This was one of the many things I loved about my father. Not only did he make so many bits and pieces (although, at the time, I'd have much preferred shop-bought things like everyone else), but he saw beyond the here and now and decided to put a time capsule into the cement of his homemade shed for someone to read in years to come. This was what I admired so much. His mixture of practical and visionary.

Would Dad buy a home assembly shed from the internet if he was here now? Probably. Although he always seemed to do things differently from everyone else. Certainly he did things that my friends' dads didn't do. He swore, and aped about. In the summer he'd fill a basin with cold water in the garden. We had to put our faces in and see how long we could hold our breath. When we went on holiday he'd walk along the bottom of the seabed doing the breast-stroke movement with his arms – pretending he could swim when we all knew he couldn't. One autumn he got a group of Adrian's friends together, Robin Ings, John Commerford, Martin Phillips amongst them, and started up their own football team. All those boys came back to see him at our house, even when Dad was an old man.

He'd been a pilot in the war and kept his old RAF jacket up in the loft with its strange wires and plugs sewn into the lining. He had stories he repeated over and over about his young life during the war years. One was about a woman who got into a train and when a man slammed the door catching her hand in the door, her hand fell off and landed in another man's trilby. He usually chose to tell us this anecdote, with various embellishments, while we were eating. Adrian nearly choked with laughter one lunch time on Mum's jam roly-poly pudding. But the hilarity around the table was tempered by Mum's anger because Adrian had spat out the pudding she'd so lovingly made.

Most of my dad's stories illustrated the carefree, daredevil days of his youth when he got up to all kinds of crazy things with his friends in the RAF. Photos of him at that time show a handsome dark-haired pilot. Even in semi-detached suburbia he managed to maintain that aura of glamour. Unlike any of our neighbours, he had a job that provided us with a brand new car every year…and he put a time capsule in a garden shed.

At the top of our road a gate led to Bluebell Woods where trees arched above a wide path flanked on either side (at the right time of the year) by a carpet of bluebells. One spring when our grandparents were visiting – a rare occurrence since we usually visited them – Adrian and I rigged up a secret teddy bears' picnic in the woods, surreptitiously taking our teddies to a clearing and seating them in a circle. We then took Grandpa up to the woods and pretended we had no idea how the bears got there. Grandpa, being of the child-friendly variety – he once owned a toyshop and a dolls' hospital – was convincingly duped.

But without adult company Bluebell Woods could transform from benign nature walk into sinister shadowy forest where big boys sometimes inexplicably drove motorbikes along the paths and even wove in and out of the trees, and where I first remember being really terrified, even though Adrian was with me. We were on our way home after collecting bluebells to give to Mum for her birthday when three 'big boys' came up behind us.

'Just keep walking,' one of them threatened. 'We've all got guns and I've got a gun pointed at your backs. If you don't keep walking I'm going to shoot you both.'

I could sense Adrian's fear as we quickened our pace, neither of us daring to look round. We'd seen enough episodes of *Rawhide* to imagine the feeling of the barrel of a gun in the small of your back. I could almost smell the smoke, and as soon as we exited the Bluebell Woods gates we ran for it, dropping our flowers behind us.

'Don't tell anyone what happened,' Adrian warned me with as much menace as the big boys' threats. I longed to share this frightening experience with Mum (as in years to come when Adrian snogged Sue post *James Bond*), but I could sense Adrian's shame. He hadn't been brave enough to fight the big boys, to turn round and wrestle the guns from them – which were probably cap guns from the toy shop in Coney Hall, or even more likely sticks, or just gloved index fingers.

I often felt sorry for Adrian because of the burden of being the eldest. Whenever we went out together my father always warned him, 'Look after your sister. She's only a girl.' This admonishment made me feel special, precious and worthy of looking after, although the word 'only' struck a pre-women's lib chord somewhere deep in my psyche. For Adrian I suspect Dad's warning made him wish he could go out on his own without the responsibility of making sure I returned in one piece.

Now I'm very much alone and feeling a little nervous as I put my brother's key into his front door. I'm like an intruder, but thankfully don't feel as bleak as I'd thought I might, arriving without him to greet me.

The flat smells as I remember it – a musty, warm kind of blokey smell which is both reassuring and cosy. I've always felt relaxed and at home here. I usually prefer old properties, whereas all three flats Adrian has owned have been new builds. But he's made each of them homely.

From the hallway I go from room to room, making sure there's no one here. No burglars or squatters. Each room has a selection of lights and dimmer switches. Adrian likes his lighting. A matching pair of double-seater sofas face each other in the middle of the sitting room. The sofas are a light grey colour but are now stained with spots of blood. A pine coffee table sits between them, the sides of which are marked with cigarette burns. His television is a ten inch portable with an orange surround and is only watchable from one of the sofas. I'm sure he watches TV a lot but whereas we've had a wide-screen plasma for a few years, he still keeps this antique with its limited selection of channels and distorting green glow on BBC1.

Three of the walls in the sitting room are yellow. The fourth is taken up with huge windows and a glass door that leads to a balcony. The windows have yellow Venetian blinds which are permanently open. On the balcony two plastic garden chairs huddle beside a collection of pots containing dead flowers and shrubs. Adrian's living room shelves are covered in nick-nacks. Things he's brought home from his travels. The walls are decorated with pictures, prints mainly and the many masks he's accumulated from all over the world. He has racks of CDs: The Steve Miller Band, Stevie Winwood, Pink Floyd, Bobby Darin, The Rolling Stones, as well as many differently decorated ashtrays and oriental bowls. Lots of Egyptian style artefacts that he may have got in Egypt or in the British Museum. Figures, more ashtrays, and masks. Two over-sized chess pieces, a king and queen made of plaster of Paris, sit side by side on a shelf.

Dominating the living room is a print of a Picasso painting, *Buste de Femme au Chapeau*. The picture takes up half the wall

29

and screams the primary colours, red, blue and Adrian's favourite – yellow. He has an ashtray decorated with the same image. At the other end of the room two lithographs of deckchairs blowing in the wind on Brighton Beach hang side by side. A drinks trolley next to these pictures is home to bottles of spirits – Armagnac, vodka, brandy, whisky and some soft mixers, as well as a large pack of Marlboro cigarettes, the duty-free kind you bring back from holiday. The outer packaging has been broken and some taken out. The top is covered in a layer of dust.

From the living room I go past the kitchen and the tiny bathroom, into the spare bedroom. Adrian inherited Dad's DIY skills and has carried on the family tradition of building fitted wardrobes and book shelves in both bedrooms. His books are history books, autobiographies, three books about Shakespeare, one about the Globe Theatre, travel guides, historical novels by Hilary Mantel and Alison Weir, most of Ian McEwan's novels. Unlike Dad, he loves fiction. The spare bedroom contains a double bed and his office equipment. Two First Aid manuals are laid out on the floor open at the relevant pages for *Minor cuts and abrasions* and *Treatment for severe bleeding*. These pages show diagrams of tourniquets and complicated bandage folding techniques. Had Adrian begun swotting up on the rudiments of first aid at this late stage?

I go into Adrian's bedroom. Although I know Carol, one of Adrian's girlfriends, has been in to clean up the bed and the spots of blood following the incident with the broken wine glass, the mattress and some of the walls still have blood splattered on them which makes the room look like a crime scene.

Hanging on the end of his bed is a yellow tie decorated with Egyptian hieroglyphs. In the hallway between the two bedrooms is a picture Adrian made from a collection of cigarette cards showing old footballers. Another picture he's made consists of twenty packs of Camel cigarettes arranged Andy Warhol style on a plain background. This hangs at the far end of his bed opposite a collage of photographs of old black and white film stars. Greta Garbo, Loretta Young, Elizabeth Taylor, Cary Grant, Vivien Leigh, Errol Flynn, Mae West, Gregory Peck – all these icons watch over him every night as he sleeps. Above his bed is picture of a red heart.

The curtains in both bedrooms are old, faded blue velvet ones that don't fit the windows. These curtains have travelled with him since the seventies.

Everything (apart from the blood) is as I remember it from my last visit. But it's dirty. The carpets are covered in a film of dust. The kitchen floor is greasy, the units in need of a good scrub. My mother was right. The flat does need a woman's touch. Adrian had to let his cleaner go when he took redundancy from his job at BT, so this dirt has accumulated over the past couple of years. I now realise he may have been too unwell to keep things together.

I switch the TV on and catch the end of *Deal or No Deal* where a woman called Violet deals at twenty-eight-and-a-half grand when she had a hundred thousand in her box. After *Deal or No Deal* I clean up a bit and risk a cup of tea. I fill the kettle which looks as if it's been in situ since the 1980s and idly open the freezer only to promptly panic as I can't close it properly. If Adrian's fridge is like a hotel mini bar with its various bottles of wine and beer occupying the door space and two magnums of champagne in the main body, then his freezer is like the North Pole in a box. I wouldn't be surprised to find the odd penguin in there, although there's no sign of any actual food. No frozen peas or pizzas. No emergency supplies of Findus meals for one or stocks of bread. The interior is clogged with ice. I begin hacking the ice with a kitchen knife in order to shut the door, only to notice ten minutes later that I've perforated the white plastic sealant around the edges. This seems like a really bad

31

thing to do. I toy with the idea of phoning Peter to ask his advice but decide against this. Hopeless woman messing up kitchen appliances in someone else's home – maybe not.

Instead I ram a chair up against the door and then I change into one of my Primark skirts before heading back home. London is boiling compared to Frome and my thick jeans are making my legs feel like spit roasted sausages. Before I leave I make sure everything in the flat is turned off, and fumble for Adrian's keys.

As I take a last look around, I catch sight of Adrian's scarf and umbrella hanging on the hook in the hall. His winter trademarks. I feel my tears welling. A red and white Yasser Arafat type cloth hangs there too, a souvenir of the time he worked in Riyadh. I wipe my eyes and make sure I've got the paying-in book which is the main reason for my visit. In the kitchen I'd noticed a pile of unopened NatWest statements. A man who leaves bank statements unopened is a worried man – or maybe someone who prefers online banking? I'm pretty sure Adrian doesn't do his banking online. I blow my nose, close the door behind me, and double lock the Yale as per his instructions.

On my way back to the station the East Putney streets are scented with wafts of purple and white lilac. I walk past the millionaires' semis with their metal grilled windows on the suburban back streets leading towards the traffic lights, past Whitelands College in West Hill. London suddenly seems like a city for young people. I realise I don't belong here any more. I'm no longer a part of the lifestyle in the way I was twenty-odd years ago – before I took the route of country wife ensconced in rural Somerset.

I change trains at Earls Court and sit down opposite two young men who are talking loudly in a theatrical way. I soon gather they *are* theatrical. They're talking about opening nights and scripts.

'I'd *love* to meet Carol,' one of them gushes. 'I'm *so* sure we'd *really* get on!'

'I'd *so* love to meet Carol too!' his companion enthuses.

What's this all about? How do they both know about Carol if neither of them has met her? Possible I suppose, and this non-meeting of Carol evidently isn't a problem. They are both smiling, chatting so happily.

My mind backtracks to Adrian and his women. When he had the heart op I realised he had two girlfriends, both called Carol. Carol (without an 'e') his girlfriend from at least thirty years ago when he lived in Cheltenham, and Carole (with an 'e') who, until recently, was his cleaner. Carol (with no 'e') has supported him through this week in hospital – and she will no doubt support him in the next weeks, months, years…? I consider her to be my closest ally in all of this.

I'm heading for Waterloo mainline, but the tube train I'm on stops at Westminster and shows no sign of starting again. The doors remain open. Most people carry on reading papers or staring into space. A few look concerned. Eventually an announcement informs us there's been a passenger incident. I feel deeply anxious, an anxiety instilled in me during the IRA bombings in Central London. Two girls wearing identical stripy tops are talking about getting off and walking to Waterloo mainline so I follow them off the train.

At the exit these girls stop to take photos of each other by the river. I don't like to stop as well in case I seem like a stalker. Anyway, I recognise where I am now and carry on across Westminster Bridge finding myself on the other side of the river outside St Thomas' Hospital. This is where Adrian was born. Where his life began. I notice a couple of BUPA adverts on advertising hoardings. BUPA was where Adrian worked as a statistician for ten years before travelling to Saudi Arabia. There seem to be reminders of my brother jumping out at me everywhere in this bustling city.

At Waterloo station I bump into a smattering of Ascot types tipsily striding across the concourse. They look out of place amongst the commuters and other young people with knapsacks who litter most of London. With the chaps smarter than smart in grey morning suits and top hats, the gals sporting haute couture dresses, they look like a group of *Brideshead Revisited* party revellers who've accidentally stumbled into a dreary Lowryesque landscape. Ah, but how Adrian adores the races. The gee-gees, as he affectionately calls them. I think of him in his bed wearing his hospital gown and wonder if he'll ever sip a glass of champers or place a bet at Ascot again.

I pray he will.

After two hours on the mainline train I climb into my car that's been waiting patiently for me at Westbury station for what seems like half a lifetime. It's so good to be almost home, almost able to relax. The CD compilation I have in the car was made up by my daughter, Emily, and includes the Coldplay track, "Fix You". As I drive, tired and drained through the dark tunnel of trees out of Westbury on my way back to Frome on the last lap of my day's journey, no song has ever seemed more relevant and poignant.

Tears stream down your face, when you lose something you can't replace, Chris Martin sings.

They do…and I'm afraid I may be about to.

When I get home I look up the word 'lesions' in the dictionary.

I feel as if Adrian's fate is sealed.

Monday 25th June 2007

The rain has been relentless all weekend and I wait for my sons, Jack and Ed, to return from this year's Glastonbury mud bath. In the morning on my way home from dropping the girls at school, I see mucky people everywhere in dirty vans travelling back from Worthy Farm. Part of me asks 'What makes them do it?' Another part wonders why I've never been myself.

Today is the day the doctor at St George's said they'd have the results of the biopsy on Adrian's lung tissue. I've already overslept, having gone to bed late last night after staying up to catch The Who headlining Glasto. They played all the oldies, anthems from the years I shared with Adrian when we were growing up in Bromley. "I Won't Get Fooled Again", "My Generation". I wonder whether Adrian managed to get the hospital television hanging over his bed to work and whether he'd watched Roger Daltrey and Pete Townsend doing their old-men stuff. Roger says something about hoping to die before he gets old. Childish words, so glibly sung. They still manage to belt out their classics without a hint of irony.

Last night, snuggled in the living room next to Peter with my hot chocolate and biscuits, I felt tearful. Tears fuelled by music from innocent days gone by. I remembered seeing Roger Daltrey performing in the old *Woodstock* film. Also the Isle of Wight Festival in 1970 when I was eighteen and tagged along with Adrian and his mates. That was the year Jimi Hendrix played. He came on late at night. Music of various standards and styles had been playing non-stop since we'd arrived on the island, but when Hendrix hit the stage it was as if someone had turned the lights on after a power cut. He was magical. A few weeks later, over the breakfast table, Dad read out the headline from the *Daily Telegraph* telling us he was dead.

When Jack and Ed eventually arrive home I ask them if they caught The Who on Saturday night.

'Who?' they ask in unison. They don't do the Pyramid Stage.

It's approaching noon, but I can't face ringing either the hospital or Adrian. After walking the dog I get a message on my land line asking me to ring him. I still can't bring myself to – I'm afraid of what I might hear. My day's all behind and I don't have lunch until two, after which I have to go out to put money into Adrian's bank account. His finances are a mess, but at least I still have enough from Mum's legacy to top him up. When I get home he phones again.

'Bad news, I'm afraid, Ali,' he croaks.

'Oh?'

'They've told me I've got cancer of the lung, kidney and liver. I've only got twelve months to live.'

I pick up a pen from my desk and scribble on my phone book then stare at the photo on the windowsill of myself and Adrian in our berets.

'Oh, no, Adrian. I'm so sorry.' I hear my voice saying these words although they don't seem to be coming from me. 'Are you sure? I mean…maybe you could get a second opinion… Is there anything you want me to do?' I'm clenching my fist again, nails digging into the palm of my hand.

'They seem sure. Sorry to lay this on you, Ali. I'm alright about it. I'm quite philosophical. Quite stoical.' I've noticed he likes the word 'stoical' and has been using it a lot recently.

'Yes?' I say in disbelief. 'What are they going to do? What treatment are they offering?'

'I'll have chemo. Actually, I think they want me out of here.'

'Typical,' I say, recalling the way the hospital in Bath tried to discharge my mother two days before she died.

There's a pause. 'I'd like to take you up on your offer,' Adrian continues. 'I'd like to move into the flat in Frome.'

Suddenly I feel scared, though I'm not sure why since I was the one who suggested Adrian leave London and move to Frome.

'Yes, I'll sort everything out,' I say, annoyed with myself for using the phrase I seem to fall back on when I don't know what else to say. I'll sort it out. Don't worry. Leave everything to me. I'll fix you. I'll try to fix you, just like Chris Martin said. Just wait and see. Tomorrow is another day. I'm turning into a modern day Scarlett O'Hara.

In the evening when I tell Peter this awful 'twelve months' news I have the same pain across the bottom of my breast bone I had during the stressful months when my mother was dying. Over dinner, Peter recalls an acquaintance in Frome who also was given a year to live.

'You remember that guy who worked in the dairy? Towards the end he walked around the streets smiling at people and looking lost. He couldn't work and I suppose he didn't have anything else to do. Eventually I realised I hadn't seen him for a while. Then I heard he'd died. He was only in his thirties. Strange because he was called Adrian too.'

At seven I go to my tennis lesson, a sport I've only recently taken up. Adrian has always been the tennis player in the family. He had tennis coaching at St Christopher School in Letchworth, where he boarded from the age of eleven.

I arrive late and the other students are already practising their serves. For June the weather is strange. The trees flanking the tennis courts are dark and menacing and an autumnal wind catches the leaves, blowing them around the nets. I smile, talk, hit the ball as hard as I can, my secret hidden inside me like a poison. Who can I tell that I've just found out my brother will be dead this time next year? I hardly know these people. But my world has changed within the last twenty-four hours. Adrian has been given twelve months to live. What can this be like for him? I still have no idea what it's like for me.

Tuesday 26th June 2007

Although I suggested Adrian move into our Frome flat, I'm worried that there are four steps up to the front door, and, more importantly, we have tenants living there. I'd have to give them six weeks' notice. I decide to spend the afternoon visiting the many estate agents in Frome. I start by looking for rentals for Adrian and end up looking for a flat for him to buy. A spectacular refurbishment in North Parade, perhaps? I can imagine the old Adrian living in this sort of place, but what about the new, sick version? He'd have to climb a steep hill to get home from anywhere. For 'anywhere' read *the pub*.

In the evening Mac rings. Mac is one of our old friends from the Bromley days who now lives in Bristol. He and Adrian go back a long way. They shared flats together in the seventies in Muswell Hill and then in Brighton. Mac has been to St George's to visit Adrian earlier today.

'I think Adrian should go away,' Mac says. 'Do something with the little time he has left. I told him as much. He seemed worried about travel insurance but he shouldn't be thinking about stuff like that. Just go off and have a good time.'

'I've considered this too,' I tell him. 'And I must admit travel insurance was the first problem that came to mind.'

'Nah,' Mac says. 'Don't bother with insurance – just go!'

I remember the insurance forms I had to fill out for my mother whenever I took her away on a cruise. *Tick boxes for heart disease, cancer. Have you been given a terminal diagnosis?* Those sorts of questions seemed ridiculous then. Questions for other people. But maybe Adrian would like to go away on a cruise now. Maybe Carol or I could take him. I'm free for most of August. And this is the wettest, most miserable June in my memory. How cool it would be to sail round the Med one last time together. Our lawn is lush, thick grass and candles, still outside from my birthday party at the beginning of the month, have puddles of rainwater around the wicks. A rose tree, given to me by my friend Jill Miller, remains unplanted.

'Plant it straight away,' she told me. Jill, who runs a cancer charity in Frome, had breast cancer seventeen years ago. I might need the help of her counselling service soon. She's one of the cards up my long and baggy sleeve. But her rose tree remains unplanted and I'm beginning to wonder whether it will survive.

At night I can't sleep. This is the third night I've been up until two in the morning. Would Adrian want to go on a holiday? Can I realistically find him somewhere to live in Frome? Should I convert our study into a bedroom for him? Would he want to live here as part of a large family when he's been alone for so long? Mac said Adrian could be out of the hospital by Thursday, which only gives me one clear day.

Panic sets in as I toss and turn the night away.

Wednesday 27th June 2007

Jack and Ed paid fifty pounds for an antiquated caravan to sleep in for the duration of the Glastonbury Festival. They've just been back to Worthy Farm to collect this monstrosity which is currently parked in the road outside our house. What will the neighbours think? The boys carry bin bags of mud-caked clothes indoors, dumping them in the back hallway in the general area of the washing machine.

Later, as I sit in my study, I overhear Peter telling them the news about Adrian. Or at least, I overhear him telling Jack and his girlfriend, Willow. But has he told Ed? I don't want to have to tell him (or anyone else, really) that my brother, his uncle, has been given a death sentence.

For so long my life has been protected from the tragedies that seem to pepper the lives of others. Even my mother didn't die until she was well into her eighties. Has my bubble of safety finally burst? We have even recently fallen out with our neighbours. Despite living in harmony with them for nineteen years – they gave us rhubarb, we gave them apples; we had them in for drinks at Christmas, they invited us for cups of tea on the lawn in the summer; we kept an eye on their house when they were on holiday, they brought us presents back from exotic places – we are no longer on friendly terms. In the past couple of years they've accused us of climbing a ladder with a box of matches trying to set fire to their (stone built) house, injecting poisonous fumes into an air vent in their kitchen, and spraying graffiti on their garage walls. My brain glazed over ages ago where they are concerned. The idea that a member of our family would do any of these things is ludicrous. Occasionally I fantasise about jumping up and down, waving maniacally and

41

making rude gestures into the camera of their closed circuit TV surveillance network. Yes, we live next door to a couple who have a closed circuit TV surveillance network and believe we are trying to kill them.

I try to put this rather disturbing couple out of my mind, but sometimes when I'm driving home, as I turn the corner at the bottom of the hill, before I get to our cluster of houses, I'll experience a horrible feeling generated by their hostility which casts a cloud over my homecoming.

Thursday 28th June 2007

Martin rings early morning to say he's just back from France. Martin is another of Adrian's friends from Bromley.

'Mac rang me to tell me the news about Adrian,' he says. Martin and Adrian were both part of the group of five-year-olds who pitched up at Wickham Common in their short trousers and bottle green jumpers in 1955. Martin, Adrian, John Commerford and Robin Ings have remained friends since. Last year Adrian joined them in a reunion weekend at Martin's house in France to celebrate fifty years of friendship.

After primary school Adrian went to Bromley Grammar School, whereas Martin, John and Robin went to Beckenham Grammar. Although Adrian seemed happy at Bromley Grammar, somewhere along the way things went wrong for him. The first sign all was not well came during the Autumn term. Although not privy to the details of their anxieties, I was aware my parents were worried about him.

One afternoon he came home from school crying. In my safe world upstairs in my bedroom where I drew in my sketchpads, dressed my dolls in clothes my mother had made, and wrote little books about families with thirteen children, and glass fairies who lived at the bottom of the garden, I could tell something was amiss in the rest of the house. I was excluded from most of what was going on, in respect for Adrian's feelings I thought, but gathered from my mother's reaction that something bad had happened to Adrian at school.

Appointments with a child psychologist followed and although I longed to be included I was left at home, reduced to being babysat by Barbara Barker's mum. But I listened to everything the other members of my family talked about when they came home. The psychologist had asked Adrian how much pocket money he got and whether he'd considered asking for more. This question exploded into my quiet little life. Were they implying Adrian wanted more pocket money but was afraid to ask? Was my father mean? Or was he intimidating? Should I be asking for extra pennies? Things seemed a bit frightening. A letter arrived from Bromley Borough Council asking my parents if they'd like to accept a place for Adrian at a boarding school. Dad, who was a fan of private education and social advancement, immediately accepted this offer, though without the agreement of my mother.

By the beginning of the next school year Adrian was no longer a pupil at Bromley Grammar where he'd proudly worn his new uniform the previous September. At a time when local councils seemed to have a bottomless pot of gold, Dad had signed on the dotted line and, with their financial support, agreed for Adrian to attend a 'progressive' boarding school in Hertfordshire.

In 1964 my life changed. At the age of twelve I became like an only child when Adrian left home to board at St Christopher School in Letchworth. By this time I'd started at Bromley Technical High School for Girls which was a trek and a half from where we lived. With a twenty minute walk to the bus stop from our house, followed by a forty-five minute bus ride to Bromley South, a train to Bickley and a mile long walk up Chislehurst Road to the school, I came home tired, with just enough time to eat and do homework before bed. I soon got used to our altered home life and when Adrian came back in the holidays he seemed like a glamorous creature I hardly knew.

That first Christmas Adrian arrived home with an LP called *Please Please Me* by a new group called The Beatles tucked under his arm. In later years he returned wearing green desert boots and purple loons. Each term his clothes would be more colourful, his hair longer and his sideburns more bushy. At St Christopher the boys were allowed to grow their hair while all the boys at the state schools back in Kent still had short back and sides. For the first couple of hours after he got home I'd be too shy to even speak to him.

At my own school, however, I laid it on thick, boasting to my friends about weekends visiting St Chris. Listing the names of the best looking boys I'd met, I basked in my second-hand spotlight of fame and fortune. We made the drive to Hertfordshire three times each term and these visits began to shape my world. St Christopher School in Letchworth was without a doubt the most romantic and wonderful place I'd ever been.

At Bromley Technical High School for Girls the only males were the gardener and the gardener's assistant. Most of the girls in my class half-heartedly lusted after the gardener's assistant who looked to be about eighteen, even though we knew in our hearts he was short and covered in leaves. At Bromley Tech we wore a navy blue uniform with yellow and red piping on the blazers. We had different hats for winter and summer (felt and straw), a specified three-quarter inch stitching on our plimsolls spelling out our names in red cotton thread and our initials embroidered on our navy blue knickers.

At St Chris there was no uniform. The kids wore anything. Jeans and baggy jumpers mainly. At my school we arrived at each lesson on time in mortal fear of detention for lateness, whilst in Letchworth lessons were optional and the pupils showed up if they felt like it. The kids called the teachers by their Christian names.

St Christopher was a Quaker, vegetarian, progressive, co-educational, experimental boarding school which was home to the offspring of diplomats, television stars and other rich or famous people. Michael Winner went there. Kenneth Allsop's children were all there. Rupert Davies, TV's pipe-smoking

Maigret, had a son in Adrian's year. Even Doris Lessing briefly sent her daughter there. At sports days a well-known actor from *Z Cars* watched his children run their races. For his seventeenth birthday one of my brother's friends received a Silver Cloud Rolls Royce as a present from his father. And at St Christopher School, Adrian flourished. By the time he was seventeen he was head boy.

I had no idea what the words Quaker (except for the oats), vegetarian (nobody I knew *was*), progressive (progressive rock hadn't yet come into being) or co-educational meant. I would, however, have given the pink flowery wallpaper from my bedroom, my Karl Denver LP and the ownership of my Dansette record player to be a boarder at St Christopher School along with my brother. But no matter how many times I asked my father over the next six years, the answer was always the same. He couldn't afford to send me there. My father sold brake linings for a living – he was no TV star or millionaire businessman. Ninety per cent of Adrian's fees were met by Bromley Council. So Adrian was educated at a private school whilst I slummed it with the masses. However, in retrospect it's interesting to note that the male equivalent of my school, Bromley Technical High School for Boys, produced the icon that is David Bowie. I don't think St Chris could match that one.

Martin was one of the friends who always caught up with Adrian during the school holidays. His would be one of the many bikes parked outside our house at the end of each July.

'Fucking hell,' Martin says now when I tell him the prognosis we have been given for his friend. This, as I now remember, is what he always used to say – even before everyone else said 'fuck' all the time. But of course he's upset. His emotion is contagious and I can't carry on the conversation. We both gulp and I have to put the phone down on him. I realise it's not only I who will be losing someone they love.

Friday 29th June 2007

I managed only four hours' sleep last night. This morning, Margaret, who lives at the other end of the village, phones to see how things are. In 1992 when I had my premature twins Margaret came to my house to help me with them every week day except Fridays (when she volunteered at the local hospital). She got me through the impossible months the following year when I had six month old twins and the aftermath of a hysterectomy. She stood by me through the death of my mum and now she looks after our dog whenever we go away. I tell her the grim news about Adrian and the one year left to live.

Margaret's reaction is amazing. She's so positive. She tells me about her friend, Edwin, who is still going strong even though he's had cancer for some years and is over eighty.

'At least they're going to treat him. And he's up and about. And he's going home.' To my dear friend Margaret this is all very good news.

I feel compelled to pass Margaret's positivity on to Martin in the email I send him later, hoping it will cheer him too.

While out with Billy I receive a text message from Adrian which he's sent me by mistake since it's clearly meant for his business partner, Phil. The text thanks Phil for visiting him last night, mentions the latest abortive terrorist attack in London, and ends, *Told prob going home 2 day – get the champs out. A.*

Adrian would never say this to me. Surely champagne is the last thing he needs. I immediately go into tutting mother mode.

Saturday 30th June 2007

I wake this morning refreshed, thinking about Margaret's words. They're still like medicine. After listening to her I'm prepared to believe everything *is* fine. To believe the proverbial glass is now half full. Adrian's glass.

But what happens if he starts drinking again? Will he last a whole year?

Today is the annual Winchester Writers' Conference. I've been to this for the past five years. I remember the first time I went to Winchester clutching my newly finished manuscript of the first novel I'd written for my Master's degree, savouring the early summer sunshine and the break from domesticity.

Now I dare to call myself a writer. I'm a mother, a wife, an un-domestic goddess, gardener, taxi driver, nurse, worrier. All those things. But when asked what I do when introduced to new people, I say I'm a writer.

When the girls were eighteen-month-old toddlers and I was a frazzled mess I saw an ad in the local paper promoting a new evening class in Radstock. The article had the tempting heading, 'Do you want to be an author?'

Did I? I'd always thought I might.

I'd graduated in English and European Literature from Essex University when I was twenty-one, subsequently had lots of odd jobs, then worked on a magazine called *Practical Householder* which was part of the IPC group. A year later I made a career U-turn and became an Education Welfare Officer in Peckham. After I had Jack I changed jobs and became a Student Services Officer in Hammersmith and West London College. My career had been chequered, but even in my twenties and thirties I could foresee that my smattering of different experiences might come in handy one day if I wanted to write.

In 1986 when Jack and Ed were little I started my own business. Housemaids Domestic Cleaning Services consisted of me juggling a gang of cleaning women against a list of clients who wanted their houses cleaned, either because they were working, were rich, had enormous houses, or suffered from obsessive-compulsive disorder. Six years down the line, when I was an in-patient in the Royal United Hospital Bath waiting to have my twins, I had all my work folders with me. I'm embarrassed to admit I even interviewed a prospective cleaner from my hospital bed.

When I travelled to Radstock on that October evening for the first week of the class – Writing For Profit And Pleasure – I felt less than presentable. I hadn't had time to feed everyone by half-six *and* wash my hair. I didn't have anything decent to wear – but I knew if I didn't go to the first class then I probably wouldn't go at all.

For years I'd felt incomplete. As if I didn't have a career of any substance. Nothing I'd achieved work-wise matched up to what I could have done, given my education and the hopes of my parents. But whenever I thought about writing I decided there were already too many writers. Thousands of books in libraries. Millions of words written in massive chunks of newspapers. More than anyone could ever read. How could there be room for me?

I soon dismissed those worthy and self-deprecating thoughts and arrived ten minutes late to the writing class. The early evening autumnal sun streamed through the plate glass windows of the college and for the first time in my life I felt I'd discovered a hobby I loved. The tutor set homework and I remember sitting on the sofa at home after I'd put the girls to bed, writing a short piece about them when they'd woken up that morning. I wrote less than three-quarters of a page, but even those few lines seemed a mammoth task. I described the girls' 'pyjama clad arms' as they stretched towards me, begging to be the first to be lifted out of their cot.

Those Wednesday night classes became the focal point of my week in terms of intellectual stimulation. I lived from Wednesday to Wednesday and struggled through the holidays when the classes weren't running.

Eventually *Woman's Weekly* magazine bought one of my stories about a woman who makes a New Year's resolution to be more friendly to the people she sees every day on her way to work. The fiction editor rang to tell me they wanted to buy it and I danced around the room after I'd put the phone down. I was officially a writer. Someone wanted to pay me for something I'd written. Something I'd made up was going to be read by thousands of people. Before long I was the one teaching the evening class with the late summer sun streaming through the plate glass windows onto a group of people, several of whom were just like I'd been years before.

Meanwhile I'd sold Housemaids Domestic Cleaning Services and used some of the money to enrol on the MA Creative Writing course at Bath Spa University. As part of this course we had to write the beginning of a novel. My novel was about a woman who was in love with two brothers. It was this manuscript I took to Winchester in search of a publisher in 2002.

Now, instead of driving to Winchester to listen to people talking about books and publishing, I've opted to drive to Westbury (again) and I'm boarding the Paddington train. I have with me my twin daughters, Emily and Frances, some yellow plastic gloves and a packet of J cloths. We're on a mission to clean my brother's flat in preparation for his discharge from hospital. If only I could bottle Housemaids Domestic Cleaning Services and put them in my bag too.

Once on board the train I choose a window seat, and settle in. The girls, now fourteen, sit together in front of me. Not long ago they would have fought to take turns to sit beside me. I miss those times but enjoy the peace of being alone, gazing out of the window as the Wiltshire fields turn into sparsely built up areas and eventually into towns.

At this point I still don't know where Adrian is. He might be back in his flat if he was discharged from hospital yesterday, or he might be in St George's still, although I suspect the former. There's no answer from either his mobile or his land line and I don't have the hospital number with me.

On Paddington station we stop for lunch in a mock wooden Traditional Cornish Pasty Shoppe. An hour later, full of traditional Cornish pasty, we take the tube to East Putney arriving at Adrian's flat around three. I feel we should knock on the front door just in case he's there. When no one answers I open the door with the key I still have, and so begins our detective work.

Although Adrian is not here, the evidence points to the fact that he has been. Three NHS hospital carrier bags and some food in a Somerfield bag lie abandoned on the floor in the living room. Ham, eggs, milk, bread, wine and a tin of evaporated milk. All the components of what I know to be my brother's staple diet. Some of these things should be in the fridge. I feel uneasy about this, but decide to leave them where they are, like a policeman leaves evidence well alone, and sit down for a rest before starting on cleaning the kitchen. When I've recharged, I clean the outsides of the unit doors, wipe the radiator and the skirting boards. I'm enjoying myself. It's satisfying cleaning something that really needs a good clean, but all the time at the back of my mind I'm wondering where the hell Adrian is and, the more time passes, the more I have an increasingly unsettling feeling that something isn't right. The blood spots on the walls are disconcerting reminders of just how worrying things had become before he was admitted to hospital. I find three blood soaked towels and a T-shirt also caked with dried blood in the laundry basket. This is a lot of blood.

I'm quite happy to leave the girls chilling in front of the TV but I persevere with the cleaning, all the while worrying about Adrian. He knew we were coming today, yet he's not here and hasn't contacted me. When has my brother ever let me down in the past? He hasn't. This is so unlike him. He is one of the most reliable men I have ever known. He's *the* most reliable man I have ever known.

I carry on scrubbing.

At two a phone rings. It's Adrian's mobile in the pocket of his black leather jacket which is hanging on the back of a chair. The girls are still lounging on the sofas. All three of us look at the jacket, wide-eyed, as if we hadn't noticed it there before – which we hadn't – and yet none of us moves to answer the phone. Wherever Adrian is he obviously doesn't have his mobile. The land line then rings and I pick up. On the other end is Bryony who proceeds to tell me what's happened.

'I've had a phone call from a friend called James…' she says. Bryony is a quietly spoken, calm person who is another of Adrian's ex-girlfriends. '…James had a phone call from Carole telling him Adrian collapsed in the pub last night and is back in St George's.'

Bryony gives me Carole's number, so I ring her. Carole says she's in a shopping mall nearby but will come to the flat as soon as she can.

She arrives within the hour, small but forthright she sits opposite me on one of Adrian's sofas. In her strong cockney accent (I love hearing a real London accent again) she explains what happened.

'I was in the pub last night, you know, The Gardener's Arms, with Adrian when suddenly he couldn't breathe. The landlord and all the regulars rallied round. They wanted to call an ambulance but Adrian – being Adrian – was adamant they didn't and asked me to come with him in a taxi back here. So we got here, and I managed to get him up the stairs and sat him down – where you're sitting now – but he wasn't getting better. I was quite scared, to tell the truth. I rang the ambulance even though he told me not to. He was having trouble breathing. I thought, oh my God, he's going to die if I don't do something. I'd only bumped into him by chance in the pub in the evening. He'd been there all day.'

So, he must have been discharged from St George's, bought the food – presumably asking the taxi driver to wait while he went in the shop – dumped his bags in the lounge, and walked out again. At first I'm outraged because he went straight to the pub after being discharged from hospital. But then I think about his life coming to an end. Does it matter what he does now?

'I went with him in the ambulance,' Carole continues. 'He was in such a bad way the paramedics had to give him electric shock treatment more than once to re-boot his heart. One of them said something about all his organs shutting down. I said to the ambulance men, "He's got a sister in Somerset. Don't you think someone should contact her?"…'

'Nobody did contact me, though,' I say and we bemoan the shortcomings of the National Health Service.

After Carole has left, the girls and I abandon our cleaning schedule, cancel the dinner date we'd arranged with Jeannette, and head for St George's.

Irrationally, I decide to save the twelve pound taxi fare and take the tube to make use of the free tube travel that comes with the tickets I bought this morning. Not a good plan, since, although St George's is not far from Putney as the crow flies, by Underground it's a long circuitous journey with at least twenty stops. Our ticket also covers the buses but, because the London bus routes are a mystery to me, I absurdly plump for the Underground route. We've already been on the tube for a good half-hour when we rattle along on the Northern Line and arrive at Kennington. While we are stationary an announcement tells us Tooting Broadway station is closed due to 'an incident'. Another incident. The world seems to have gone mad with incidents and terrorists. I feel uneasy, although I try not to reveal my unease to Emily and Fran. I keep smiling and chatting before making a snap decision to get off the train at Kennington and exit the London Underground system. We emerge from the tube into the dull sunshine and afternoon heat of Kennington Road where we board a bus which seems to be heading in the general direction of Tooting.

The bus journey is horrendously hot, packed with sweaty bodies swaying and bumping together. We pass through Brixton where the rows of shops make me feel as if I'm in a different continent, hairdressers showing pictures of exotic hair styles and plaiting, African markets glittering with gaudy trinkets.

I feel sticky, anxious and uncertain that we're on the right bus. I'm so used to Frome, inner cities feel alien to me. Nevertheless, I've noticed Londoners are very friendly and polite. People who serve in shops, for example, are affable and tend to smile a lot more than they do in Frome. Is this because they are afraid? Are they smiling in case I've got a bomb in my handbag?

I tell the girls we should get off the bus as we seem to be quite close to Tooting, but two boys, who must have heard what I was saying and realised we are en route to St George's, put us right and tell us to stay on until the next stop. London is suddenly more genial, even if the bus drivers don't give you a chance to ask where the bus is going before snapping the doors shut on your heels and driving off.

By the time we get to Tooting High Street we are hungry and naively I plump for an Albanian burger bar where the girls choose burgers and I force down a hideously fat-soaked meal of ribs and chips. The ribs are like leftover, spat-out lamb gristle which has been marinated in lard and then put out in the rain for a week. This culinary experience is aggravated by the fact that the man serving doesn't understand the word 'glass' when I request a drinking vessel for my can of Fanta. From looking around me, I suspect this restaurant is only frequented by friends and relations of the owner. I drink my Fanta from the can, having managed to secure the aid of two straws but feel quite ill after this meal, although the girls seem to cope with theirs. If I'm sick at least we're heading for the right place.

We reach the hospital as dusk falls. The sky is a shimmering grey, promising the end to one of the few really hot summer days of the year. I'm exhausted and fearful of what we might find, especially as we don't know which ward Adrian is in. I just can't recall what Carole said.

'Richmond Ward,' Fran says with a click of her fingers.

'Brilliant! You're right,' I say. And in Richmond Ward we find him.

The first thing I notice about Adrian is the oxygen mask he's wearing – you can't really miss it – and the fact that he looks so ill. Then I notice his hands. His fingers are a strange colour. A yellowy-brown, as if they're nicotine stained. Although my brother used to be a heavy smoker – my God, isn't smoking cigarettes the root of his problems? Damn Sir Walter Raleigh. Couldn't he have been content with the potatoes? – I'm sure Adrian hasn't had a cigarette since his last farewell puff on the balcony when he was admitted here for the heart bypass. On closer inspection I realise the discolouration on his hands is in fact…faeces. Despite all the signs around the hospital *Beat the Bugs, Wash your hands before and after entering the Ward*, etc., my brother is lying in a hospital bed with his hands covered in shit.

He's semi-conscious and lifts a finger towards his right eye as if to rub it. I lunge towards him, grabbing his finger just in time. A male nurse, the only visible member of staff on the ward, is busy changing the bedding of another patient, so I clean

Adrian's hands for him with a paper towel I've dipped in water from a sink near his bed. It's now almost ten pm and we aren't supposed to stay too long. This is just an assessment ward. The nurse arrives at Adrian's bed.

'Are you going to wash my brother?' I ask. 'Only he appears to have...poo on his hands.' Why doesn't the English language have a comfortable word for the product of human defecation? Faeces sounds too pompous, poo too childish, shit too rude. The nurse seems harassed.

'I'm going to wash him now,' he replies, swishing the curtain around the bed. I get the hint but I'm reluctant to leave so soon.

'Is it possible to speak to a doctor?' I ask.

'You can try the nurses' station,' he says pointing us towards the door.

Verity Jones is a registrar who I manage to find at the change of shift. She takes us into a meetings room off the ward where we can talk in private. During our conversation I discover she's from Freshford near Bath. She's pencil thin in black regulation trousers and her skin is flawless. She's young and, although not necessarily pretty, she becomes attractive as soon as she starts speaking. I imagine her at a party with other medics, juggling plates of canapés and glasses of white.

'How can I help you?' she asks.

'What I really want to know is what's wrong with Adrian? How has he ended up here?'

She describes the effects of an irregular heartbeat which has been brought on by excessive alcohol consumption. She exudes passion for her job and is very generous with me.

'After excessive drinking the heartbeat can go out of control. He's here so we can treat this condition.'

'In view of his situation I suppose he was just drowning his sorrows.'

Verity looks bemused. 'What *is* his situation?'

'He was only discharged from Rodney Smith Ward yesterday. Surely everything is in his medical notes.'

'I haven't had a chance to read his notes.'

'My brother has cancer and has been given a terminal prognosis. He only has a year to live.'

'Ah. I do apologise. I'm so sorry. I deal specifically with hearts,' she explains. 'Adrian was brought in with a heart problem and it's my job to stabilize his heart. We don't always have the time or opportunity to read every patient's notes.'

'He must have gone straight to the pub the minute he got home from here yesterday!' I feel I should be disapproving since his actions have brought him back here.

'Don't be too hard on him,' Verity goes on. 'The sort of news he's had is a huge amount to take in. You can't blame him for behaving erratically. And if he's alcohol dependent then he's likely to turn to alcohol in a crisis.'

'Alcohol dependent? *Is* he?' I'm shocked. Alcohol dependent sounds like a down-and-out sitting on a park bench nursing a bottle of meths.

'Yes he is. But the medical definition of alcohol dependency is quite low,' she explains. 'In other words you wouldn't have to drink a huge amount to be clinically described as alcohol dependent.'

Despite the bleak news she's giving me – that on top of all his other woes, my brother is, at least in the terminology of the NHS, an alcoholic – I like her. This young woman who's crossed my path on this hot June night in the middle of St George's Hospital in Tooting. Other people are trying to get hold of her if her bleeper is anything to go by, but she doesn't attempt to terminate our conversation. Instead she skilfully leaves that to me, giving me a sense of my own importance. We are all important, Adrian, myself, Emily and Frances who are in the room with us. The situation we are in, matters. If not, then what is the point of her job? It's Verity's job to help.

At quarter past eleven, before leaving, we look back on

Adrian. He's asleep now and I watch him for a moment. He's not the man he was. He's frail, ill, vulnerable. But the tie of love outweighs everything. My brother is a kind and gentle man. A funny man, a clever man. An individual. A one off. But he's lost his way. It's my own eyes I have to wipe now.

'Come on, Mum,' Em says. 'I think we ought to go. That nurse over there is giving us a funny look.'

Sunday 1st July 2007 – morning

I leave Emily asleep in her half of the bed we shared last night and re-launch myself into cleaning. The phone rings a few times. Stan from The Gardener's rings to see how Adrian is. Bryony rings for an update and I tell her the details of how Adrian got discharged and then readmitted to St George's within the space of twenty-four hours.

'Silly boy,' she says.

All morning the old Roger McGough poem keeps going through my head. *Let me die a youngman's death. Not a clean and inbetween the sheets…*

At lunchtime Jeannette and Kyria arrive. They've brought an upright Hoover as I'm finding Adrian's Henry hard going. I worked with Kyria and Jeannette when I was an Education Welfare Officer in the seventies and we've remained friends since.

One of the remits of the job of the Education Welfare Officer was, and still is as far as I know, to persuade disaffected children to attend school. When I started the job I was based in Peckham until I was transferred to Kensington. The areas were more similar than one might imagine. Both had families living in appalling conditions where the pervading smell was of rotting garbage and urine. These were homes, given my middle-class upbringing, I previously had no idea existed. During my time as an Education Welfare Officer I met parents who'd been imprisoned for murder and others with mental illnesses which could have put me at physical risk.

As Education Welfare Officers, once we'd employed all reasonable means to get the absentees back to school, if they still

THE MAN WHO DIDN'T GO TO NEWCASTLE

failed to attend, we were expected to begin court proceedings. The first family I took to court were the Chapmans, a mother, father and two sons living in a ground-floor council flat in the Walworth Road area of Peckham.

The Chapmans were desperately hard up. Mr Chapman lost his job in the print when multiple sclerosis took hold. He'd sit hunched in a wheelchair – always welcoming me into his home – but anyone could see he was a beaten man. His wife was a small busy lady who'd offer me a cup of tea and maybe a biscuit. She could do nothing to get her two sullen teenage boys out of bed and into school.

I met her in the anteroom of the court on the day of their hearing. My role was an impossible mixture of persecutor and comforter. As I stood up before the magistrate and read out details of the meetings and conversations we'd had about school attendance I felt like a traitor. At the same time as grassing them up I was supposed to support and guide the family throughout their ordeal.

I'll never forget the frightened form of Mrs Chapman as she greeted me at the court in Walworth. Looking smaller than ever outside the confines of her home, she sat in her best clothes, with a brown plastic handbag perched on her knee. It was probably her best bag that she'd taken out of the wardrobe and dusted down for this occasion. Not even an occasion to enjoy. For some reason it made me think of my mother's crocodile skin handbag from Mappin and Webb which she kept wrapped in tissue paper. The Chapmans were fined. One of the boys had a couple of present marks in the register as a result, but not for long.

Another family that stuck in my mind were the Warlocks from Lakeside Road, the most deprived, impoverished and frightening area on my Kensington patch where at least one murder was known to have taken place in the past year. The Warlocks were a first generation West Indian family with five

60

children who lived on the top floor of a dilapidated council house.

Mr Warlock was a dapper little man, a tad old for his role as father to such young children, who appeared worn down with the struggle of dealing with the authorities. His wife, who suffered from schizophrenia, was twice his height and easily three times his width. When Mrs Warlock spoke to me, which wasn't often, she did so facing the wall in the dingy half-painted purple hallway of their Lakeside Road flat.

'What you want, Missy?' she'd mumble at the wall. I'd answer with my spiel about school attendance and how important it was for her children to be in school, quoting numbers of unexplained absences with the inevitable threat of prosecution. Of course, nothing I said had any impact on Mrs Warlock.

It was the Warlocks who contributed to my decision to leave the job. A case conference with Social Services agreed the four older children should be taken into care in order to get them into school. I could see they were a weird, unconventional family, but they were a family. I despaired at the way Social Services tried to impose their own middle-class values and didactic ethics onto people who had a right to be who they were. I may have been wrong, but some of the Local Authority homes were as dodgy, if not more so, than the family homes the children were coming from.

Today I'd imagined Kyria and Jeannette would drop the upright Hoover off and have a cup of tea and a chat, but they've come with their metaphorical working hats on and get stuck into cleaning my brother's flat like regular Kim and Aggies. How did I get such brilliant friends? They even mop the balcony, although this elicits a torrent of complaints from the downstairs neighbour who says she's getting flooded. Whoops. Oh well. At least Adrian has the most spotless balcony in the block.

While dusting the bookcase in his spare room I pick up a pack of photographs and notice some are of a holiday Adrian spent in Wales in the seventies with a group of friends. I remember this trip vividly, although mainly from the distress at being left out. Adrian was in his first year at Warwick University studying pure and applied maths. During the summer vac a big team of West Wickham-ites rented a cottage in Wales and just hung out. How I longed to go too. But I was still a schoolgirl and not part of their gang. The closest I got to being included was waving them off as Adrian drove away in the strange yellow van he'd acquired whilst in Leamington Spa. The van, rather oddly, had a bathroom tap fixed onto the front of the bonnet which at the time seemed 'far out' but on reflection, why would a van have a tap on the bonnet? Could it have been previously owned by a plumber? One careful owner. Faucet included. All I saw of the Welsh holiday were the photos Adrian brought back of the 'team' looking as wild as characters in *Lord of The Flies*, with their shirts open and bandanas tied around their long hair, making V signs at the camera.

Next I come across a photo of Den, one of Adrian's old uni friends who I haven't thought about for years although I send his family a card every Christmas. Maybe I should write to him now? Should I be letting people know what's happening to Adrian?

The soft burr of Kyria still hoovering in the living room soothes me as I continue my cleaning. Propped against the skirting board is another photo which has been blown up and mounted on cardboard and shows Adrian, myself and Mac walking down a lane in London. It's from a later era, a few years after the Welsh farmhouse trip.

In fact it's a trip of a different kind. More the chemically induced variety. All three of us wear broad smiles which caused my mother to comment on the whole batch of photos we took that afternoon.

'What lovely photos. You all look so happy. It's so nice to see you enjoying the sights of London together in the sunshine. You spend much too much time sitting in darkened rooms listening to records.' None of us liked to spoil the illusion by telling her we were high on hallucinogens at the time.

I only took acid once and the only person I would have considered taking it with was Adrian. The trip itself was good fun. I mistook an emergency exit door in the Tate Gallery for a work of art, which seemed hilarious. And we all had to be guided across the road by my (non-tripping) boyfriend, Bruce, in Piccadilly Circus – equally side-splitting. But as the drug began to wear off, when brightly coloured pavements stopped melting into each other and we'd tired of cracking up at the sight of a random ice cream van or shops selling gentlemen's underwear, we went into a pub where Adrian started crying into his beer. We knew we were coming down. He'd taken acid before. He started talking about his future plans, saying he'd decided to buy a sports car, drive it round London, burn himself out. But another of his plans was to sever all ties with our parents.

'I'm not going to see the folks any more,' he said.

'You're not serious, are you? Surely,' I challenged him. 'They'd be devastated.'

Adrian seemed upset. Mac told me to back off. And so ended the trip. I didn't see why Adrian wanted to break away from our parents but his relationship with them had always been a grey area for me. I never fully understood why he'd left home to board at St Christopher, and I'd never dared ask, since this seemed a taboo topic.

On the back of the photo of us tripping, which I'd mounted on cardboard and given Adrian as a Christmas present, is a little sticker showing a blonde child in a red cape carrying a basket. On the sticker I've written *To Adrian, love from Ali* and a hand written poem. Well, not a poem as such – it's the lyrics from the third verse of "Brain Damage" from *Dark Side of The Moon* by Pink Floyd.

And if the dam breaks open many years too soon
And if there is no room upon the hill
And if your head explodes with dark forebodings too
I'll see you on the dark side of the moon.

And if the cloud bursts, thunder in your ear
You shout and no one seems to hear.
And if the band you're in starts playing different tunes
I'll see you on the dark side of the moon.

What made me copy those words in 1973? How could I ever
have guessed I'd be reading them thirty-two years later in such
circumstances? They seem strangely pertinent now. Did Adrian
shout and no one seemed to hear? *Dark Side of the Moon* remains
one of his favourite albums to this day.

Sunday 1st July 2007 – afternoon

K yria and Jeannette pack up their cleaning gear and are off in a whirl of hugs and kisses, humping the Hoover down the steps back to Kyria's car. Just before the girls and I leave, there's a knock on the front door. It's Adrian's neighbour.

'I'm Gary. From the flat upstairs,' he says pointing upwards. 'I just thought I'd come to check everything's alright. I haven't seen Adrian for a while.'

Gary is tall, camp and confident, with in-your-face glasses. I give him a brief summary of Adrian's plight. I'm surprised at the amount he knows about Adrian as Adrian has never mentioned him.

'I'm really sorry to hear about that,' Gary says. 'I've noticed him decline over the past couple of years. He used to be really fit and played a lot of tennis. But recently he's been looking a bit stooped and not as smart. I wondered if he'd been drinking. Going to the pub too much…I think he might have been lonely.'

Gary's words stab me. *Lonely.* Of course he was lonely. I have an image of myself surrounded by my family at home and Adrian alone in this flat, and I'm crushed. In amongst his paperwork I've come across a letter from a dating agency called Cavendish Avenues. How many solitary days and nights had he spent in this flat and how often had his loneliness driven him towards The Gardener's Arms in search of company. How often had he then made the now seemingly sad and solitary walk home at closing time? Gary gives me his card and entreats me to ring him if I need anything. He says Mary in flat three has been worried about Adrian too. And yet I'd seen this block as being totally anonymous. But then, no one could live somewhere for twenty-two years and not know anyone. Even in London.

I lock up the flat and we return to the hospital – this time by cab. Adrian has been moved from the assessment ward back to Rodney Smith. When we arrive I have to try to compose myself, because he's behaving so strangely – trying to get out of bed when he's not strong enough to even stand up, let alone walk. He's back in the same style hospital gown with no proper fastening at the back. My previously gorgeous brother seems to be turning into a bonkers old man. Emily appears to be on the verge of tears. Starting to feel tears burn my eyes too, I leave his bedside and walk around the corner to be alone.

A student nurse, Yasmin, seeing my distress takes me off to the visitors' room where we talk for half an hour about life, our children, cancer. She thinks the current increase in cancer is fuelled by our lifestyles. Yasmin is studying to be a nurse but she's also going through the menopause, has five children *and* is a lone parent. She's the sort of person who touches your heart – even though she yawns at least three times during our conversation. Am I boring her? Or is she just worn out? But she's so kind. All these people, so kind.

After my conversation with Yasmin I return to the ward. Adrian seems calmer and has sent the girls out for a newspaper. Verity Jones arrives to see one of the other patients.

'Haven't you been to bed yet?' I ask her.

'Yes,' she says and laughs. 'It's alright, I've got the day off tomorrow and I'm going to Wimbledon. How are you getting back to Frome?' she asks.

'We'll get the train later,' I reply. 'Enjoy the tennis!'

I realise we're talking about Wimbledon in front of Adrian. One of the highlights of his year. Tennis, the love of his life. He's even been a member of the Wimbledon club. His flat is full of

Wimbledon memorabilia – T-shirts, towels, programmes, lots of tennis racquets and balls.

My mind slips back to the summer of '83 when Peter was working abroad and Adrian had won, through his club, two tickets to the men's finals. McEnroe was playing Chris Lewis, an un-seeded New Zealander, and Adrian invited me to go with him. As a non-tennis fan, I felt a bit of a fraud going to such a historic match but, at that time, McEnroe was as much a media star as a tennis player. Adrian drove to West Wickham to pick me up on a boiling June day. I left Jack with my parents and we sped off to Wimbledon in his Alfa Romeo.

Three things strike me about that afternoon. Why Adrian asked *me* to share the tickets; how extraordinarily smaller the centre court was in the flesh than it appeared to be on TV; and the fact that, despite Adrian being a huge tennis fan, we left as soon as the main match was over and didn't bother to stay to see some of the other stars take part in doubles matches. In those days Adrian was always on the hop. We whizzed off from Wimbledon to a nearby pub, downing a quick half, and then to another pub before speeding back to West Wickham.

I felt as if I'd been caught in the eye of a hurricane. It was a nice feeling and I was flattered to have been chosen to go with him – but I do remember wondering what woman could keep up with his lifestyle on a permanent basis. Maybe none.

Now my poor brother appears confused and old before his time. He renewed his tennis club membership in May but, in light of his current situation, this seems an optimistic and unnecessary expenditure. I suggest he watches the tennis on the TV suspended above his bed, but he can't find the television card I bought yesterday. I can't find it either so I begin the rigmarole again of trying to reconnect Adrian's television. The whole television scenario takes ages with me phoning, going up and down the corridors asking disinterested members of staff where the television card machine is, giving out my credit card details willy-nilly to complete strangers. I have to get this telly sorted for Adrian before I go. Eventually everything comes together and we get a picture on his screen.

Frances has the remote and is triumphantly ready to tune in to Adrian's choice of programme.

'What would you like to watch, Adrian?' she asks.

'Nothing,' he replies, deadpan.

I resist the urge to laugh. After all this palaver, he doesn't even *want* to watch television.

'I suppose I could watch *Rome* at nine.' One of his other loves – history.

Why would he want to watch TV anyway? Everything is beginning to get to him. Things have changed. Before, we were working towards the discharge and now…now we have taken a big tumble downwards on the ladder leading to…what? Perhaps he will be able to step upwards again. I *will* him to be able to step upwards. After all, he seems to be on a lot of medication at the moment. Once he gets out of here and off the strong drugs things will improve. They must. They will.

Before we leave his bedside, I hold his hand. When did I last do that? When we were three or four perhaps? In those innocent primary school days when I still believed I'd marry him…

Sunday 1st July 2007– evening

We leave Tooting and take the tube to Paddington. The Westbury train from Paddington mainline is packed and the only spare seats we can find are in a First Class carriage. When the ticket inspector comes round we upgrade for just ten pounds. Brilliant.

I settle into the journey, cosy in my soft, wide, elitist seat, but soon decide I need some refreshment and recall something the ticket inspector told me – as a First Class passenger I'm entitled to a freebie at the buffet counter. I hurry off down the aisle, swaying with the carriage. Even First Class carriages sway. At the buffet car I order a tea. This is my first mistake. I don't show my upgraded ticket *before* ordering my tea. Instead, I show it *afterwards*. The waiter presents me with two teas – the one I ordered before showing my ticket, and the one I'm entitled to for free.

'That will be one-pound-eighty, madam,' he says, charging me for the first cup of tea.

Two polystyrene cups sit on the counter. 'But I only want one,' I say, 'and I understood my drink would be free as I'm travelling First Class.'

'Yes,' he patiently explains as if I am primary school age, 'but to get your complimentary beverage you have to show your ticket *before* I pour it.'

'But what difference does that make?' I persevere, even though it's clear I've already lost the battle before it began.

'You have to show your ticket *before* I pour the tea,' the jobsworth repeats.

I survey my two teas – my free tea, and the one costing one-pound-eighty.

'Can I just take the free one?' I ask. And in fact, they are just two cups of boiling water as I realise now I have to insert the tea bag myself before adding the milk too. So, we are quibbling over two plastic cups of hot water. I look around at the queue of fellow passengers forming behind me. Some are smiling with a supportive 'yes we know, and we do sympathise, but basically we're relieved this is happening to you and not us' kind of look.

'Anyone want to buy a cup of tea?' I ask weakly. A few people snigger but there are no takers. I carry both 'teas' precariously back towards our seat. Maybe one of the girls will want the spare tea…I mean, cup of very hot water. Very hot water which, as the carriage lurches to one side, splashes my hand. Ouch.

During the course of the journey I realise we aren't on the Westbury train after all. We have to change at Bath. It's already dark when we sit tired and huddled round a table together in the waiting room at Bath Spa station. A sad-looking boy is curled up in a chair by the window. It's Sunday night, so still technically the weekend and my mood is lifted by the arrival of a young couple who breeze in looking dressed up for a party. They sit (thankfully) behind my daughters where they can't see them and the girl produces some complicated paraphernalia from her bag, laying various bits of paper and powder on the table. They then snort some white powder…

Today is the first day of the new smoking ban in all public places. These two youngsters don't seem deterred by the security cameras everywhere on every station in the UK filming our every move – and now also presumably making sure we don't surreptitiously light up the odd Silk Cut.

So…no tobacco allowed in public places as of today, but cocaine? Fine, just carry on snorting. They'll be handing it out free to First Class passengers next. Oh, but do show your ticket *before* snorting, madam…

Once home I tell Peter the news of our London escapades. 'It all sounds a bit seedy,' he says.

The July issue of the local parish magazine lies on our kitchen table. I pick it up and skim through the pages as I drink today's last, and least stressful, cup of tea. I think to myself as I read the news of the local villages, yes, this is my life now – news of bell-ringing rotas in the churches, of book clubs and gardening tips, the June weddings in the village. There's even a report of a church service in one of the adjoining villages held specifically for pets that was attended by eight dogs, four cats, two kittens, one lamb and a horse.

'Dogs,' the report says, '*ranged in size from a St Bernard downwards. All of the animals behaved impeccably, not even a bark out of place.*' Can animals go to heaven, though? I thought they didn't officially have souls, so what's the point in them taking part in acts of worship?

Okay, the news in the parish mag isn't particularly relevant to me – I don't belong to the book club, haven't met the happy couples getting spliced, and Billy didn't attend the bestial church service – but nevertheless this is my world and I realise it has been for a long time.

The person I am on July 1st 2007 doesn't even flinch at the report of a church filled with livestock.

Monday 2nd July 2007

I'm glad to be home and back to working on the critiques for the Frome Festival Short Story Competition. While I'm typing away on the computer, Welsh Phil phones to say he's just home from his holidays and is worried about Adrian.

'I spoke to him earlier on his mobile and he says he's not feeling too good and won't make the pub quiz tonight.'

I knew my brother could be the master of the understatement but this is ridiculous. The man's in hospital with heart malfunction, cancer of the lung, kidney, liver and pancreas. He's acting bonkers, wearing a paper nightie and disposable pants, and he's apologising for not going to the pub quiz tonight. Now I've heard everything.

I met Welsh Phil when Adrian was in hospital last time. He turned up at Adrian's bedside when I was there, although I hadn't twigged then just how important their relationship was. In fact Phil and Adrian are close friends and drinking buddies who go on a pub-crawl every Saturday night. On the phone Phil comes across as such a genuine person, it's impossible not to warm to him. With his lilting Welsh accent and his deferential, hesitant manner, Phil comes up trumps.

'What about a convalescent home? When Adrian leaves the hospital?' he says. 'I mean, I don't know what you had planned? And I don't want to interfere at all. It's not really any of my business but maybe something like that would help him recover his strength a bit and then...I mean I don't really know...it might help?'

'What a great idea!' I say.

As soon as I put the phone down I google convalescent homes and come up with two in Wells.

Later, I phone Adrian while I'm waiting in Asda car park for Emily and Frances to meet me after school. He croaks in reply as I tell him my plans as suggested by Phil and I can't hear him properly, but he does say he's much better. This is such good news. He is going to climb back up that ladder again after all.

I'm still waiting for the girls when the sky turns purple and then gun metal grey. The rain is as sudden as it is heavy. So heavy I put the windscreen wipers on, even though I'm stationary. I can't ever remember a summer like this. And I don't only mean the weather. The girls arrive bedraggled and we whip round the supermarket with our trolley.

Adrian rings in the evening, keen to talk.

'I had a nightmare and all the staff came running to my bed. I've also got pneumonia,' he says and then coughs as if to give weight to this new revelation. I wonder what else there is he could have wrong with him. And yet at the same time I'm not sure what to believe. Has he really had a nightmare or did he perhaps try to get out of bed the way he did when I was there?

I can't see any point in pursuing this and so I sympathise and then change the subject to our previous discussion about convalescent homes.

Pushing him forward, pushing him away from St George's Hospital. Always pushing.

At night, before I go to bed, with the bathroom door locked, I cry in the shower. I cry and I cry. The water runs through my hair, down my face, into my mouth, and I cry some more. I cry as I remember what Yasmin, the trainee nurse said to me.

'Let it out. Better out than in. If you keep it in you'll make yourself ill.'

Yasmin, one of the London angels.

I do what she told me. In the privacy of the shower in my bathroom. Boy, do I let it out.

Tuesday 3rd July 2007

Adrian thinks he'll be discharged in a few days' time and I'm worried if I don't take action and get him into a convalescent home he'll just end up back in St George's again – via the contents of a wine glass or ten. When he's discharged this time I'll have to go up to London – or someone will – to look after him until we can sort out a nursing home. At the flat there will be no one to look after him. My mother's prophesy comes true.

Once I've got the girls off to school, I sit down in front of the computer…and think. During my last visit to the hospital Adrian told me about a peppercorn subscription he's been paying into a private health insurance scheme called Benenden which he joined when working for the Civil Service in his twenties.

'I'm sure this Benenden has a convalescent home. It's in Kent but I'd like to go there. PDQ,' he said.

'Kent! But you'd be miles away from us and…everyone,' I said, unable to think of anyone we still knew who lives remotely near Kent.

'But it will be free,' he said. 'I've been paying into this scheme for years.'

I could tell where he was going with this. He wants to get his money's worth. Maybe all those subs of one pound a month would now be his salvation.

'But you've got money,' I told him – not for the first time. I know for certain he has numerous shares both in this country and abroad, as well as other savings accounts, and ISAs. I also know he hasn't been working for a couple of years, is classified by the DSS as a 'Jobseeker' and that he regards himself as skint. But he's got savings for a rainy day. How much rain does a man need?

'You could cash in some of your shares,' I suggested, skirting around the obvious fact that he's not going to need them soon and so he might as well spend, spend, spend. This was hard to point out, though. His voice was gravelly and he seemed so low.

I discover the Benenden home is in North East Kent and decide to ring them later.

Meanwhile I go to town and run into a few people. In Frome there seems to be lots going on. Everyone is talking about the Frome Festival. The festival we've worked towards all year begins this Friday. I am the person who organises the Frome Festival Short Story Competition and the prize-giving lunch which takes place in twelve days' time. But will I even be there? This no longer seems a definite.

When I get home I ring Benenden. They say they have a hospital but not a convalescent home.

'I could research suitable convalescence for your brother as he has been contributing to our scheme,' the Benenden employee tells me.

Adrian will be glad to hear this.

Later, Charlotte, the Discharge Nurse at St George's, rings me to say Adrian has told her he'll be coming to Somerset to be near me. I feel glad, touched to hear he's chosen to be with us, and yet afraid at the same time. It is up to me now to play an increasingly positive role. I ring Carol. She is such a nice person. I can see why Adrian has stayed friends with her for so long.

His relationship with Carol goes back to the seventies, a period when our lives were separate though intertwined. At the beginning of the decade when Adrian was still at Warwick he visited me a couple of times at Essex University where I was an English undergraduate. I remember him swaggering down the path away from the lecture theatre block with his two friends, thinking there was no one at Essex quite as glamorous.

After he graduated from Warwick, Adrian lived in a flat in

Muswell Hill. Those were the days when we rolled joints on LP covers, and smoked to the sounds of the Steve Miller Band, and Pink Floyd. After graduating I moved into the Muswell Hill flat when he moved on to start a new life in Cheltenham with two friends in a rented Georgian apartment on the London Road. I lived in Cheltenham too for a while. At that time people seemed to drift around. Jobs, flats, friends, lovers – were easy-come, easy-go. In Cheltenham Adrian fell in love with a local lass called Angie. Later he swapped Angie for the more stable Carol, who I'm talking to now.

We discuss the possibility of Adrian going into a convalescent home.

'But those places are so expensive,' Carol says.

'Money is not the problem,' I say, again reluctant to point out that Adrian might as well spend everything he's got.

'But they are incredibly expensive,' she persists.

'He can afford it. Adrian has got money tied up in various places.' Once more I ask myself, what is this money for if not to spend now in his hour of need? Adrian tends to be in this same mindset as Carol. He's been hard up for a while trying to set up a business, but he seems to be overlooking the savings he's stored up for his retirement. It's the old rainy day thing again, and it's pretty well pouring down from where I'm standing.

'I suppose he could sell his flat in Putney,' Carol suggests.

'But selling property can take months,' I say. 'Shares can be cashed within hours in any bank. Money should be the least of his problems.'

I phone Adrian during the afternoon but there's no answer. He phones me back at about ten on our land line and Ed answers. Ed (who is twenty-one) hasn't spoken to Adrian for some months. I can tell by the expression on his face that he's shocked by the change in Adrian's voice. Ed's trying his best, but it's obvious he'd rather hand the phone over to me.

Adrian is ringing to see how I got on with Benenden.

'They're going to look for a good convalescent home for you. We need to get you strong again. You need some nursing care where someone is looking after you, helping you build up your strength.' I speak these words but feel in my heart this won't be the case. I'm aware I'm saying 'convalescent home' when what I really mean is 'nursing home' and I know from my experience when Mum had dementia that most nursing homes are unsatisfactory places. What will become of him? I can't bear this pity I have. I can't bear feeling sorry for him. It's breaking my heart.

During the daytime I'm fine. From the hours of nine in the morning to nine at night I am practical and clear headed, but by the time night comes the unbearable sadness overwhelms me. Adrian ends the phone conversation because he's tired. His voice is getting ever weaker. He finds it exhausting just to speak.

I go upstairs to say goodnight to the girls. The *ITN News* has concentrated on recent terrorist attacks and Emily is anxious.

'Look, darling. Think about it,' I try calming her, 'have you seen any terrorists in Great Elm recently?' The idea is so absurd we both laugh. But I don't mention the 'shoe bomber', Richard Reid, who strangely enough did live in Frome. And he was originally a South Londoner, born in Bromley...

Wednesday 4th July 2007

I try phoning Adrian in the morning while I'm out walking the dog, but his phone is switched off. I'm about to try again in the evening when Carol rings me. She's upset following a visit to the hospital earlier on.

'I'm talking to him and then he keeps drifting off mid-sentence,' she says. I remember now that Carol is a big talker. I've always thought one of the reasons Adrian likes her is because she's so garrulous and I too find her easy to get on with. Neither Adrian nor I are big talkers. 'I think he's sedated. And now he's got a drip in his arm. I feel quite upset about it all. Anyway, I just thought you ought to know. I can't imagine how many different drugs he's on.'

I ring the hospital and a nurse on the ward duty desk answers.

'What actual treatment is my brother getting?' I ask. 'I mean, is he on lots of drugs? Is he going to have chemotherapy?'

'No, he's not due to have chemo until he leaves. Then he'll come back as a day patient. At the moment he's having injections of Fragmin which thins the blood.'

This explains the drip, I suppose. I ask to speak to Charlotte.

'Do you have any idea when my brother will be discharged again?' I ask her.

'He's not due to be discharged because he's still being treated with antibiotics for a lung infection.'

Is this the pneumonia? Surely it must be. Is the drip in his arm for antibiotics rather than Fragmin? Stupidly I ring off without asking these questions, because, suddenly, there are just too many. Everything seems such a mess. So difficult to get my head around. But I have to remind myself to count my blessings.

I have a house I love, a family I love, a job I love. And tomorrow I collect my tickets for our holiday in Portugal at the end of July…

Thursday 5th July 2007

I ring St George's yet again to find out when Adrian will be discharged. Charlotte says they don't know because he's still on antibiotics.

'I'm thinking about having him transferred to the Benenden Hospital. It's a private hospital in Kent and is part of the Civil Service insurance scheme Adrian told me about,' I tell her. 'I'm sure they will take him there.'

Even if it is in Kent I feel he'll be better off in a private hospital than in St George's, but when I ring Benenden they say part of their hospital has been shut down. Currently they only offer diagnostic and surgical wards. So they can't help us after all.

I eventually speak to Adrian at eight-thirty at night. It's getting harder to understand him. When I tell him about the Benenden set-up he sounds angry.

'Look, I've been paying twenty-five pounds per month for twenty years into this scheme. That's six thousand pounds.'

When he first mentioned Benenden he said he was paying a pound per month now it's increased twenty-five-fold. The conversation is disheartening. He finishes the call without saying goodbye, which is hurtful and so unlike him. He seems a bit more lucid now, but is very tired. Will he get better before he gets worse? Another thing he slips in before he ends the call – the doctors are doing tests to check whether the cancer has spread to his bones. How can he take any more of this? Although, he also said 'they *think* I've got cancer' – which is pretty much what this whole nightmare is all about. It's fair to conclude he's not sure what's happening because of the drugs he's on. Given the circumstances, is this really such a bad thing?

I ring Charlotte back to tell her Benenden is not an option after all. Instead I'll go ahead with finding a convalescent home near Frome.

Crysse, my writing buddy, rings me. We talk about the 'Lying Competition' on Sunday which is part of the Frome Festival. I've put my name down for it without knowing what it is. I realise as I talk to Crysse that the other literary bods presume I won't be taking part in anything in the festival because they've heard about my brother. But what can I do? Sit at home and think? Surely I will be there and I resolve to get to Body Basics tomorrow for a workout. In the afternoon I have a radio interview on FromeFM.

Friday 6th July 2007

Day one of this year's Frome Festival.

I ring Adrian whilst walking Billy to touch base before I go into town for the radio interview. Christine, one of the presenters, wants to talk to me about the short story competition. Afterwards she's going to read one of my stories on air. It's only small-time, small-town stuff, but my life seems so full and, in contrast, Adrian's so horribly bleak.

His voice is still very hoarse and I have to strain to catch what he's saying. Actually, he's repeating what he said yesterday, that they are testing him for bone cancer. But he has walked to the hospital shop with the aid of a stick, which is good news.

'I've found a convalescent home in Wells. Peter and I will come up to London to collect you as soon as they discharge you from St George's,' I tell him.

'I'm not sure what to bring with me…' he says and I realise this is a massive step for him. A native Londoner fleeing to the country. He's lived in his flat for over twenty-two years. It's full of stuff. Adrian is not a man who has ever de-cluttered. What should he bring with?

'Don't worry,' I reassure him. 'It's not as if we can't go back again if you need anything.'

After we've rung off I carry on over the stile, along the path by the river that leads towards the duck pond. Today the river is high and swirling fast. Mushrooms of white foam nudge the banks. Over the last few weeks the rain has turned the water in cascading liquid mud.

I think a lot when I'm out with Billy. At this moment I'm thinking: *How have we got to this awful situation in such a seemingly short space of time?* My thoughts echo the words my mother spoke a few weeks before she died when I was driving her to Bath hospital after she'd broken her arm. I stopped the car outside the crematorium to adjust her seat belt as she seemed to be slipping towards the floor. She was little and frail, confused and in pain.

'Why have you stopped here?' she said looking out of the window at the big black sign for Bath Cemetery. 'How did I come to this?'

The entrance to the crematorium was the only space without yellow lines on the long narrow road leading to Bath. As I drew up I realised this was a ghastly place to stop.

She was taken to the same place in a different car eight weeks later. I didn't have an answer at the time for my mother and had long given up trying to answer her questions. Now I have no answer to my brother's plight. How has he come to this? The answer is, I don't know.

At the pond Billy paddles in the water and barks half-heartedly at a duck. I'm wondering to myself what would this be like if things were reversed. Would Adrian help me if I was sick? Except I wouldn't be dependent on him as I have a husband and children. But I'm sure he would do what he could.

And what will it be like for us, having him here in the West Country, so close to my family? I think back to his relationship with my four children. With Jack and Ed he's been happy to play the role of the somewhat intellectual uncle. Imaginative Christmas and birthday presents have always been his forte. A card game based around the Seven Wonders of the World, an Egyptian version of Snap, a board game with ghouls and ghosts. But when I had the girls I felt, for Adrian, I'd somehow gone a step too far. As a mother of *four* children – and the new arrivals were premature twins – I'd moved too far outside his orbit. Although as the girls grew older he became more engaged with them. As soon as he could talk to them and have a joke, everything improved.

I took them to stay in his flat for a weekend when they were eight and he made a huge effort, showing us the London sights he thought would capture their imaginations. I had no idea until then how fascinated he was with the British Museum. He told me he'd devoted hours during his lunch breaks exploring every room in the building.

We posed for photos by Mummies and Egyptian relics and then travelled back, giggling in a bicycle rickshaw. The following day he lugged our suitcases around so we could visit the London Dungeon unencumbered. Although, he did carry them to one of his favourite pubs and waited for us there…

My radio interview goes well, even though they get the order of the story and interview mixed up. Jill Miller (who founded the charity, Positive Action on Cancer) is there and asks me how I am. I say 'fine'. What I don't say is 'I'm bloody awful, my brother is dying of cancer and has been given a year to live. I'm in a state of shock and going through the worst few months of my life. You're probably one of the only people I know who'd be able to help me…' But I can't say this. Jill would be too sympathetic, too kind. I would lose my composure and start sobbing in the FromeFM makeshift recording studio. Instead I tell her I'll be at her charity 'Pamper Day' at Orchardleigh House on the Tuesday.

Back home the men say they listened to my interview on FromeFM while they were at work and it sounded good. I settle down to write the last of the critiques.

The weather continues to mirror this nightmare of a summer. But curiously, despite the sadness engulfing my heart, I feel strangely content deep inside. Maybe the bleakness of Adrian's situation has made me more aware of the good things in my own. And I'm never better than when there's lots going on. I now have to focus on the festival events I'm involved in. I need a microphone for the prize-giving lunch at Orchardleigh

Golf Club on Saturday week. On the first Sunday I'm going to help at the library at an event called the Just Write Day and Wendy and Ellie from the library have offered to share their lunch with me.

Saturday 7th July 2007

Today is turning out to be my worst day. It's the beginning of the festival and in the morning I walk round town with Crysse, enjoying meeting and talking to the writers who are taking part in the Writer in Residence competition where they sit in shops and write. Over lunch one of my other writer friends mentions her novel has just been accepted by a publisher. Suddenly feel left behind, old, and annoyed with myself for not spending more time on my writing. Then I remember my parking ticket is running out and rush to my car just in time to avoid a fine from a man in a high viz jacket and peaked cap.

Before going out in the evening I speak to Adrian. He has Carol with him but obviously wants to talk. His voice sounds worse – it's almost impossible to hear what he's saying and I've started to feel my own voice going in sympathy.

Adrian wants me to take him back to the flat to get some belongings once he's discharged. I have to keep reminding myself he can do whatever he wants. He can leave the hospital, he can go home, he can move out of London, or stay put. He's neither a criminal nor a prisoner. He's just reliant on other people more than usual.

I'm happy with his plan for me to help him pack his belongings but I worry I'd have to drive up to London if I'm to bring him home. I don't mention this though.

'And there's something else which seems very odd,' he says. 'I can't spell any more.'

'Maybe it's something to do with the infection in your lungs,' I randomly suggest, though I'm struggling to find an explanation for such a bizarre development.

'I think it's to do with the drugs,' he says.

So basically, his end, there's nothing going on except various things getting worse. In the evening Peter and I go to the Food Fest in Frome market place where rows of marquees offer dishes from around the world. An Indie band are playing in the car park. We can't agree on which country's food to try. Peter has been playing golf all day and is tired. I spot a few people I know but for some reason I don't want to talk to anyone. We end up in the Indian restaurant we often go to at weekends.

When we get home Margaret rings. She's been researching the local nursing homes for me, which is so kind but I just haven't got the heart for it all. I tell her I'll talk to her another time.

By bedtime I feel empty. Empty with envy for my friend whose book is to be published. Empty because we didn't join in the festivities of the Food Fest. Empty because I couldn't be bothered to speak to anyone tonight.

I resolve to make more of an effort in future. The *Third Frome Lying Championship* is tomorrow (it's the first one, but therein lies the joke). I've said I'll take part, but I haven't prepared anything, so I'll have to use an old short story called *Stainspotting* which is a comedy about a woman who's obsessed with cleaning. But I feel as if I've lost faith in my writing. I haven't done anything new for so long.

Sunday 8th July 2007

I arrive at the library, fired up and full of enthusiasm for the Just Write Day. Most people are in a writing workshop so only a few hopeful authors are hanging around, clutching manuscripts to their chests, waiting to meet literary agent Jane Judd.

After lunch I attend a talk by publishing guru Julia McCutchen. I'm fidgety and can't seem to relax, but this turns out to be one of the most interesting talks I've been to for a while. Julia is professional, unexpectedly spiritual and incredibly focused. In the evening I send her an email to ask for coaching to help me sell my novel, *Two Blackberry Lane* – when I've finished it. I phone Adrian to tell him I'm coming to London tomorrow and will get some of his belongings from the flat. He wants his black leather jacket and keeps telling me where to find it – but I know where it is. 'I put it away in the cupboard in your bedroom,' I tell him. He continues suggesting other places to look for it. 'We cleaned up. I put everything away,' I repeat, but he persists in suggesting places where I might find it.

'It might be on a hook in my bedroom.'

'Okay,' I say. 'I'll look for it there.'

His voice is stronger today. He says he wants to get out of St George's but they won't let him out because of 'litigation'. That doesn't make sense. I think he's got the wrong word. I resolve to talk to Charlotte.

He also tells me the ward he was in has moved due to refurbishment, and he's now in Trevor Howell Ward. 'We've moved,' Adrian says, which I find unnerving since it makes him sound as if he's part of the hospital set-up. It's amazing how quickly we can become institutionalised.

'I'll see you tomorrow,' I tell him.

As soon as I walk into the pub where the Lying Competition is taking place, I regret going. Clearly all the other contestants will be *speaking* their lies whereas I've just printed off an old story to read.

After it's over, the judges call out the results. Cringe. I've won a bar of chocolate as I am in third place out of only four entries, even beaten by the organiser, who strangely seems to be a competitor too.

I get into conversation with a young man called Sam, who is recording the event for a radio station in Warminster. He makes a point of asking me lots of questions but later I feel oddly aware of him watching me, and feel unsure of what to say to him again. He's quite attractive. Perfect nose, dark, almost black hair, bright blue, lively eyes.

As I get up to leave Sam leans over towards me. 'I'm going to the Cheese and Grain after this. There's a good band on. We can get in free if you'd like to come with me.'

'Yes, okay,' I say.

Outside a few of us gather in a huddle on the pavement. Sam looks at me. 'We can go in my car,' he says.

I consider what this implies. Could he be asking me out? I'm old enough to be his mother. Possibly even grandmother. I'm wearing a wedding ring. Surely he couldn't see me as a pick up. Suddenly I feel uncomfortable about going to the Cheese and Grain with him, not least because someone might see us.

'I'll drive myself. I have to go down to the centre of town anyway to get some money from the cash point.' The more I think about going to the Cheeser with this man, the more worrying it becomes. I have to make a quick decision.

I catch his eye. 'To be honest, I don't think I should come – thanks for asking me, though. I think I should go home,' I say rather more firmly than I'd intended. He looks taken aback and a little hurt. At least I think he does. The whole episode is a shock and reminds me of the 'me' many years ago – before marriage and children. What would I have done then? Gone, of course. Maybe ended up in bed with him. But I'm not that person any more. Anyway, why is he single? If he is single, of course. And if he is single, then why is he interested in me? There's a much younger girl who was sitting at my table. He could easily have come on to her.

When I get home, I'm so glad I didn't go to the Cheese and Grain. The girls' uniforms need ironing and Fran says she thinks she may have asthma. I'm a mother – and a wife. A middle-aged woman. Behave.

I sit down with Peter to watch TV before bed.

'I must really love you, you know,' I say.

'Why?' he says barely diverting his attention away from the news.

'Because I've just turned down an invitation to go out with a gorgeous thirty-something Adonis.'

Peter grunts or farts or something and then switches to the History Channel. And then to the tennis. Wimbledon is on.

'Federer won. Isn't that great!' he says, teasing me. He puts his arm around me and gives me a hug, knowing full well I don't give a monkey's about Federer.

'I'm extremely pleased for him,' I say.

Later when we're in bed Peter asks me why I'm going up to London again tomorrow.

'Is it for any specific reason? I mean Adrian's not being discharged yet.'

I have to think for a moment before answering. Is Peter annoyed at the amount of time I'm spending in London? His question makes me pause and mull over this sequence of events I've created.

'To help Adrian, I suppose. And because I'll be busy with the festival for the next week or so. Really because I have a free day.'

Am I neglecting everyone else in my family?

Monday 9th July 2007

I have a cunning plan. I take the train from Warminster to Clapham Junction. The penny has dropped that Clapham Junction is not only nearer to Putney than Paddington, but this route is much cheaper. Once I'm aboard the train though, I realise it's committed to stopping at every outback station between Wiltshire and the metropolis.

When I eventually arrive at Clapham Junction, I discover it's not a tube station, but only a mainline. I'm surprised at myself for not knowing this – especially as my father was from Clapham.

I take a bus, even managing to work out the correct side of the road for Putney, arrive at the flat and find it is, of course, still clean! I eat some sandwiches I bought in Somerfield, watch a bit of TV, find the paperwork relating to Adrian's shares, collect his mail and then get a taxi to the hospital. The taxi driver is suited and booted and, believe me, it is hot – and has been since the weekend. 'You must be hot!' I say to him via his rear view mirror.

Adrian's in a new ward in a bed by a grubby window which takes up the whole of the outside wall. A hospital social worker, Lucy, is sitting on a chair beside him. Adrian's face is white – like thin paper.

I introduce myself because Adrian doesn't introduce me. And yet this was one of the things I've always loved about visiting him. He'd introduce me to his friends in such an affectionate way. 'This is my sister, Ali.' He made me feel as if he was proud of me. Now I sit down beside Lucy and gradually become drawn into the conversation.

Adrian seems wrapped up in his anger. Something's upset him during the ward move. As the conversation progresses I gather he went AWOL during the course of the move because he wanted to watch the men's final.

'Look,' he says to Lucy. 'These bastards can't tell me what I can and can't do. I've played tennis for forty years. I used to belong to Wimbledon tennis club.'

Lucy looks taken aback and unsure what she should say. She and I both express our sympathy. Neither of us can figure why Adrian shouldn't have watched television in the family room while the ward was being moved anyway.

'I'm new here,' Lucy says. 'But I'll look into all this for you.'

'I travelled a lot in the eighties,' Adrian says picking up on her Antipodean accent. 'I've lived in the Middle East and I've been to Malaysia, Australia, New Zealand. Where are you from?'

Lucy tells Adrian the name of her home town – Craggy Rock or some such – and he seems to know it. 'I'm sure I've been there. It's a very beautiful part of the world.'

This exchange makes me think three things. Firstly, I'd forgotten just how much travelling Adrian has done. While I was popping babies, he was exploring the globe. Secondly, I've never been anywhere further south than Athens, and thirdly, what makes someone like Lucy swap Craggy Rock for Tooting? But of course I know the answer to the last one. We move away from our homes in order to find ourselves. To understand who we are and where we fit into the world as a whole. Maybe one day Lucy will return to Craggy Rock a more fulfilled person for having braved the NHS, Tooting branch.

I want to talk to Lucy in private and suspect she may feel the same, so we pretend (for Adrian's sake) to go in search of tea. We end up sitting in the day room. I begin first.

'Why shouldn't Adrian go into the family room to watch television when they moved the ward? Why is he losing his voice? When will he be discharged? '

Lucy doesn't have answers. Why should she when she's just

landed from a different hemisphere? However, I become concerned when I discover she doesn't know what the DSS is either. She's a social worker in a huge London hospital and she isn't familiar with the abbreviation DSS. This is not right.

'But I do think you should get power of attorney,' she advises. 'And sooner rather than later.'

On my way back to Adrian's bed I bump into Yasmin, the trainee nurse with five children. I take her hand and tell her I've been thinking about her – which is true. She says 'You're looking better,' which I hope is also true.

Lucy and I reconvene at Adrian's bedside. He's calmer now and Lucy quickly tries to move the conversation on to the topic of his finances, which is clearly in her remit to address.

'I left my job in 2004. I've been in the process of setting up my own business since then. But officially I'm a Jobseeker.'

Being a Jobseeker has been one of Adrian's pet themes since he took a redundancy package from BT in 2004. Initially this new, somewhat absurd status seemed amusing as he was eligible for cheap entries to cinemas, had no intention of seeking a job, and had to make sure he was in London on Tuesday mornings to sign on. Now his job-seeking status seems less diverting. Surely no one has ever claimed a less fitting moniker.

As we try to steer the conversation towards a solution for his apparent lack of cash Adrian is keen to hammer home his status with the DSS.

'Do you know what that means? I'm a *Jobseeker*,' he repeats to the ever-ignorant Lucy.

I actually feel like crying at this point.

After he recovered from the heart bypass, Adrian returned to work at British Telecom where he was a statistician. His job was to forecast trends, but the stress of the job caused him to negotiate a redundancy package after a year. When he left he planned to set up a consultancy business with a work colleague,

Phil Gullifer. Eventually Phil Gullifer also left BT and they created a company together, Twenty-Four-Seven. Not only does Adrian have two Carol(e)s, he also has two Phils. Does he like to have two of everything?

Phil and Adrian enjoyed the conception, the procedure of setting up the business, even though the work they'd hoped for didn't pour in. Adrian has piles of Twenty-Four-Seven business cards by his computer. I found one of these cards on Mum's hospital locker after he'd visited her just before she died. I imagined him showing it to her, leaving it with her, proud – even though she was semi-conscious, foetal, incontinent, almost gone. Maybe somewhere something had registered with her. Despite his earlier post-acid resolve to burn out and not see the folks any more, Adrian's love for our mum went very deep. He was still trying to impress her in her final hours.

Most of Twenty-Four-Seven's business meetings seemed to take place in pubs and they had plenty of company outings to the races and restaurants. But 'the biz', as Adrian calls it, didn't work out as planned and after a couple of years, in order to have an income, Adrian was signing on. He'd recently been for interviews for jobs way below his qualifications. He'd been knocked back, of course. One rejection letter was on his desk in the spare bedroom. The letter thanked him for coming for an interview, but regretted the post had already been filled. I wished in my heart that he hadn't allowed himself to be subjected to this particular humiliation, but this is one of the provisos of the Jobseeker's Allowance. The recipient has to prove that they are genuinely seeking employment. The efficient way he'd pinned the newspaper ad for the job on the rejection letter somehow made it worse.

When Lucy's gone I get out the paperwork relating to the shares Adrian has in various companies throughout the world. How can one person have so many small amounts of money invested in so many different places? I shuffle through various documents and share certificates trying to persuade him to choose which to cash.

'Do you want me to have power of attorney?'

'No,' he says emphatically. 'I haven't lost my mind.'

'Okay, but we need to cash maybe just one of these shares. You need about ten grand to settle your debts so you won't have to worry about money.'

But we get nowhere. He doesn't want to part with any of the shares and keeps studying bits of paper, then other bits of paper and then reads the first bit of paper again. But he's drugged-looking too. His eyes are rolling. He looks totally awful.

'I don't need my flat any more. You can arrange to have it rented out.'

'So, you've definitely decided you won't be going back there.'

'It's up ninety shares,' he says.

'No,' I correct him. 'It's up thirty *stairs!*'

As I stuff all the share certificates back into my bag, his mobile rings. It's Carol.

'Mum's here,' he tells her. I shake my head at him.

'No, it's not Mum – has she been here?' he asks me, as if to gloss over his mistake but actually making it worse.

'No,' I say. 'Mum hasn't been here.'

A nurse appears with tonight's dinner menu. Pea and ham soup, followed by corned beef hash, with vanilla ice cream for afters. I recall the hundreds of times we've eaten together in various restaurants in different parts of the world. In 1998 Adrian and I took Mum on a cruise. The Mediterranean Medley on the P&O cruise liner, the *Oriana*.

Mum had a romantic attachment to the sea, which went back to her childhood. Having been born into an army family and brought up in India she'd travelled at regular intervals back and forth from India to Plymouth. Since Dad died she longed to sail again.

The three of us shared a cabin on the *Oriana*. How wonderful it was to cruise for days then wake up one morning with the sight of land, either a busy port or a sun-baked island. Adrian showed up at the formal meals each night in a white linen jacket and red tie. After dinner we went to the quiz, teaming up with people we'd met on board. I hadn't much experience of quizzing but thanks to Adrian's extensive general knowledge we won four bottles of champagne.

Whether floating around Monte Carlo, Barcelona, Gibraltar, Venice or on *terra firma* in Florence, London, Bath, Frome, in all the different places we'd eaten out together he was always the same, giving his order to the waiters confidently polite, charmingly inquisitive. On the *Oriana* his favourite haunt was the Cricketers Bar where he'd hang out after Mum had gone to bed. He struck up a friendship with the head waiter, who greeted him each evening with a wide smile and a knowing nod when Adrian ordered his favourite tipple, a large Armagnac.

Now he scowls at the nurse and can't decide on a pudding. The dinner arrives only to turn cold as he fiddles with the TV hanging over the bed. Since his ward change we are now back to square one with the television reception. Despite the amount of money Carol and I have spent on various cards and phone calls (over thirty pounds), because he keeps moving beds, the screen is once again blank. Meanwhile his food becomes more inedible, he gets more frustrated and I sink further into desolation. Eventually he gives up and lies back on the bed. I kiss him goodbye – I have a train to catch – and as I do so, I feel his shoulder bone through the hospital sheet.

Before leaving I stop at the nurses' station and ask to talk to one of the doctors.

'There's no one available. There's been a crisis upstairs,' a nurse tells me. I try to envisage a crisis upstairs. I have a crisis here in my heart and the doctors are all keen to speak to me – or so I've been told. Perhaps they will ring when I get home. The nurse asks if they have all my details on their computer.

Yes, they do.

I leave the ward feeling much smaller and more insignificant than when I arrived two hours ago. I trail along the meandering corridors where different names jump out at me from the rows of closed doors. Resuscitation Unit, Cardiovascular Treatment Area, Diagnostic Imaging Centre, PET Scans, Craniosacral Therapy room.

Outside I take a taxi and get the same driver we had at the weekend when I was here with Emily and Fran. He remembers my name but neither of us can remember where he took us. I think it was Leylands on the Saturday night. He says, 'Yes, but I didn't see your face.' He's nice. I like him. It's good to come across someone I know in the midst of this big, unfamiliar metropolis. As we drive past the vast black railings of the cemetery by the hospital he asks who I've been visiting.

'My brother.'

'Is he going to get better?'

I catch sight of the flowers on the graves behind the bars. 'No. He's not going to get better,' I reply. Then I feel embarrassed by his silence. Should I have wrapped my reply up into an acceptable piece of information? Pretended he's a bit better today? Some people would.

We're still passing the graveyard – it looks to be about three acres of headstones, flowers and paths. How long before Adrian is here, I wonder? A year? Maybe a bit more? Please don't let it be here. Please let him get away from this place. He's said he wants to come to Somerset rather than stay in London. Please God, let him. I leave my taxi driver at Clapham Junction.

'See you again!' he says. I feel I'm making friends in a strange kind of a way. The taxi driver, Verity, Yasmin…

On Clapham Junction station I buy Ed some Bonjela as he's got a mouth ulcer. It feels so important to get something for Ed. To still think about everyone else in my family. I wait on the platform for the Westbury train. One of the trains listed on the information board is going to Liphook and Liss. Such memories these two place names evoke. We lived in Liphook briefly when Jack was little. And Ed was born in Liss.

This is to be my last trip up to London until the Frome Festival finishes on Sunday. As I board the train home I cherish the thought of tomorrow's Pamper Day at Orchardleigh House.

Tuesday 10th July 2007

My kitchen table is awash with documents. I've sorted Adrian's paperwork into piles of share certificates, details of savings and bank accounts, and – the biggest pile of all – his bills. Sifting through these I see he's been using a credit card which is throwing up hundreds in interest.

And there's some correspondence from the dating agency.

Adrian came to our house last June when Mum's name was to be mentioned during the Sunday church service. Mum died in June 2005 and her ashes are interred in the grounds of St Mary's Church in Great Elm. Dan, the vicar, comes to the house every year and slots a scrap of paper through the letterbox inviting us to this service.

The night before the service Adrian got drunk and told me he'd signed up with a dating agency. This is one of the only times I've ever seen him really tipsy. It was after midnight and he was standing in the doorway that leads from our kitchen to the living room, swaying with a glass of whisky in his hand.

'I've arranged a date with a woman called Elsbeth,' he said. 'She sounds really interesting. She's a music teacher. Plays the violin and she's got a horse. She looks lovely. I'm looking forward to meeting her.'

Although surprised, I was pleased he was looking for a permanent partner. But I worried any prospective girlfriend wouldn't see the attractive and much sought-after person my brother used to be. The boy who brought beautiful girls home from school, the object of my school friends' fantasies, the envy of all the ordinary boys who lived nearby. Instead she'd see a stooping, prematurely ageing man who drinks too much.

A letter I find amongst his paperwork confirms my fears. It's very polite but says the agency hasn't heard back from his last introduction. I take this to mean she didn't want to meet him again. I can't dwell on this for long. But there are other letters from the same agency giving profiles of women he might be interested in dating. And one of Adrian himself.

ADRIAN'S PROFILE

Adrian is an attractive man both in looks and personality. He is fifty five years old and at 5'11 he is tall, slim to medium build with grey silver hair and blue eyes. Adrian is a Statistician by profession who has just recently set up his own company. He is a single man who lives in the South West area of London.

Educated to degree level Adrian is intelligent, articulate and interesting company. He is a well balanced, rational and socially aware gentleman with a compassionate and sensitive nature. Adrian is a confident man who has an easy going, warm nature which belies strength of character which has served him well professionally. Adrian's interests include art exhibitions, horse racing and playing tennis. He enjoys trips to the theatre, dining out and appreciates good wine.

Adrian would be looking to meet a lady with a similarly lively mind who has lots of different interests. She would be honest, reliable and feminine; a stimulating conversationalist with interesting ideas and opinions. As Adrian is keen to see more of the world and a lady who is keen to travel would be a definite advantage. Adrian has a good social life and a job he enjoys but feels that he would really like to meet a lady with whom he could build a happy lasting relationship with. (sic)

While I'm sorting through all this Adrian rings me. He sounds much better.

100

'I'm close to making a full inventory of all my finances. It's taking a while because some of them are tied up on secret internet sites,' he says.

Secret internet sites! This sounds a bit James Bond.

Then 'I think I want to stay in London,' he carries on. 'I'm not going to rot in some old fogey's home in Somerset.' His phone cuts off.

Let me die a youngman's death. Not a clean and inbetween the sheets... Again the Roger McGough poem runs through my head. Perhaps he'd rather just pass out in the pub. An inbetween the pints death...

After lunch I clear the table and drive to Orchardleigh House to the PAC Pamper Day. A woman from the WI who used to know my mother is in charge of catering.

'My husband used to cut your mother's grass,' she says as she pours me a cup of tea. 'I read one of your stories the other day.'

I'm intrigued and momentarily flattered. 'Oh really. Which one?'

'Err...I can't remember...Is your mum still alive?'

'No, she's not, I'm afraid,' I say, grabbing my tea and moving on. I climb the sweeping staircase to one of the bedrooms where I'm booked for a massage. Half an hour of bliss.

Back home Fran is painting a sign for the short story prize-giving event for Saturday. She's sprayed pink paint and glitter all over the garage floor.

Wednesday 11th July 2007

This morning I have my house dream. The dream is always the same – I have sold Moons Leaze (the house we live in) and there's no going back. In today's dream the house we're moving to is poky and dark with lots of cupboards all over the purple walls. It's nightmarish. I know I can't get Moons Leaze back and my home now seems like a wonderful, lost land. In contrast, the house we're about to move into is ghastly. As usual, my relief when I wake and realise I've been dreaming is beyond ecstasy.

After breakfast I walk the dog. When I'm in the big field where the cows sometimes are – though thankfully not today as I don't fancy being flattened by a herd of charging cattle – I phone Carol. The conversation lasts all the way through the field, and back. Maybe the cows are elsewhere, but the cowpats I have to dodge prove they have recently been *in situ*.

We talk about Adrian, of course.

'He's taking twenty-seven pills per day. We worked it out when I was in there yesterday. That's a hell of a lot of pills. No wonder he's acting strange,' she says. We touch on his money problems again and then I tell her he's decided not to come to Somerset after all. 'I understand his take on this,' I say. 'Why would he want to drive away from everything familiar and go to die in the middle of Somerset? Most people like to be at home when they're ill.'

As I get home Adrian rings me but I'm in a hurry to get to my teaching job at Center Parcs. He won't be able to ring me there either as there's no signal.

'I can't talk now,' I say. 'I'm going out.'

'You'll have your mobile with you, won't you? I'll phone you later.'

'I'm teaching, though. So I have to switch my phone off.' I don't like to go into details about the location of my teaching job in the luxurious fake tropical setting of the Center Parcs holiday complex at Longleat, and anyway he doesn't ask.

After the class I have a swim in the outdoor lagoon followed by my regular slide down the wild rapids.

Thursday 12th July 2007

Charlotte rings me to arrange a meeting at the hospital to discuss Adrian's future. I agree to next Tuesday. I leave a message on Adrian's mobile but he doesn't ring me all day.

Margaret comes round in the afternoon. I ask her if she's got any old beds we could borrow in case Adrian changes his mind and decides to come here after all. She says she hasn't.

I can feel him changing from day to day, getting more unsettled. Is this the weaning off the booze? He certainly seems to be fighting something…

Saturday 14th July 2007

My big day in the Frome Festival calendar: the prize-giving for the short story competition at which I am the MC and the general person on whom everything hangs. Yikes.

This year I have been dreading it and wake up with a headache. But I have a new Nougat dress which has been altered to fit me and once I've poured myself into this fabulous garment I feel good. I feel great.

From the moment I hammer Fran's pink sparkly sign into the ground outside Orchardleigh coach house, to the time I drive away home, everything is hunky dory. The do is a success. The sun shines on Orchardleigh from noon to two pm even though it's been cloudy and dull up to, and after, the event. If there is a God, maybe He's looking down on me.

Sam from the Lying Competition is at the prize-giving, reporting again I suppose. He looks even younger in daylight. A bit of a smooth Brad Pitt type but with dark hair. I can feel him staring at me as I line up with the winners and judges for a photo shoot. I feel about twenty. This is extremely flattering – I think – unless perhaps he's trying to work out which of his mother's friends I remind him off. Or which of his grandmother's friends I remind him of...

Our judges this year are delightful. The lovely Debby Holt and Booker short-listed novelist, Gerard Woodward. Both are charming guests and both angle their talks on the short story, focusing on the competition, which is perfect since many of the audience are wannabe writers. I give my usual speech with a bit of inside info about this year's entries. We had lots of stories about dogs and cats, quite a few ghost stories and rather too many with vegetable themes. Marrows, cucumbers and swedes are best avoided, I advise, if entrants want to impress the judges. Everyone chuckles and then claps as the winners accept their cheques. This year, for the first time, we finish the event with an actress reading the winning story. At the end of the afternoon, reporter Sam comes up to me and asks if I can help him with some poetry he's writing. I'm relieved to be able to say 'no'. I have absolutely no expertise in the field of poetry.

Today I don't make contact with Adrian at all. I rang him yesterday and the day before but haven't heard back. Maybe he needs a rest from me. Perhaps I've been too pushy. Again we are so different. If something needs doing then I like to get stuck in, whereas he tends to mull things over. He's still considering moving to Salisbury at some point, which is something he's been thinking about for the past twenty years.

Adrian may never now be able to move to Salisbury but I feel certain he wants to try to move back into his flat for the last year of his life. I really do understand this and will support him any way I can.

In the evening I doze on the sofa – worn out by the day. The house phone rings but I let it go onto answer phone. Later when Peter is back I listen to the message. It's Phyllis, his mum – in tears – saying her best friend Bessie has died. Bessie, a little roly-poly Scottish lady who has for years, ever since I've known her, been one of my favourite people – the sweetest of women, with a mischievous glint in her eye and not a bad bone in her body. Poor Bessie, and poor Phyllis who will miss her friend's company enormously.

Nonetheless, I feel inexplicably happy. I'm relieved the prize-giving is over and went smoothly. A few emails arrive from prize-winners and fellow Frome lit types thanking me and praising the prize-giving event. I think about what we literary bods have achieved over the few years the festival has been running. From starting with nothing we have put on so many events. Without meaning to, I find myself mentally planning next year's competition. Lots of questions buzz around in my head. Who can I invite to be the next judge? Should I put the price up for the critiques (I've written eighty-four)? Shall we do the prize-giving at Orchardleigh again?

What am I like?

Sunday 15th July 2007

Last night I dreamt Adrian was buying shares in Dainsbury's, which, he explained, was a subsidiary of the more famous supermarket chain, Sainsbury's. Also I dreamt I was in London but hadn't thought about going to see Adrian. I then decided to visit him with a girl, who could have been anyone, but was no one I recognised.

I awake feeling dizzy and sick. What's wrong with me? Something I ate?

I ring Adrian in the afternoon. He hasn't rung or texted for days. He can't speak well and sounds sedated but he's worried about his shares again. He's now saying he wants to cash them in and give the money away.

I get a text from Carol saying Adrian rang her earlier as he wasn't feeling well. I'm hurt because he didn't ring me, but force myself to be logical. Would he have rung me before all this happened to say he wasn't feeling well? Certainly not. All the same, I'm beginning to feel rejected.

Carol goes on to suggest she stays with him in a rented, ground-floor flat, if they can find one, in London. 'But he'd need to stay in a convalescent home until the 7th of August which is when I get back from holiday,' she adds.

This would suit me as we are going to the Algarve during the first week of August.

By night time I feel tired and drained, although thankfully the sickness from this morning has gone. I ring my mother-in-law to express my sorrow about Bessie but I can't carry on the conversation as it's too sad. Poor Phyllis. I can tell she's devastated. She and Bessie were nurses together, holidayed together, went to church together and shopped in Tesco's every week before sharing tea and cakes in the restaurant. I tell her I'll send a donation to Cancer Research in her memory. But what good is a cheque to Bessie? It might help someone else who's in the same boat, but it's too late for lovely Bessie.

'The situation with Adrian will be like a roller coaster ride,' Peter remarks over dinner.

If so, then I'm in the middle of a long dark tunnel. How long till I begin to see daylight at the other end?

Monday 16th July 2007

Adrian rings me while I'm out with the dog.

'Ali, I've changed my mind. I *would* like to come down to you. I'll stay in London for a bit and then move down.'

'Oh, okay.'

'You are still coming to the meeting tomorrow?'

'Yes, of course.'

'I'll see you then...'

Tuesday 17th July 2007

The day of the meeting at St George's. Rain has poured all morning but as my train leaves Warminster the sun comes out and steam sizzles from the rails. I stare out of the window, wondering what this meeting will achieve. If nothing else, at least I'll get to talk face to face with the medics who are treating my brother.

Just after Basingstoke I feel ill again. I've been reading for about half an hour, and have just drunk a cup of strong train-type coffee when I suddenly experience agonising stomach cramps and have to rush to the loo. However, finding a loo on this train isn't straightforward. The nearest is occupied, the second nearest, flooded. I'm several carriages away from my seat when I eventually find an empty, dry toilet.

I feel better by the time we reach Clapham Junction, but new horrors await me there. Three young lads are beating the crap out of each other by the ticket barrier. I'm shocked to see the ticket collector does nothing, except radio for help – although, on second thoughts, he probably has experienced this kind of behaviour before and so, sensible man. Other people stand and stare but I move as far away as possible. Violence is everywhere on TV and in movies but nothing on celluloid compares with the shock of experiencing real, in-the-flesh aggression. Unless we join the police, the prison service, or take up inner-city secondary school teaching, how many times do we witness actual physical violence in our day-to-day lives? I find it frightening.

I keep moving but at the same time can't help but look back over my shoulder. Two of the boys are still grappling with each other as they pass through the barrier (no sign of the ticket collector asking to see *their* tickets). As I watch I realise this isn't just one person chasing another but one boy is the victim who is being pursued by the other two who look intent on killing him. I exit the tube station pronto, cross the road and get the bus to the hospital.

In the ward I approach Adrian's bed only to realise it's surrounded by unfamiliar visitors. I experience a moment of panic until a nurse tells me he's been moved to a side room.

'Outside the door you'll find plastic gloves and aprons which you have to put on before entering the room,' she tells me. Presumably they are trying to protect him from any infections. I gladly oblige by donning the plastic clothing. This new room has his name on the door, though wrongly spelt. He's sitting on the bed and is looking much better. He's fully dressed and even his voice sounds stronger. I sit down beside him but this outfit, in particular the gloves, makes me feel hot and sweaty. The hotter I become, the more the tips of the fingers bulge with moisture. The room is new and completely devoid of anything homely. No television either. Adrian is understandably desperate to escape.

'I've got to get out of here. Did you manage to get any info on the homes in Somerset, Ali?'

'Yes, we can look at them after the meeting.'

I'm early for the meeting. In fact I'm the only person there at one o'clock and have to ask around for the other participants.

Everyone is assembled by one-fifteen. The meeting consists of me, Adrian, Lucy, a doctor, a Macmillan nurse and Charlotte – all, except Adrian, are wearing plastic aprons and gloves like mine. The doctor who is young, short and not especially attractive (what happened to all the tall, fit ones?) begins by introducing everyone. Then he turns his attention towards me.

'Alison,' he says. 'What do you understand to be the diagnosis and prognosis for your brother?'

I'm shocked to be asked such a blunt question in front of Adrian and immediately begin to wonder what the point of this meeting is. I have absolutely no intention of answering. Swiftly I sift through my options. I could honestly reply with a list of my brother's medical conditions and his 'year to live' prognosis, but have no desire to do so. How insensitive to be expected to talk about Adrian in this way when he is sitting in the room. I could walk out, but if I did I wouldn't be helping Adrian.

'Why do you want me to answer that?' I chuck back as coldly as I can. Everyone else in the room remains silent. The doctor pauses. Hot sun streams through the un-curtained window. I sincerely hope my reaction shows him what a prat he is. Hey, this guy needs to wise up his bedside manner, big time.

'You do realise,' he pauses here. '...You do realise we're talking about a matter of *weeks* rather than months,' he says.

Something slips inside in my world. The previously sweltering room goes cold. Adrian nods his head approvingly as if the doctor has just said 'you are Mr Adrian Tilbrook of 8 Leylands, Viewfield Road, Putney?'

I'm stunned. Did Adrian know about this prognosis? Did he lie to us all about the 'year to live'? I'm sweating buckets into the gloves and trying desperately to remember who told me the 'year' thing. Surely it was Adrian himself. I look at my brother who is sitting on the bed. I'm in the only chair and all the others are standing in a semi-circle around us. One of the reasons for this meeting I now realise is to put me straight. Adrian hasn't told any of us the truth. Lucy must have sussed this. This is why I am here. Jesus Christ. My brother has hardly any time left.

The doctor then describes the kind of tumour Adrian has in his lungs as one of the most pernicious. I look over at my dear brother. His head is bowed. He looks old and grey, lips limp, eyes small, bony thin frame in too big clothes. I wonder whether every person in the room is imagining, as I am, how they would cope with such news. Adrian is a very brave man.

113

We turn to practical matters. Where will Adrian go when he leaves St George's this time? I make it clear he's welcome to come to our house but between us we decide he'll go home initially to his flat at the weekend with Carol for support. I'm aware at this point that Carol isn't getting any say in this. The subsequent plan is for myself and Peter to collect him on Monday 23rd (or perhaps Tuesday would be better for me) and bring him down to Dorset or Somerset to be near us – to one of the homes I've found on the internet. Then when Carol is back from her holidays he might return to London if she can move in with him.

During the meeting the subject of money comes up again.

'Look, please. Forget about money,' I suggest. I have to make it clear Adrian is not a charity case. 'I think what Adrian needs is to go to a nursing home where he'll be looked after. Somewhere he can relax, eat good food and build up his strength.'

Everyone nods in agreement.

Afterwards Lucy stays behind and broaches the subject of Adrian's drinking. I can guess what she's getting at – the chances are he'll leave hospital only to be readmitted after a booze-up in The Gardener's. I see her point. The drain on the Health Service – the anxiety for his friends and family. All the same, I do feel, well, what the hell. Does any of this really matter any more?

Referring to his somewhat hedonistic past, Adrian tells Lucy he's been a bad boy. I have to admit I like this. Even in his weakened state he's taking control, and he's being funny. He's admitting he's had a good time during the course of his life, he lives as he chooses to live, even though this is where it's landed him.

'I've drunk too much and I smoked fifty a day…' he boasts. Why did he smoke so much for so long? If only he hadn't, then none of this would be happening now. 'They say the definition of an alcoholic is someone who drinks more than their doctor,'

Adrian carries on. I laugh out loud, although Lucy simply looks confused. These bloomin' Poms got some weird ideas about what's funny.

We talk about other things in general and when the topic of money arises yet again, Adrian starts explaining to Lucy what liquid assets are…

Later, Lucy and I go for a cup of tea (again). In one of the family rooms I confess to having felt jealous when he chose to have Carol at the flat with him during the meeting. I break down and cry and she doesn't try to comfort. Just waits, which seems the right thing to do. Comforting makes you feel you're doing something wrong by crying as if the other person wants you to stop.

We discuss my family holiday in Portugal which is getting nearer.

'Do you think I should cancel our holiday?' I ask her.

'If you did, would you be cancelling it for you, or for Adrian?' she rather intriguingly asks. I can't quite work out what she's getting at.

'Er…for me? But so that I can be with him. I mean supposing he died when I was away…'

'Do you think he'd want you there when he was dying?'

My God. I have no idea. I'm unable to reply.

I return to Adrian's room. He's sitting on the bed. 'There are so many books I haven't read,' he says. 'How many do you think I could read in two weeks?' I smile indulgently. 'Or, more to the point, how much beer do you think I could drink in two weeks?'

Is it really going to be two weeks? Surely the consultant didn't specifically say *two*.

We sit in this sterile, empty room with its massive dirty window looking out onto the buildings of Tooting talking until four pm. I give him the list of convalescent homes I've got from

Benenden and some of their details I've printed off from the internet. I mention one in Dorset I think looks nice.

'It's got a swimming pool, and *a bar*,' I say, reading from the description.

'Oh, I like Dorset,' Adrian says.

Yeah, right.

Adrian gives me a copy of the list of his assets he's drawn up whilst in hospital. As I'd surmised from perusing his paperwork, he has bank accounts all over the place, as well as shares, here and in the US, and something called 'loan notes', as well as ISAs and goodness knows what else. Not only has he composed this list from memory but he seems to have several nurses on his case involved in photocopying sheets of paper for him and one even posting a copy of this to me. Clearly I'm to have two copies of this document.

Adrian goes on to say he's entrusting me to put a codicil on his will. He wants me to give seven hundred and fifty pounds to The Gardener's Arms (for folks to drink at his wake) as well as legacies to some friends. I note this down but really I want to leave – the heat of the room, the convoluted money problems are all beginning to wear me down, and now he's heaping more on top. Codicils and alcohol instructions. And I'm quite keen to get out of these gloves.

But Adrian wants to chat. He enquires after everyone. I tell him the Frome Festival has now finished.

'Did it go well?' he asks

'Yes, and my prize-giving event was a success. And Ken Dodd was on at the Memorial Theatre. And we saw Paul Merton. He was good.'

'Yeah, Paul Merton used to live near me. I saw him a few times walking about. And I saw Ken Dodd play Yorick in a film version of *Hamlet*,' he says.

'Wow. Ken Dodd as Yorick? But surely Yorick is already dead in the play. You only get to see his skull.'

'Yeah. It was the Kenneth Branagh film. When Hamlet's doing the whole 'Alas, poor Yorick' speech there's a flashback to the young Hamlet playing with Yorick. Ken Dodd doesn't speak. It's just a visual flashback. It was funny though because the skull Hamlet holds up had the Ken Dodd teeth. I never saw Ken Dodd perform as a stand up, though I would have liked to.'

I nearly say 'perhaps we could go if he comes to the Frome Festival next year,' but I don't. After all, will either of them still be here next year? Will any of us? If I've learnt anything today it must surely be that life is fragile. As Hamlet realises when he holds the skull of the dead jester... 'here hung those lips that I have kissed I know not how oft. Where be your gibes now? Your gambols? Your songs? Your flashes of merriment?' We all end up as earth, loam.

Adrian starts talking about Phil Gullifer, his business partner, and I've come to realise Phil G is also someone he loves dearly. It seems Phil is moving house and Adrian tells me how good Phil's been to him.

Then he puts on his black leather jacket, the one I've brought from his flat.

'Come on, Ali,' he says, taking his walking stick. 'I want to show you something surprising!'

In this hospital, I think to myself, what could be surprising? Or at least what, readily on display, could be surprising?

'Do you mean the shop?' I ask, visualising a fairly impressive flower and newspaper shop at the entrance to the main foyer. Duh. How different we are. Me thinking immediately of retail outlets whilst my brother has something far more esoteric in mind.

Tuesday 17th July 2007 continued – The Time Stones

We walk together, through the long tunnels of hospital corridors and a glass corridor linking one building with another where we pass the doctor from the meeting (Mr Non-Existent-Bedside-Manner). I get ready to smile and say hello, but he looks away. Probably thinks I'm the next of kin from hell. Adrian leads me through a door into a memorial garden, which is laid with paving stones and dominated by a huge fish pond containing goldfish the size of trout.

'Look at the size of these guys!' Adrian says. In truth I walk nonchalantly past several ponds like this at Center Parcs every week with goldfish as big but I gaze in wonder at Adrian's fish.

After the Garden of Remembrance he takes me out of the main hospital doors where rows of taxis wait. Here he shows me something else I haven't noticed before. Twelve stones are arranged on the ground in a semicircle. Each stone has a plaque explaining where it is from and a month engraved on it.

'Stand on the stone for the month we are in,' Adrian tells me. 'We're in July, so it's the seventh stone…'

I do as he says, positioning myself on the July stone.

'Your shadow's falling on the fourth stone, so it's four o'clock!'

I look over at the stone for April and sure enough my shadowy outline falls across the stone.

'This is so amazing, don't you think, Ali? And yet most people will walk over it without even noticing it. Go round it, rushing into the hospital and then rushing out again and they would have missed something so brilliant.'

As on so many occasions in our lives I am dazzled by Adrian's passion, his fascination for things. Usually I feel the amount of enthusiasm I can express in return is inadequate. Yet his passion is contagious and I'm in awe of his excitement, especially in view of his circumstances. He has found something historic, artistic and quirky, one of the most inspirational *things*, as opposed to *people*, in the whole of this miserable hospital. A building which is home to myriads of corridors like so many tubes leading nowhere. Rooms with frightening sounding labels, grim-faced people on beds, in wheelchairs, hooked up to tubes. My brother has found something special. A bunch of stones that can tell you the time by your own shadow.

I read the inscriptions on the plaque for each stone explaining where it's from, searching for one I can identify with. Numbers seven and eight are from Dorset. Number three is from Bath. I run my finger along the Bath stone. It feels like it's mine. It's come all the way from the West Country. And it's really worn down.

Adrian says something unexpected. 'Do you know, I actually feel quite well.'

I pounce on his words. 'Adrian, they could be wrong. They might be wrong! I've known people who've been given weeks to live and are still alive years later.'

Slowly he shakes his bowed head. Almost as if he *wants* it to be true. Has he already had enough of this life? Is the mortal coil too much of a tie? I stand again on stone number seven beside my fifty-six-year-old brother who is stooped, paper thin, white-haired, leaning on a stick, and I kiss him.

'I'll have to get going soon,' I remind him. 'Do you want me to come back inside with you?'

'No, it's okay, Ali. I'll be alright.' He smiles a kind of lifeless smile and I turn to go, leaving my brother by his stones, slightly worried that he might not be able to make it back into the hospital safely.

As I walk down one of the side roads leading away from St George's I pass a pub. I almost stop to turn round. I could so easily go back for Adrian now. I could tell him to just come with me. Sod the lot of them and join the rest of us in the outside world. Remember when we were Cowboys and Indians shooting the passers-by? Let's shoot them now and make our escape. Aren't we still invincible? Whatever did happen to those leather holsters Mum made?

But I don't go back. I'm not programmed for running away or doing the wrong thing. Instead I walk round the corner, get a bus to Clapham and then a train to Reading. As the train passes over the River Thames I see a sunlit Barnes where we lived when Jack was born. Where Jack spent the first three years of his life. The train goes through Esher where my Grandpa moved when Grandma died.

After I've changed trains at Reading a lady ticket inspector arrives at my table. I've already suspected, because of its superior standard, that the train I'm on has come from Paddington and is therefore not the same one I travelled out on. The inspector has various ticket machines, chip and pin machines and other train related paraphernalia hanging about her person. Clearly she is someone who is dedicated to the world of the locomotive.

She scrutinises my ticket. 'You'll have to pay a supplement. This isn't the train you've paid for.'

'But one of the railway staff at Reading directed me onto this train.'

'Will you be making this journey often?' she asks. A bit of a non sequitur. I ponder over this one. What's the number of journeys I'm likely to make in the future got to do with my present predicament? I'm loath to jump in here since there must be a right answer and a wrong one. It's just a matter of guessing which is which.

'No?' I suggest tentatively.

'So you won't be coming this way again?'

'Err…no?'

She produces a map of railway lines and shows me the route I *have* taken followed by the route I *should* have taken. She also mentions the sum of forty-two pounds.

'You mean I've got to pay forty-two pounds?'

'No,' she snaps. 'You've *paid* thirty and so you now owe *twelve* pounds.'

'I don't have any cash on me,' I lie.

'We take cards. So, let me ask you again. Will you or will you not be coming this way again?'

I'm flummoxed. Her question seems so off the wall I can't think what to say. Maybe I should come out with something like 'well, I might be making the journey again. It depends on my brother who is dying in a London hospital. As long as he's still living I'll be going up to see him. But if he is no longer there then you can rest assured I won't be burdening First Great Western with my presence any more.' Instead I make a befuddled face at the girl next to me. We both laugh.

Big mistake.

'Right. That's it!' the inspector says. 'I was only trying to help you. You'll have to pay the whole amount now!'

Damn. She was about to let me off, instead of which I've upset her and lost out. I had no idea train fares were calculated so randomly.

'In fact,' she continues, 'it's only five pounds you have to pay as you came the *right* way on your outward journey. It's just on the *return* journey that you're on the wrong train.'

I tap my pin into her machine. She moves on down the carriage in search of her next victim, the train rattles along, and I gaze out of the window. When we arrive at Westbury I spot her again – head hunched down, striding along the platform like a corporal in a sandstorm. Where do these people come from and how do they always seem to end up working for railway companies?

At home I phone Sobel House, the Dorset home Adrian is interested in (the one with the bar). Andrea Someone answers the phone.

'I'm ringing on behalf of my brother,' I begin. 'I'm looking for nursing accommodation for him for a while.'

'Oh, I'm afraid I've just come from our other home.'

'Do you happen to know if there are any vacancies at Sobel House?'

'I don't know anything about this home, I'm afraid. I've just come from somewhere else.'

'Is there perhaps someone else I could talk to?'

'I'm not sure. I'm not usually here, you see. Sorry.'

I'm in the study and turn to look out of the window. It's getting dark. I haven't had time to close the curtains and I see my reflection staring back at me. Tired hair framing a tired neglected face. I'd scream if I had enough energy.

'Perhaps I should phone back another time, or maybe there's someone else I could speak to?'

'I'm really sorry. I don't know this place at all…I'm not sure whether there's anyone else here at the moment…'

Oh, well. Maybe she has recently visited the bar.

Wednesday 18th July 2007

This morning things seem less surreal at Sobel House. When I ring I'm informed they have a vacant room. I tell them, or at least I tell Andrea, (strangely enough, it is she of the nil information once again) that my brother is a high priority case or a 'Banding One', which is what Lucy told me to say. Andrea says this is the lowest level of banding, which contradicts what Lucy told me, i.e. that 'Banding One' is the highest banding in London terms. So will they take him at Sobel House? I hold my breath…Andrea suggests we pay them a visit.

Today four students turn up for my creative writing group at Center Parcs. One is from Wimbledon and one from a place near Reading which my train went through yesterday – Newbury? I come home exhausted from Center Parcs, and the weekly shop at Asda, to Carol on the phone in panic mode. Adrian has gone AWOL from the ward, and made his way (how?) to a bookies in Tooting to collect some money he'd won on a horse. He's been placing bets over the phone. From there he carried on to a burger bar (not the Algerian one, please) and then went on a spending spree in Marks and Spencer. Carol is with him in a pub now.

'He's in here with a glass of wine!' she says.

'Good on him!' I say and we begin to hatch a plan to get him discharged from St George's asap. He's had enough. I've had enough. This has to be the turning point. If he can get an ambulance to drop him at the flat Peter and I will drive to London tomorrow and fetch him. I should be able to arrange for an ambulance to take him home and up the steps and then we will bring him back here to Great Elm, or to the nursing home in Dorset. Anywhere but St George's. The only problem is he's given Welsh Phil the keys to his flat.

I phone Welsh Phil.

'Oh, yes. That seems like a good plan. A very good plan. But those ambulances are very slow. Very slow indeed.'

I wonder how he knows this. Maybe from experience. But anyway Operation Escape From St George's will go into full swing tomorrow, even though Carol cannot be involved this weekend. She can't stay in the flat with Adrian. It's too stressful for her – she's already got too much going on in her life at the moment what with moving house and going on holiday. I don't think she would have agreed to everything in the grand plan if she'd been at yesterday's meeting.

SOMERSET

Thursday 19th July 2007

Emotions are running high. Lucy has disappeared – she's on a course (maybe not such a bad idea) – and the hospital want to discharge Adrian as soon as possible. He's become a liability I guess since he went AWOL to collect his winnings from Ladbrokes. For speed I manage to book him into a nursing home called St Vincent's over the phone. St Vincent's is in a village not far from us...Sobel House will have to go on hold for the time being, as it's such a long way away and we haven't had a chance to visit.

I arrange for a hospital ambulance to take Adrian back to Putney this afternoon. Peter and I drive up to London around lunchtime. When we arrive Welsh Phil is waiting in Adrian's flat as he has kindly gone up there to let us in. This is the second time I've met Phil. Like a younger (and thinner) version of Ronnie Barker (but with a Welsh accent) he is a delight. He chatters on and on as we wait for Adrian to arrive, but as the hours tick by it becomes clear Phil was right. The ambulance must be taking the scenic route (via Birmingham). Tooting is only ten minutes down the road.

However, Phil helps pass the time. We discover he's against health kicks of any kind, is pro smoking, drinking and anti bike riding, jogging or anything remotely healthy.

'All those people jogging and getting in the way on their bikes,' he says with his Welsh lilt. 'They're just a real nuisance. Clogging up the pavements when you're trying to get around. And all these so called Government Health warnings. They say drinking is no good for you but it's never done me any harm. And although I gave up smoking thirty years ago it wasn't because of any health reasons. I just went off it, I suppose. I can't really remember why I stopped. I might start again though if I feel like it.' Phil chuckles and I decide he is a nice man. Adrian does seem to know a lot of nice people. I'm enjoying the way they're all so laid back up here. In Frome jogging and bike riding are worshipped on a par with wholegrain rice, yoga, solar panels and elderflower wine. This is all so refreshingly naughty.

At last, like a long awaited celebrity guest, Adrian arrives climbing the stairs unaided (except for a walking stick) with his thin, stiff legs. We all greet him and as he comes into the living room I watch Peter's expression. Peter hasn't seen Adrian throughout all this. In fact they haven't seen each other for over a year. He doesn't flinch, though later I catch him looking kind of filled up.

After Phil has gone, Adrian searches around the flat for things to take with him. He has bags full of new stuff with him. Spanking new white trainers, packets of white sports socks, chinos, T-shirts, a leather belt and a wallet full of notes. He usually only places small amounts when he's betting, so he must have had a very good horse the other day.

As we talk about leaving soon before the traffic gets too heavy Adrian looks around the flat he's lived in for the past twenty-two years.

'I need to get everything now. I might never be coming back,' he says.

'We can always come back for anything…' I offer.

The Picasso print, the *Buste de Femme au Chapeau*, hangs above the dining table in the lounge. Adrian loves this picture – it's big, dominated by the scarlet and yellow face of a large-eyed lady with strands of blue black hair showing beneath a hat which looks like an apple pie. The picture represents so much of what is essentially him. It's unusual, striking and tells a story. When we were on our Med cruise Adrian took me to the Picasso Museum in Barcelona which is where he bought this poster. He told me how Picasso had been fascinated by the Velázquez painting *Las Meninas*.

'Come and look at this painting, Ali,' he'd urged me as we dodged gangs of Japanese tourists. 'Picasso painted hundreds of different interpretations of this painting. The little girl at the front of the painting is depicted over and over in various pictures. Each version of her becomes less and less like the original. Look, Ali, isn't it fantastic!'

I studied in awe the different interpretations, some representing the whole and others individual figures from *Las Meninas*. The *Buste de Femme au Chapeau* is, I think, an interpretation of the small girl figure in the forefront of the Velázquez painting. I know what this picture means to him and he's wondering whether to bring it. If he doesn't he may never see it again.

'Bring it,' I say with a sense of urgency and a lump in my throat.

'It won't go with the room,' he replies, probably thinking of the photo I showed him of the interior of the bedrooms in St Vincent's, which are typically old fashioned flowery chintz style.

'Bring it anyway,' I manage to get the words out whilst biting my lip to hold back the tears.

Peter carries the picture down to the car. As we drive out of London, Adrian sits in the back reading the *Daily Mirror* for a while and then dozes. We speed away from his home and all his old haunts, managing to get out of Putney and East Sheen before rush hour. The roads are clear as we negotiate our way out of West London towards the M3. I sit back and relax. We've done it, we're away and it feels like the beginning of a new phase in all our lives.

We reach St Vincent's at seven and as soon as we drive up the sweeping entrance to the house I realise we've made (I've made) a big mistake. The place is large, grandiose in fact, but there's something wrong. Some instinct makes me feel Adrian will not be happy here. Two of the night staff open a door as tall as a London bus, greet us and show us to his room. It's clear as we go in that none of us is impressed. The room is small with a bathroom off it linked to another resident's room. The outline of an old lady lying in a bed is just visible in an adjoining room. The matron didn't tell me Adrian would be sharing a bathroom when I rang this morning. In fact I'd made a point of requesting an en-suite. This is not my idea of an en-suite.

As we're all hungry and there's nothing on offer at St Vincent's except sandwiches, we decide to go to a pub Adrian noticed at the end of the road as we drove up through the village. When we're back in the car he thanks us for all we have done today. We both eschew his thanks. It doesn't feel like we've done much.

The Woodman is dirty and reminds me of the pubs in the Essex countryside in the early seventies. At the side of the bar is a grotty looking sink with an even grottier looking draining board where glasses are drying upside down. This means the rims of the glasses are not in any way, clean. How did this place get past health and safety inspectors?

A woman, who'd given us directions half an hour ago, is sitting at the bar, and asks if we found St Vincent's. She tells me she used to work there – for seventeen years. But she left when the present matron arrived.

'The matron there now brought cheap labour in and standards went down.' She keeps looking at Adrian while she's speaking. 'St Vincent's isn't the right place for someone like him.' She tells me about another home, Robins House, where she, and her mother, now work. I decide to investigate Robins House tomorrow.

Meanwhile Adrian is struggling to exist in the outside world. He disappears to the Gents for a good fifteen minutes. When he comes back he says he's lost his wallet. Like other things, (Phils,

Caroles), he has two wallets, a brown one and a black one, and has lost the black one in the loo. Peter manages to find it while Adrian and I stand at the bar. I can tell he's not happy with the idea of St Vincent's. So much was riding on today – too much. I have let him down big time. He orders a glass of wine and sinks a pint of beer and then the whole glass of wine in one. He begins talking about Mum.

'Since all this began,' he says, patting his chest. 'Since I've had this illness, I've been thinking about Mum a lot. Just little things like how she found it so hard getting in and out of cars when she was really elderly...'

I don't want to join in this conversation even though I know I will regret this later as we've never really talked about Mum since she died. I'm just too exhausted to begin another journey down another emotional road.

Instead I say, 'Do you mean, before she died?' which, on reflection, is an absurd comment since she didn't climb into many cars afterwards.

All the same he answers, 'Yes.' But I can't pursue this. After the drink, having discovered there is nowhere we can get anything to eat (I resort to ordering a packet of pork scratchings) we drive back to St Vincent's.

'I'll call in tomorrow and we'll find somewhere better for you to stay,' I say, trying to deflect from the let-down of this place. 'Either here, Dorset or Robins House or Higham Lodge...' which was another home I found on the net. We are back in his bedroom and Adrian phones Phil G to tell him he's arrived in Somerset.

Peter and I drive away in the dark of the summer country night. We've kept the Picasso in the car – a symbol of the fact that Adrian will not be staying at St Vincent's. I'll sort it all out tomorrow. Find somewhere more suitable. Tomorrow is another day. I'm beginning to feel like Scarlett O'Hara again.

Friday 20th July 2007

How could I have begun to imagine yesterday what today had in store?

This morning I am on a mission. I must find somewhere for Adrian to stay other than St Vincent's. The rain pours and the streets are literally flooded as I head for Robins House to see if they will take him.

Robins House turns out to be a Regency town dwelling. Jane Austen or any of her middle-class characters would certainly have been at home here. I'm tempted to leave my calling card on a plate in the hallway – well, I'm not really – and actually I don't have one – but it's that sort of place. I'm greeted by a nurse and invited to wait in a drawing room where I am served decaf coffee in a cup and saucer with three different types of biscuit arranged in a semi-circle on a plate.

As I nibble around the edges of a Garibaldi I notice a group of people sitting in the opposite corner of the room. An elderly lady, who I take to be a resident, a younger woman – her daughter? – and two men, both dressed like undertakers. From ear-wigging their conversation I gather the men are probably financial advisers. The two men and the daughter are discussing the fees in the home, the old lady's funds and her fiscal situation. However, none of them makes any attempt to include her in the chat. She looks a game old bird. Determined not to be brushed aside, she keeps chipping in with phrases like 'the fees here went up five per cent last year', and 'I've been here since the 19th of January 2004'.

I guess she's running out of cash. Maybe she's hung on longer than expected. But why don't the others take any notice of her? From the way she's talking I imagine she may have been an accountant in her day. She's getting on a bit but she's very hot on percentages – and has a huge head of curly hair. A wig, though. Almost a hundred per cent certainty a wig.

The manager arrives. I'm led to the available bedroom – a largish bed-sitting room (complete with en-suite) on the ground floor with French windows leading out to a flower-filled garden. The room is newly decorated with luxurious armchair and decent-sized television. The place has a good feeling about it and I immediately want it for Adrian. But as I talk to Rose, the manager, she wonders about the home's suitability for my brother, as Robins House is a residential home and not a nursing home. When she asks me what exactly is wrong with him I begin the now familiar list; lung cancer, cancer of the liver, kidney and pancreas, and heart problems… I wobble a bit here and she offers me a tissue.

'Poor man,' she says. She points me in the direction of Higham Lodge, which she feels may be more suitable for his needs.

Higham Lodge is a huge detached residence which, in contrast to Robins House, looks more Bates Motel than Jane Austen. The gothic style building is located, unexpectedly, in the middle of a new housing estate. The car park is full and I'm already frustrated by the time I get to the reception desk, having been forced to abandon my car in a puddle at the side of an unmade road. There's no one on the desk, but it is lunchtime. A woman, with her elderly mother in a wheelchair, stands near the entrance. The mother who has a small pinched up bird face screeches like a parrot every few minutes. There's no way I'd inflict this place on my ailing brother.

All the same, I've come this far and so continue to wait at the reception, deciding to keep an open mind. From the desk I can see the dining room where some residents are waiting for lunch. A man with wild white hair, strapped into a high backed wheelchair contraption (bringing Hannibal Lecter to mind) who is staring with crazy eyes at nothing. A painfully thin woman sitting in her place at a dining table, shaking. A sweet little old lady, neat and tidy sitting primly at another table, who looks fine, but I know from past experience when my mother stayed in homes like these she'll most likely be in a world of her own, waiting for the maid to serve her from the silver service and then to be whisked off to a tea dance with Fred Astaire.

The most disturbing thing about these places is the thought of ending up somewhere like this oneself, although apparently only one in ten people do. I make a mental note to inform my children on no account are they ever to put me into any kind of old folks' home. Shoot me or administer poison preferably.

A woman arrives to give me the guided tour. Everything about Higham Lodge would be fine and dandy if the date was 1943. But it's 2007. The rooms are depressingly dingy with central ceiling lights, heavy old mahogany furniture, small windows and tired décor.

'I won't waste your time any more,' I say after viewing room number four. 'I think it's all a bit old for my brother. He's only fifty-six.'

As we walk back to the main reception area I notice the dining room has gained another lady resident, one of those really cheery types who call out to everyone and everything.

'Hello!' she trills as we pass.

'Hello!' the manager and I both call back. Still no sign of any food on the table, though. My mother once told me she was served with bread and butter for every meal in one of the homes she was in, and that was with fees of three hundred pounds a week. As a relative I was always wary of complaining about these things in case the staff took it out on my mum.

Armed with directions to St Vincent's I leave, at the same time hatching a plan to persuade the manager at Robins House to take Adrian there.

I arrive at St Vincent's just after two. My first visit in daylight. I realise how impressive this house is. As I wait in a vestibule which has wide curved windows, a visitors' book and a telephone, I can see through some glass doors into the main hallway which is home to a sweeping staircase reminiscent of the one in Tara in *Gone With The Wind*, and with ceilings so high they're almost beyond view. A Del Boy chandelier hangs to the right of the staircase. The hallway is tastefully decorated with fresh flower arrangements in every available space.

I wait in the vestibule, ringing the bell for several minutes before a woman appears. I ask whether I can let myself in in future as I notice the entry phone on the main door has a coded door knob.

'Goodness me, no,' she replies. 'Even the staff don't have access to the code.'

So this is Matron, who sounded really nice and keen to be of service when we spoke on the phone, but who I've already gone off slightly since my meeting with the woman in the pub last night. She certainly isn't as I'd expected. She's less engaging and a wee bit intimidating. In her forties, or possibly older, her greying hair is cut in the style of a man, she wears half-moon glasses and a navy skirt which is a tad too short for her milk-bottle knees.

'Mrs Clink, I'd like to talk to you,' she says peering over the specs. We enter her office, a room the size of a small billiard hall. Now I know how Matilda felt when confronted by Miss Trunchbull. I glance around the room half expecting to see canes arranged in order of size on the walls.

I've been rehearsing my speech for this meeting all day. Considering I am on tricky ground, having booked Adrian in here only to immediately arrange his removal, I feel nervous. My plan is to be straightforward. No messing. I'll admit Adrian doesn't wish to stay here and express my dissatisfaction with his bathroom arrangements.

However, I don't say any of this. Instead Matron calls the shots. She sits down, clears her throat and asks me what is wrong with Adrian. Yet again I trawl through his list of ailments. Cancer of the lungs, kidneys, liver and pancreas, and heart disease.

'What about the diarrhoea?' she asks. The way she puts this question is accusatory. I feel increasingly uncomfortable. I remember him having a bad stomach, but it wasn't something I'd considered worth mentioning. In view of his other woes, an upset stomach seemed insignificant.

'I thought his tummy bug had cleared up,' I reply. 'I'm sure the hospital said it was gone…' I mumble, trying to remember exactly what they did say.

'Well the hospital shouldn't have discharged him and if we'd known your brother had this bug we certainly wouldn't have agreed to have him here. We only took him because Aniela, who was on duty last night, is Polish and she didn't understand the abbreviation 'C.diff' which was written in the hospital transfer notes. English is her second language. Although she is properly trained and a very good nurse, she wasn't familiar with this particular abbreviation. If she'd understood what it meant she would certainly not have let him in.'

Suddenly in a bizarre U-turn I feel supremely grateful Adrian was allowed to stay here last night. I thank God for the twist of fate that meant Aniela was on duty. Matron goes on to explain that the infection which kept my brother in isolation in St George's is one of the most lethal superbugs.

So this is why the hospital was so upset when he went AWOL, and also probably the reason they were so keen to get rid of him. On top of everything else, my brother has contracted some horrendous hospital superbug. My heart sinks to an even lower place than it has sunk on many occasions during the past weeks.

'I've already rung St George's and given them an earful,' Matron goes on. 'And to be perfectly honest, I'm surprised the

C.diff hasn't killed him. He'll have to move to a different room. He can't possibly share a bathroom with Mrs Jackobson. If this spreads to any of the older residents it could wipe them out.'

'What exactly is this C.diff?' I ask her. 'I've never heard of it before.'

'It's like MRSA but causes violent diarrhoea. It's very dangerous. In his condition I'm surprised it hasn't killed him. He's already living on borrowed time.'

Okay, she's said this twice now. I get the picture.

Matron produces a form from her desk drawer and asks more questions. She broaches the uncomfortable subject of resuscitation. I remember this coming up with Mum. If anything *happens*, do I want my brother to be resuscitated? Of course my initial response is 'yes'. Obviously. I mean, she is asking if this person I'm related to and love very much has a heart attack, do I want them brought back to life? The answer is straightforward. Yes, of course I do. But it's not as simple as it might seem. When I had to make this decision for Mum, I was told the process of resuscitation usually means force i.e. breaking ribs, often causes a delay in oxygen reaching the brain, and can leave the patient in a vegetative state. Would I want my brother to go through this? Thanks, but no thanks.

Matron carries on with her list. Is she enjoying herself? Or is it revenge for lumbering her with a new inmate who's carrying a deadly superbug?

'Of course his heart is weak and if his kidney is impaired too then this could lead to heart failure or heart attack.'

'Aren't they the same thing?' I venture.

'No, not at all…'

She launches into a lecture on the difference between heart failure and heart attack but I've stopped listening, because I can't stop thinking. I'm overwhelmed by this new information about the C.diff. This explains a few things – why Adrian was in the loo for such a long time when we were in the pub yesterday evening, and why he was in a private room in St George's which I'd naively imagined was for his own safety to keep him away from infection. How ignorant I've been, and how uninformative St George's Hospital in Tooting.

'I've been wondering,' I tell her when she's finished her lecture on the possible malfunctions of my brother's heart. 'I've been wondering about my holidays, and whether we ought to go to Portugal or cancel.'

'Would you like me to ask him?' She says this in the same business-like tone.

'Yes, please!'

Despite her lack of compassion I feel as if a weight has been lifted from my shoulders.

After all this interrogation what I really want to know is how Adrian is.

'Well, he's been in bed most of the day,' she says as if this is quite unruly. 'And he hasn't eaten anything. One of the nurses is washing him now.'

Eventually I am dismissed and allowed to go into the room to see him. He's lying in a foetal position, a curve of bones under a thin blanket. There's an opened book beside him, a biography of Shakespeare by Peter Ackroyd with a picture postcard from Bali marking his page. So at least he's been reading. He says 'hello' but we don't really converse. He must be so tired from yesterday's journey and all the events surrounding such a life-changing day. Plus the C.diff must be making him weak. I leave after about half an hour, telling him I'll return after lunch.

Once I've left I can't see any point in dining alone in a pub and then going back to St Vincent's. Adrian probably needs to rest. I carry on driving through heavy rain till I get home and have tinned tomato soup instead, watch most of *Countdown* and eventually drift off to sleep in front of the telly.

In the evening Margaret and I go to the theatre in Frome to watch a play put on by the school. It's a spoof about *Big Brother* contestants. The plot is clever and it makes me realise I've started looking differently at youngsters recently. They are *life*. They aren't intruders who are there to fulfil our adult needs or do what we tell them to do. They already own the world – whereas a lot of us old uns are past it.

When I get home Peter tells me about a programme he watched on TV about a man who made maps relating to small areas in the Lake District.

'It was really good. All about walks in the Lake District. This man, Bradshaw, was famous for the walks he wrote down that people still follow in the fells and the dales.' Somehow, while he's talking, I realise we are a good couple. It's our twenty-sixth anniversary on Tuesday – which he won't realise as we've never celebrated it in the past – but does that matter? We got married five days before Charles and Diana. At least we've lasted a lot longer than they did.

Saturday 21st July 2007

Rain pours. I splash along the road on my way to see my brother. On the news people are living in floods. Taking boats to work. Some kids are even trapped inside a school. Houses are sinking. Whatever happened to global warming? Or is this its result?

No one answers the door when I reach St Vincent's, so, as I have Billy in the car, I walk him round the grounds. I amble across lawns where croquet would surely have been played a hundred years ago by the family who lived here, saunter under the gnarled branches of ancient apple trees, and end up beside an ornamental pond which is surrounded by a slippery, uneven stone path. All very dangerous, especially for the elderly and infirm. But there's no one around. No sign of life here at all, except a shadowy face at one of the windows which I catch sight of as I eat my sandwich in the car. On closer scrutiny the window reveals an old woman sitting in an armchair, eating and staring out at nothing. This is surely survival at its most basic level.

The sight of this woman reminds me of something my mother said. Describing one of the other old ladies in the last home she was in, she said, 'She's like me. Just waiting.'

I didn't need to ask what they were waiting for.

Leaving Billy in the car I try once more to gain entry to the house.

Still no one answers and then I notice a sign giving a phone number which I ring. Eventually I am let in by Sister, a pleasant-faced lady who leads me to her office.

'There's a few rather difficult questions I have to ask you, Mrs Clink,' she says over her shoulder as we walk along the corridor.

We sit down in her cramped office – a mere cupboard compared to Matron's domain. She begins by asking about my family.

'Well, there's myself, my husband, my two sons and my twin daughters. We are Adrian's only family. He's my brother and he doesn't have any other relations alive except me.' My voice falters at the last sentence.

'It's alright,' she says, 'I know exactly how you feel,' she hesitates, 'although to be perfectly honest, I don't really know how you feel because I've never lost anyone close.'

I'm sorry…? At least she's being honest. She produces a sheet of paper with lots of questions she's already put to Adrian and his answers which Matron has filled in.

Is he able to talk about his diagnosis / prognosis – yes.
Does he wish to be cremated – yes, at Putney Vale cemetery.
Does he want a priest with him at the end – no.
Does he want his sister to cancel her holiday – no.
Does he want his sister by his side holding his hand all the time at the end – no.

Harrowing questions. My God, is this really necessary? I imagine Matron sitting on his bed jauntily ticking her boxes. And I feel rejected by his answers. The ones about the holiday and the hand-holding. But then why would he want to spoil our family holiday? I'm positive he wouldn't. And why would he want to inflict more pain on me by asking me to be there when he dies? My feelings of rejection are irrational.

'Look, thanks for all this,' I say blowing my nose, 'but Adrian really wants to move somewhere else and my husband and I don't think this is the right place for him either.'

Before I leave her, I ask the Sister to write down for me the full name of the hospital superbug, so I can look it up on the internet. It's called Clostridium Difficile. C.diff for short, she explains. The word *difficile* is used because the bug is difficult to categorize.

On a windowsill outside Adrian's new room is a box of plastic gloves, a pile of aprons and some antiseptic spray. I spray my hands, don the plastic gloves and apron, spray my hands again, then knock and open the door. The room stinks of fresh paint. Adrian is in bed with the curtains closed. We start talking about moving as soon as he's clear of the bug. The research the woman from Benenden carried out has thrown up a nursing home in Bournemouth. Adrian seems keen to decamp to the coast.

'But the Bournemouth home isn't by the sea,' I tell him, remembering those summers on beaches in Bournemouth. 'I've looked it up on the net. It's in the town. And it would be a lot further for me to travel to visit you.'

'I don't mind where it is. I just want to get out of this place.'

We chat about money and Bournemouth. When he asks me to go to a shop for him I leave, relieved to escape the foul smell of paint in his room.

I return a couple of hours later and it's harder than ever to get in to St Vincent's. Again the outside bell brings no response. I try the phone numbers listed until eventually after ten minutes a young nurse appears. I ask her for the code on the door hoping to circumnavigate the rules of Matron.

'Even we don't know the code,' she says.

Oh, well, it was worth a try.

I return to the hot smelly room and the skeletal figure of my brother on the bed. I've been home to collect our kitchen radio, a phone charger and a digi box, which I leave on the floor by the TV, hoping Phil G, who is due to visit tomorrow, may be able to sort out. Then I realise I've left the remote at home.

We sit together, me in the armchair and Adrian in the bed, watching the golf, although he's watching and I'm reading the paper. He refuses a meal from a nurse at five-thirty. Surely this is too early for an evening meal. I'm beginning to get the impression Adrian hasn't eaten anything since he's been here.

He hobbles out to the loo several times and returns, gingerly arranging himself back into bed. I explain to him a couple of things Matron and another nurse have told me about C.diff but he doesn't seem interested.

'I've had enough,' he says. 'I just want to die.'

'I'm sure you'll start to feel better soon...' I try, but my words seem so limp. So inadequate. So unlikely...

We then have a disjointed conversation about the rigmarole of his finances. The conversation is going round in the usual circles and getting nowhere. The room is so hot, dark and still smelling of paint.

'I'm beginning to feel sick,' I say.

'You can't be feeling as bad as I'm feeling,' he replies. Fair enough, but I leave St Vincent's feeling low. In the car on my way home I play the scene I've just been in over in my mind. The C.diff is already taking its toll on Adrian. I must remember the old Adrian. The real Adrian. The one who's become lost in the midst of all this shit. I force myself to cast my mind back, to visualise him as he used to be. Eventually, as I drive towards the mini roundabout at Badcox I see Adrian walking towards me, wearing his old brown leather jacket and his Wimbledon T-shirt underneath. 'Hi Ali!' he calls out. 'Are you alright? How's it going?' I see him relaxed on one of the loungers on the deck of the *Oriana* with the latest Alison Weir or biography of Oliver Cromwell propped on his chest. I see him helping Mum to her seat in the restaurant, explaining the menu to her. I see him unwrapping a Christmas present in our lounge – a book, a new checked shirt, a bottle of Armagnac – 'Cheers Ali, Peter!' He holds up the gift to show his appreciation...and then watches as the kids open the latest card game or Sims computer game he's trekked around Regent Street to find for them.

But of course I don't see these things – except in my mind's eye. I will never see them again.

Sunday 22nd July 2007

What a difference a day makes. I know that song! Emily and Fran come with me to St Vincent's today. The weather has changed to warm sunshine with just a smattering of white fluffy clouds.

'He's sitting outside,' one of the nurses says when we arrive. This sounds like good news, although the emphasis in her voice implies Adrian shouldn't *be* sitting outside. *Outside*? In the external quarters? Experiencing contact with fresh air? Goodness me. Whatever next?

'He's not supposed to leave his room, but…' She trails off. She obviously fears he'll spread the C.diff to the other residents. Other residents? Apart from the staff, I haven't seen a living soul since I've been coming here, except for the shadowy figure at the window.

We find Adrian sitting on a veranda at the back of the house. Alone.

'The nurse seems a bit worried about you being out here,' I tell him.

'Yes I know.'

'Because of the danger of infection. But who are you going to infect? I mean it's not as if there's anyone else around.' I'm trying to be supportive, even though actually I do understand their concern. There must be some other patients hidden away somewhere.

'The others are all in bed. Or, they've seen what it's like here and they've fucked off,' he adds.

I leave the veranda, which is in shade, and walk down the stone steps leading to the lawn. From here I look up at the house. A square Georgian building of massive proportions.

Once somebody's country pile. As the sun heats up I lie on the grass with the girls, and wonder how many other people have enjoyed this lawn in summers gone by. I look at Adrian too sitting on one of the garden chairs. He's so much better, it's unbelievable. He's dressed and has walked outside unaided. Thursday's journey combined with the C.diff must have knocked him for six and now gradually he's getting better. Thank heavens for antibiotics, and the healing power of rest, and time.

We give Adrian the papers and all the other bits and pieces we've bought him on the way here but I realise we forgot to buy an indelible pen to mark his belongings. Name tags are essential in places like this. I'll never forget the sight of Mum sitting in a chair dressed in another resident's clothes. And – equally shocking – walking past the room of one of the other old ladies who was wearing a skirt that was so distinctively my mother's. She'd made it herself – the pattern and remnants of material were still in her sewing cupboard.

Emily goes off to look for the nurse to see if we can borrow a pen but returns saying the nurse has been rude to her.

'Oh! So I'm expected to do this as well am I?' the nurse shouted at Em before throwing the indelible pen at her.

Adrian is quick to empathise with Emily. 'The staff here are useless. Almost as bad as St George's. I asked for my bed to be made this morning and it took them two hours to get to the room. I asked for a pillow and the nurse brought some pills. You ask for a pillow and all they bring is more fucking pills. I want out of this place!'

Martin Phillips rings in the evening – he's trying to organise a visiting rota with Adrian's other friends so he's not left alone while we're in Portugal. Everyone is being so kind. But I'm still worried about the holiday which is getting uncomfortably near. I know Adrian told Matron he doesn't want us to cancel, but I fear if we go away he will be stranded in St Vincent's longer than necessary. He has to have two clean swabs before he can be deemed to be free of the C.diff. Nowhere else would take him with the infection and he is resolved not to move in with us. The all clear will probably come while we are away, thus delaying his release.

I decide to ask him again about our holiday.

Monday 23rd July 2007

CLOSTRIDIUM DIFFICILE IS THE DEADLY SUPERBUG YOU HAVE NEVER HEARD OF UNTIL NOW.

You are nearly 2.3 times more likely to die of Clostridium Difficile than MRSA in England and Wales and Clostridium Difficile has been linked to:

- 1214 deaths in 2001
- 1428 deaths in 2002
- 1788 deaths in 2003
- 2247 deaths in 2004
- 3807 deaths in 2005

Clostridium Difficile (so called because when it was first discovered it was difficult to grow in the laboratory) is a cause of diarrhoea, which is usually acquired in hospital. Although in most cases it causes a relatively mild illness, occasionally and particularly in elderly patients, it may result in serious illness and even death. The bacterium produces two toxins which are responsible for the diarrhoea and which damage the cells lining the bowel. In addition, the bacterium can form spores which enable it to survive in the environment outside the body and which protect the organism against heat and chemical disinfectants. Source – Wikipedia

I log off and phone Matron.
'How is Adrian today?' I ask.

'I haven't had a chance to see him yet but I think he had a good night.'

'I'd like to get him a laptop as he's feeling a bit cut off – the mobile phone signal isn't always good and there's no land line in the room. Maybe we could have a land line put into the room?'

'Oh, I doubt that would be possible.'

'Why?'

'It's not something we could do. And I think your brother is in denial about what he can and can't do. He thinks he can live independently which, as we both know, is not the case...'

'Oh?'

'He's talking about moving to a flat or another nursing home. But he has another week on antibiotics and then when the course has finished he has to have three clean swabs before he's deemed to be clear of the infection.'

'I thought it was two swabs.'

'No, three.'

I'm beginning to suspect that, despite everything, Matron wants to keep him there. After all, at eight hundred pounds per week, paid four weekly in advance, he's worth thousands in fees.

Jill Miller phones in response to an email I sent her last week, asking for help in finding somewhere for my brother to stay. But already the circumstances have changed. C.diff is now the key player.

Before driving to St Vincent's I take Billy for a walk to Heaven's Gate at Longleat. As far as I know, the name of this precipice is taken from a poem, *Aubade* by Shakespeare, which begins, "Hark! Hark! The lark at heaven's gate sings..." I can't hear any larks but standing here looking down onto the magnificent grounds of Longleat House I could be on the top of the world. If I took a run for it I can almost believe I could fly. We could both fly, Billy and I, gliding above Longleat House, waving at the giraffes, the gorilla on his island and the monkeys who are busy dismantling windscreen wipers from sightseers' cars.

I sit down on a bench leaving Billy to amuse himself with his relentless exploration of the undergrowth. This is a place where people take stock of their lives and the world. A place to ponder the meaning of it all. A couple of elderly men are on the next bench and one is trying to point out two giant footprints on the grass to the other. I can see the 'footprints', although the man's friend clearly can't. They are like two size 45 imprints of a giant's shoes in the grass. Maybe God popped down during the night. I'm presuming here that God would have very large feet if in fact He had feet...

After Heaven's Gate I head for St Vincent's. Today I get in with ease. The Brobdingnagian door is opened by a middle-aged man in shorts. I can't work out whether he's staff or visitor. If the latter then he's the first I've seen since I've been coming here. I go straight to Adrian's room, tie the apron round my waist, squirt alcohol gel on my hands, squeeze into the gloves, squirt more gel. Since reading the Wikipedian description of C.diff I am taking this infection more seriously, although I'm glad to be able to take these precautions outside the room where Adrian can't see me.

Depressingly, he is back in bed as if yesterday had never happened. His face is gaunt. His body reminds me of the victims of Auschwitz who were filmed at the end of the war. He seems low, but not angry. I sense he's been mulling things over.

'Thanks for coming, Ali,' he says without making eye contact. 'Thanks for everything you've been doing for me.'

I brush off his thanks. Nothing I have done has been difficult. He's the one who has suffered.

We chat about life in St Vincent's.

'The people here bring a new meaning to the word slow,' he says. 'And when they do bring something they never get it right. I asked for some water, and someone brought some but placed it just there.' He indicates a spot just out of his reach. 'The service here is pretty awful, but at least it's not as bad as the typically three hour wait for anything at St George's.'

I bring up the subject of our holiday.

'I don't want you to cancel,' he says more than once. We have already put in motion a rota of visitors for while we are away. Phil G, Welsh Phil, Bryony, Martin, Margaret, Jack and Ed.

'Phil G's coming tomorrow,' Adrian says, although I had thought he was due on Wednesday. 'I've told the staff my business partner is coming and I've ordered lunch for two to be brought to the room.'

Mmm... I think he's going a tad OTT with the whole business partner thing, implying they're having some kind of high powered executive/boardroom meeting.

'So what did they say? Are they going to serve you with luncheon for two?'

'They said 'no' – because of the '*protein*',' he says.

'*The protein*? What on earth do they mean by that?'

'No idea.'

I wonder, did they perhaps say 'because of the *quarantine*' and he misheard the word as 'protein'? Anyway, I don't know how Phil G feels, but I actually wouldn't eat a peanut in this room with all those C.diff spores floating about.

Back home I feel in such a bad place. During my visit Adrian apologised for being grumpy over the past few days. In a way this is more upsetting than when he's being bad tempered. A grumpy man is easy to dismiss. A repentant one, a lot harder.

Everything is crowding in on me. My brother is apparently dying and I can't believe it. I can't take it in. I can't talk about it. I have no idea how it will happen, this *end of life*. I sit in the kitchen with a cup of tea. The *Buste de Femme au Chapeau* is propped against the wall still awaiting a more permanent resting place. Wide-eyed, her gaze bores into me. Eyes like nuggets of coal. Thick black lashes – like tears. Tears stream down her face. Apart from books and clothes, this is the one possession Adrian brought with him from his flat. His one luxury item, apart from the Bible and Shakespeare. I really want him to have this picture in his room at St Vincent's. It belongs with him, not here in my kitchen. But I'm afraid to take it in case it implies permanence.

In the evening I collect the girls in town and do a drive thru at McDonald's. Em has put the Coldplay CD on and again Chris Martin croons the words of "Fix You" which for me has become the anthem of this summer. As the girls munch on cheeseburgers and slurp Coke, I chew things over in my mind. Tomorrow is the last day of school before the summer holidays. What will these holidays hold for me? I am in a play with a certain outcome. I love my brother. Why can't I fix him?

Okay, I realise I might not be able to fix him, but I ask two things: one – he's still alive when we get back from Portugal; and two – he doesn't suffer any more.

(And three – *I wake up tomorrow morning and find out none of this has happened.*)

Tuesday 24th July 2007

Our wedding anniversary. Adrian was Peter's best man. We got married in cold drizzle but today is hot and sunny. On the journey to school I enthuse about our forthcoming holiday in the Algarve with Kyria and her daughters.

'I can't wait. Don't you think it will be brill?'

Both girls are unenthusiastic. They seem cautious about the heat.

'I hate being really hot. Will it be really hot?' Emily doesn't like being really hot.

'And I'm allergic to the sun.' Fran is allergic to the sun.

Hey ho…

Within seconds of arriving home I have a phone call from the school telling me Fran is wearing white shoes.

'But she had a note,' I say to the woman on the other end of the line. 'I'd written her a note to explain she was wearing white shoes because her black ones were wet.'

'She's in Time Out and will have to stay there for the rest of the day unless someone is able to bring her black shoes into school.'

'I can't believe I'm hearing this. It's the last day of the fucking school year.'

Oh my God. I've just sworn at a teacher. Should I say more? I plough on. 'I've got enough to do today without this sort of thing! Can I please talk to my daughter?'

Fran's voice comes on the phone, little and scared.

'I'll bring the shoes, Fran. But I've just got to wait in for Dad to come home because he wants me to do some typing for him.'

'Okay.' Fran says, still sounding nothing like the child I dropped off twenty minutes ago.

Peter arrives home to do some paperwork. I tell him about the white shoes debacle.

'The school is picking on small things because they've lost control over the big issues. It's like the police focusing on car crime when the rest of the population is killing each other.'

He's right. I leave for the school, comforted by my husband's logic, and armed with a pair of tatty, soggy black dolly shoes I've failed to dry properly on the radiator. As soon as I reach the school campus I notice a boy in a group of five or six other kids who's wearing *white* trainers. I stomp towards the reception, making my way to the glass booth where a member of the office staff sits.

I grab the receptionist by the neck and haul her through the gap in the glass. 'Get my daughter, now!' I scream, 'And while you're at it you can get that bitch of a teacher who put her in Time Out for wearing white shoes. It's the last bloody day of term for fuck's sake.'

In fact this is not what does happen. The real version is as follows:

'I've come in to bring my daughter's black shoes because she's been in Time Out for wearing white shoes.' I'm holding up a bag containing the shoes. 'And...and I've... *just seen a boy wearing white shoes.* Why is my daughter in Time Out when other children are walking around in white shoes and aren't in Time Out?'

By now I'm in tears. Behind me a delivery man is in the process of delivering a pile of about twenty cardboard boxes that reach the ceiling.

'What's your daughter's name?' the receptionist enquires, as if I'm a routine visitor who is not snivelling into a tissue.

'Frances Clink in 9S.'

I snivel some more and eventually the receptionist ushers me away from the delivery man, and everyone else (including one of my neighbours who just happens to be the head of sixth form) who's milling about in the reception area. I sit down at a paper-strewn desk in the glass-fronted office, put on my sunglasses and give my nose a good blow, while she makes futile attempts to phone the teacher concerned.

'They're all in an end of term assembly,' she says, holding the phone away from her ear.

'Get her to ring me, then,' I blurt as I slam my carrier bag down with Fran's socks and shoes in it. 'Tell her to ring my mobile,' I say *en passant* having decided to make a quick exit before I humiliate myself further.

I drive out of the school, taking the right turning when it should have been the left – for the journey to St Vincent's Nursing Home to visit my brother – who quite often wears white shoes instead of black if he can manage to get out of bed and put them on, and who is dying of cancer and who only has a few weeks left to live. So where do white shoes, black shoes or any other sodding colour of shoes come into the scheme of things?

For once the front door of St Vincent's is opened by a nurse before I've even had a chance ring the bell. Matron and another woman are standing in the cavernous hallway. Matron greets me and immediately brings up the subject of the laptop.

'I'm sorry, Mrs Clink, but yesterday I told you the wrong thing,' she confesses. I'm momentarily stunned since she doesn't seem the sort of person to back down on anything. 'You *could* have a land line put into Adrian's room...'

As she speaks I see Adrian walk across the far end of the hallway towards the back door.

'...or you could pay to have broadband put into the room, but to install broadband would take about two weeks. And, well,' a little laugh here, 'it doesn't seem worth it. I mean he's only got about two weeks...'

'He's only got two weeks? Is that what the doctor said?'

'Well, yes. They said he's got 'weeks rather than months' when he was in St George's, didn't they? And that was at least a couple of weeks ago. When we had broadband installed in the office it *took* two weeks just to do the job.'

I learnt from experience when Mum was in a care home not to fall out with the staff. If I argue with Matron there may be repercussions for my brother so I take my leave of her and follow Adrian out to the garden to give him some things I've brought for him. He looks loads better than yesterday. He's dressed in a plain white T-shirt, an un-ironed maroon shirt (one of those Christmas presents from me in a different life) and his old tan coloured leather jacket. (Not the black suit-type style leather jacket I've seen him in recently and have come to associate with this time of his life.)

He's sitting at a table below the veranda hunched up in this now familiar pose, a glass of white wine beside him.

'Oh, thanks for all the things, Ali.' He takes the bag from me. 'Sit down. I've got some bad news for you.' He produces a notebook and pen so I guess we are going to talk money. As far as *real* bad news is concerned, we've already had bad, worse, and the worst (and more piled on top). Surely things can only get better.

'Do you know anything about Life Insurance Policies?' he asks. I don't, as it happens, because, although I'm sure we've got them, Peter has always dealt with that sort of thing. He continues, describing two policies he has connected to his mortgage. From what he's saying he seems to think I'd go on paying the premiums on these policies after he's gone. This is unbearable to put into words, but I try to follow what he's saying.

'You could end up in trouble and even go to jail.'

What is he talking about? Surely the whole point of life insurance is that it pays out after your death and covers the outstanding mortgage.

'And you might stand to lose 50k.'

I still don't know what he means. He's drawing squiggles and numbers on the pad and says he will get Welsh Phil to look up the numbers of the Life Insurance Policies for him when he's next in the flat.

What I want to talk about is our trip to Portugal. Two things have changed the way I'm feeling about this holiday. One was a fleeting look on Margaret's face the other day which showed me how surprised she was to hear we were still going, and the other was Matron's comment just now about 'two weeks'. Supposing he has only got two weeks. How can I leave him for one of them?

'I'm still a bit worried about the holiday to Portugal,' I begin. 'Would you prefer it if I just cancelled it. I mean, we're insured. We'd get every penny back.'

'I don't want to make you do something you don't want to.' As he speaks his body is twisted away from me and he's looking down at the path.

'But would you prefer it if I didn't go?' I press him.

The big answer comes...

'Yes.'

I feel my holiday crumble and die. I'm already mourning the loss of the sun, swimming and spending time with Kyria and her twin daughters who we were meeting out there. But regret dwindles and dies equally quickly, and is replaced by relief. I'm relieved I no longer have to worry about who will visit Adrian during the week we're away. I don't need to worry about a holiday I'm not in the least prepared for. I haven't ordered a single euro and haven't foraged for a single bikini, sun hat or bottle of sun oil. I can relax and be here to help Adrian. Anyway, the hotel was in Praia de Oura which is near the area where the little British girl, Madeleine McCann, was snatched in May, so already has a slightly bad taste to it...

'The holiday wasn't a big deal,' I gabble. 'Peter doesn't want to go anyway because he's in the middle of doing up the bathroom. The girls don't really like hot climates, and it was way over-priced. Two grand for a week, self-catering. I'll cancel it when I get home. We'll get the money back on the insurance.'

While we're sitting together in the sunshine beneath the leafy veranda a nurse arrives with a tray of lunch.

'No thanks, I don't want anything to eat,' Adrian says. Matron appears and in fact I've been aware of her hovering in the background for a while. Her office windows are behind where we are sitting.

'If you're drinking alcohol then you should be eating,' she lectures Adrian, nodding towards his glass on the table. 'Remember what happened when you were in London, when you went out drinking and ended up in hospital with heart tremors?'

'No, don't worry. I'll be careful,' he says gently, so calmly and politely. His charm is far superior to the one it's bestowed upon. I know in this moment how glad I am I've decided to cancel our holiday, how pleased I am to have my brother near me in Somerset. I'm proud of the person he is. His charm, his bravery, his individuality. I won't even think about the Algarve again.

I leave St Vincent's, collect the girls and drive to Trowbridge so they can buy new clothes to wear to a party tonight. Later I drop them at the surprise party they've planned for Em's friend, Rosie. As I drive away I see Rosie with Georgia and Ruby, two of their other friends, walking along the street. These girls are only fourteen – Rosie is fourteen today – and they are all dolled up in the latest garb – too much make-up, denim shorts, cut off tights, wide belts. Georgia and Rosie wave when they see me – I wave back at them…and I have a little weep. I weep because Georgia waves with such a lovely smile, and because Rosie smiles too with a growing-up smile of confidence where before there was only childish shyness and uncertainty. I weep because

Rosie is walking towards the surprise party the others have arranged for her with no knowledge of where she's really going. Apparently she's been told they are just going down town to hang out in the skate park (dressed like that?!) and I weep because of their sheer anticipation of life and what it holds for them. Lastly I weep because my brother whom I love dearly is turning into a skeleton in front of my eyes and because he is dying.

Wednesday 25th July 2007

The front page of today's *Daily Mail*.

HOSPITAL SUPERBUG SOARS BY 22 PER CENT IN JUST THREE MONTHS

Cases of a deadly hospital superbug which thrives in filthy conditions have soared to record levels.

In the past year, almost 56,000 vulnerable and elderly patients have caught Clostridium difficile – a stomach bug that can be halted with simple soap and water.

Between January and March alone, 15,592 people were infected with the bug – a staggering 22 per cent rise on the previous three months.

The true toll is likely to be even higher, as the figures cover only the over-65s who account for 80 per cent of infections.

The figures from the Health Protection Agency highlight the failure of numerous Government drives to halt the rise of a bug which is spread by dirty hands and bedding.

In the early 1990s, just over 1,000 patients a year fell victim to C.diff. Today, more than 1,000 are infected each week.

A bigger killer than the MRSA superbug, C.diff claimed 2,247 lives in 2005 – a 69 per cent rise on the previous year. The latest figures do not record the number of deaths.

But experts in infection, patients' representatives and politicians said the Government was guilty of a "spectacular failure" to halt the rise of C.diff and described hospital hygiene as "sorely defective".

Chief medical officer Sir Liam Donaldson said the failure of doctors and nurses to wash their hands was a key factor behind the superbug crisis.

A Healthcare Commission report to be released today blames pressure to meet treatment targets and cut waiting lists for lapses in infection control in many hospitals.

Clostridium difficile exists naturally in the stomachs of many healthy adults, where it is kept under control by "friendly" bacteria. The problems start if the balance of bacteria is disturbed, perhaps as a result of taking antibiotics for another infection.

Once the "friendly" bacteria are killed off, the C.diff is able to multiply and produce the toxins which cause diarrhoea and, in the worst cases, a potentially fatal infection of the abdomen.

The spread of the bacterium, via hardy spores, is swift.

But it can be combated using simply soap and water, while powerful disinfectants can keep hospital floors bug-free.

The rain is back. Phil G is due to visit Adrian today. After I've been to Center Parcs I drive to St Vincent's. On arrival I'm ushered into the office by Matron. She has Adrian's bill for the next month. I don't open it but at a quick guesstimate it must be over three grand.

'We have two kinds of contract,' she explains as she hands me the envelope. 'Short term and long term. Obviously Adrian will be short term.'

'Has anyone else been in to see him today?' I ask, intent on changing the subject.

She shakes her head with a little snort, as if to say *of course not!* So Phil hasn't made it.

'No, he hasn't had any other visitors,' she says. 'And he hasn't made any effort to get up and groom himself...' (what is he, a horse?) '...which I thought he would have done as he was expecting his business partner to visit.'

'Well, maybe he didn't feel like it...'

'Oh, and he's complained about one of the staff. He claims she was rude to him. I wonder if you could find out who it was. He didn't seem to want to say...'

Following the national media's sudden interest in the C.diff bug, I am uber-fastidious when I go into the room. Gloves, apron and lots of disinfectant gel.

Adrian's lying in bed again. I have a theory.

'Adrian, have you noticed? There's a pattern emerging here. Sunny days you're up and looking better, rainy days you're down and back in bed.'

'Yes, you're right. I hadn't thought of it like that before.'

So, the weather is playing a significant role in his progress, although there isn't a lot he can do here when it's raining, except stay in bed, read or watch television.

'Matron said someone has been rude to you.'

'Oh, it doesn't matter,' he says shrugging it off. Instead he wants to discuss money again. He's back on the subject of his Life Insurance Policies and explains they are endowment policies. He wants me to decide what do to – cash them in or not. I still don't understand what he means.

'It's up to you,' I tell him.

'No, it's up to *you*. I'm not interested in money. I don't want any Armani suits.'

I don't know how to respond. Talking about designer suits is so much at odds with his circumstances – and anyway when has Adrian ever worn designer clothes?

Another thing he won't give up on is his recent request for some ice.

'I asked for some ice and the nurses say they don't have ice. *'Computer says no',*' he says, imitating the recent *Little Britain* catch phrase. 'They're all in the fucking nineteenth century here. They're not going to install broadband. They haven't even worked out how to make ice.'

We settle down to watch TV. He continually watches *Sky News*. There's been so much rainfall there are floods all over the UK.

'The whole country's fucking sinking,' he says and in a way it seems he's right. The rain, the cold, floods – everything seems to reflect what we are going through.

The news continues. People are floating, we are sinking, Madeleine McCann is still missing. Adrian harps back again to his finances.

'I'd like to sell my flat to you for a fiver,' he says.

'That's probably illegal,' I say.

'It's mine. I can sell it for what I want.' This seems logical but must surely be prevented by some law or other. He gives me a list of little things he wants me to buy for him and then he says he wants to change his will.

'In what way?' I ask.

'I don't know,' he says. 'I haven't got it with me. I've lost power over my life.'

This is so oppressive. Surely he had everything properly organised, will-wise. What about the DIY will the Malaysian nurse witnessed in St George's? He must have thought things through then – and that was only four years ago.

He goes on to talk about pain and discomfort. The cancer pain is getting worse. When I was looking for a home for him everyone told me to make sure I found somewhere offering palliative care – now we have ended up in a place that doesn't. I've failed on the basics. But someone from Dorothy House – a hospice near Trowbridge – is coming to see him next Wednesday. They are the local version of Macmillan Cancer Support. He seems to be looking forward to this visit.

Before I leave, Adrian asks me to do a couple of things for him.

'Do you think you could find out on the internet any information about lung cancer and how it kills you? Oh, and C.diff too. And I'd like to look into having some kind of massage.'

I'd suggested the idea of a massage after seeing an ad in our parish magazine for a peripatetic masseuse.

'Maybe I could do the massage myself?' I say.

'But not with the rubber gloves on. It wouldn't work well with rubber gloves.'

Do I detect a note of annoyance at my attempts at hygiene? He's right, though. Perhaps I could wait until the infection has gone and rubber gloves are no longer required.

At night I search the net for information on lung cancer. There are some very unpleasant photographs of patients in the last throes but no descriptions of what gets you in the end. I've already googled C.diff and decide not to go there again. I don't print any of this off.

By the end of the day I feel bleak. I'm sinking, Adrian is sinking faster and, as he pointed out, half the country seems to be going down with us.

Thursday 26th July 2007

Another wet, cold July day. Fran and I go to the travel agents to deliver our letter confirming cancellation of our holiday. I buy a V-shaped pillow and a plug-in heated pad for Adrian from Argos, which makes me feel I'm doing something useful.

When we arrive at St Vincent's, I find Matron to seek her approval of the plug-in pad since my past experience tells me electrical appliances in these places have to be approved before use.

Matey seems the type who doesn't like to say 'yes' to anything per se. She observes the heated pad with furrowed brow, and is clearly trying to think of a reason to send it packing but sadly its plug is moulded onto the wire so she has to admit it's okay.

Then she hesitates. 'The problem with this,' she says indicating the pad, 'is that the cloth cover might get dirty…' She's not using the word 'diarrhoea' but somehow she's managing to shift that word from her brain to mine in a kind of thought transference. '…the cover of the pad might get *dirty* and then you would have to *wash* it.'

So how is this small piece of material any different from anything else my brother has in his room? All the same, I agree with Matron. I will be the one to undertake the onerous task of washing this nine inch square piece of fabric, should dirt make its way thereon. She seems happy with this. I give her a post-dated cheque for three thousand two hundred pounds for the next month's fees and she's positively cheery.

I find Adrian still in bed (it's a rainy day) but he seems brighter. I've brought some ice but apparently the staff have already got some in for him. Progress indeed. But no newspapers. He's been here for a week now and we asked for a *Daily Mirror* to be delivered on the first day – a newspaper from Monday to Saturdays being part of the package on offer – and still no paper.

I go back out to buy him a paper from the local garage, while he watches the end of *Columbo*. Then we sit together. I read the paper while he's watching an Agatha Christie film. He seems a lot more relaxed – but then there is a glass of wine by his bed.

During the ads, he tells me a doctor called this morning because he wanted extra pain relief. This doctor told Adrian the cancer had 'moved' (does this mean spread?) about halfway down his chest. I wonder how he can tell this, but anyway he's prescribed some steroid pills to 'take the heat out'.

'He also mentioned morphine but I'm not keen. He said it would be just a tiny amount at first and then gradually *as things get worse*... He didn't need to go on...' Adrian says.

Adrian is also worried about the C.diff because he finished the course of antibiotics today, and he still has diarrhoea.

This is indeed worrying.

Friday 27th July 2007

Adrian rings me in the morning to ask for the latest Alison Weir novel. In town I buy the book, *Innocent Traitor*, and head to St Vincent's with the dog and lots of bits of paper. Adrian is sitting in the garden but it's getting chilly. He has a glass of wine on the table in front of him and is propped up with three cushions, which he's borrowed from a row of folded wheelchairs stacked at the back door. A male nurse comes out with a blanket and, as if he's on a cruise and this man is the waiter, Adrian asks him to bring him more wine. Adrian is still good at asking for what he wants, which I find both practical and time saving. There's nothing worse than trying to work out what someone wants when they are self-effacing and don't want to bother those around them. With the blanket cosied around his legs he starts talking about money again. He's trying to explain the insurance policies attached to his mortgage. I still don't understand what he's getting at. And he's stopped smiling.

'I want you to go to Putney and get my will from the flat. What I don't want is for you to be in a mess after I've died. This is all for you. I don't give a shit about any of it.'

'Why don't you just make a new will?' I ask.

'No. I want you to get the old one. It's up to you now. I don't give a shit.'

But he does (give a shit) because he wants to alter his legacies. It's cold and blowy so we go inside. Adrian is unsteady on his feet and is leaning on his stick. He says he can hardly walk now. I help him by carrying his wine glass.

In his bedroom the sickening smell hits me at once. A foul mixture of paint and too much central heating. He tries to hang up his jacket and it slips to the floor.

'Fuck it, fuck it,' he says.

Although it's not directed at me, I'm uncomfortable with his anger. I hang up the jacket for him and start making the bed. The sheets have small bits of poo on them. Now *I'm* angry. Isn't cleaning bed linen an integral part of nursing care? This is a nursing home after all. I help him into bed. He's so tired. On my way out I tell one of the nurses about his dirty bed linen and ask her to change it. I return to the car feeling confused about his money issues and let down about the sheets. Shouldn't eight hundred pounds a week entitle him to clean sheets?

Saturday 28th July 2007

I've got the girls passes for Center Parcs today and after dropping them off I turn round and make my way to St Vincent's. The day is warm and sunny and as I arrive I can see Adrian outside at his usual table under the veranda. I'm surprised and pleased to see Phil Gullifer sitting next to him. I don't know Phil very well, in fact I've only met him once before at Mum's funeral. But I feel fond of him, probably because Adrian is. If I'd known him earlier we might have been friends. Over the years when Adrian talked about him I wondered what he was like. I soon realised he is a rather charismatic man and I saw within minutes of meeting him exactly why they are such good friends.

I decide to back out, though. I think Adrian needs to have time alone with his friend. I've brought a packed lunch so I sit at the bench on the other side of their table and tuck into my cheese and pickle on brown. As I do so, I notice Phil's reaction to Adrian. He's trying to lighten things by making jokes. For example, when Adrian takes off his shirt because of the heat Phil says 'I hope you're not about to streak across the lawn.'

But at the same time, Phil is being careful, bending to his friend's every whim, passing him a pen, filling up his wine glass, agreeing with everything he says. They are talking about Adrian's computer, which is to go to Phil because it holds all the data from the business. In the conversation, Adrian refers to this business as 'my life's work', meaning all the stats he has on the computer. But is this really his life's work? I'm sure he's achieved a lot more than this in other ways. But then, come to think about it, I've heard myself say the same thing about my two unpublished novels...

Maybe we're not so different after all.

As I'm about to leave, Phil is standing on the lawn looking up at the house.

'Imagine all the people who lived here in the past,' he says. 'What an amazing family house this must have been.'

'That's exactly what I always think when I'm here,' I say. 'This house would have belonged to a reasonably wealthy family at one time. Just one family in such a huge house. It must have been a fabulous place to live. Plus all the staff people used to have.'

I take my leave of Adrian and Phil and drive to Trowbridge to buy some nail clippers and a T-shirt for Adrian. Trowbridge is grim. Even for a determined shopper like myself there is little to tempt me. New Look is full of tunics which are in fashion this summer. Who decides what we should be wearing? Tunics make me look pregnant.

I donate some of our old clothes and junk to the Help The Aged shop which was Mum's chosen charity, then regret not keeping them for the Dorothy House shop in Frome. After putting some rubbish in the recycling bins I sit in the car and write out cheques for Adrian's gas and electricity bills. When I can't think of anything else to do I return to St Vincent's. By the time I get there Phil has left.

I give Adrian the nail clippers and the T-shirt and help him into bed. Phil's visit has tired him but lifted his spirits. Exactly the function of a good visitor. I say goodbye, waiting for eye contact but he hasn't been doing much of that recently. His eyes roll and his body leans away from me. But he does look at me (albeit briefly) and says 'thanks' with a half-smile, a dead smile, that takes in his lips but not the whole face. A smile nonetheless.

My next job is to collect the girls from Center Parcs. There's no phone signal there and I can't find them so have a swim in the outside tropical pool on the off chance of spotting them on the rapids. As I splash about I think of the enjoyable things I have in my life. Adrian has nothing to look forward to, except maybe getting out of St Vincent's. But whatever our circumstances I suppose we still look forward to something. Perhaps Adrian looks forward to seeing me and his friends. Perhaps he looks forward to his glass of wine, to the heat of the sun on his skin – when it finally appears. And of course no one knows how long any of us have got on this earth. I could be squashed by a falling tree, or eaten by an escaped lion from the Longleat estate this afternoon.

However, neither of these happens. At the Center Parcs shop I buy a massage glove, oil and two massage brushes. I can give Adrian a massage even with the rubber gloves on if I use these. I find the girls outside the ice cream parlour and we go home. In the evening Fran and I experiment with the massage oils. I decide I'll definitely do this for Adrian. I have to keep planning and doing things to try to make his situation more tolerable. Trying to fix things for him.

Before I go to bed I google my name. The last time I did this, about a year ago, I was horrified to discover I was listed as a tattooist on a website for local businesses. The site even gave detailed directions to my house with a map to help potential customers find me. I want to make sure there are no new sites giving me an alter ego. Thankfully the reference to me as a tattooist has been deleted, but I notice a new entry by someone calling themselves 'Womag'. This seems to be a magazine writer who's written some comments on her website about my two latest stories in *Woman's Weekly*. Of one, *Chapter Thirteen*, she says 'this is wacky,' and also describes it as being 'laugh out loud'. She dissects another of my stories, which appeared in the same magazine called *Things That Make Me Cry*, and was about a shopping trip with Emily. She goes on to comment on the unusual structure I've used in both stories. I'm so chuffed. I must get back into writing and set up my own website.

In bed I read yesterday's paper where I see an advert for a

competition to win a week's holiday in the apartments we were due to stay in in Praia de Oura.

    I show Peter. 'The catch is you have to go tomorrow,' he says. 'It's probably our holiday they're trying to get rid of.'

Sunday 29th July 2007

I've persuaded Fran to come with me to the flat. On Westbury station we meet a woman called Deb who used to be one of my students and is on her way to a writing course in Wales.

I tell Deb I'm going to London for the day to 'get something,' which probably sounds rather enigmatic. She might be wondering what I'm getting in London. The will, in the back of the white filing cabinet in my brother's flat in Putney. That's what.

We board the Paddington train and settle into our seats. As the train hurtles along towards London the sun burns my arm pleasantly through the window. The thought of Kyria and her girls in Portugal flits through my mind, and then flits out again.

At East Putney Fran's ticket won't work in the machine at the exit but she manages to get out of the gate and we scuttle off towards Viewfield Road.

We arrive at Adrian's flat, which is becoming increasingly familiar and doesn't have the effect of making me tearful and sentimental today – probably because I'm not alone. I find the things Adrian wants – his will and some other bits of paper, and whilst I potter about, Fran, who is suffering with a headache, has a rest on the sofa.

We don't stay long. Long enough to grab the will and the half-full bottle of Armagnac Adrian asked me to get. Back at East Putney both our tickets work fine, so we are on our way homeward.

On Paddington mainline concourse we stop off at a Sushi bar for a late lunch. I've noticed this bar before, and have always wanted to try it. Customers sit in a circle whilst little pots of exotic food travel around on a carousel in front of them. It's a bit like collecting your luggage at an airport. If you don't grab it fast enough and miss your preferred dish, you're left red-faced wishing you hadn't tried.

We sit down ready to brave the possible humiliation of grasping unsuccessfully for our lunch. We manage to get what we want and anyway, a menu is involved, so it's not as random as I'd imagined.

While we're eating, a girl on the other side of the Sushi track starts crying. Tears stream down her face. When Fran goes up to the till to pay she comes back and says, 'Apparently the girl crying had a text that upset her. I overheard one of those women talking about her.'

'Maybe she's been stood up,' I suggest.

'Or maybe someone's died,' Fran says.

'But surely no one would send a text to say someone had died.' After I've said this I remember the emails I sent out to make sure everyone knew my mum had died, and to avoid embarrassing conversations in the street. But an email is different. I mean, *a text!*

We arrive home at ten bearing one last will and testament, several other bits of paper and having braved the Sushi bar on Paddington station. Mission most definitely accomplished.

Monday 30th July 2007

Wandsworth Borough Council will foot the bill for Adrian's stay in St Vincent's Nursing Home. A lady called Louise rings me from Wandsworth with this amazing news. We will be refunded every penny we've paid. Wow.

When I arrive at St Vincent's Adrian is sitting outside with two women from the kitchen (cooks?) who are trying to persuade him to tell them what he'd like to eat. As he's hardly eaten anything since he's been here they've decided it's time he did, suggesting omelettes, cheese salad, ham salad, shepherd's pie, beef risotto, rice pudding, apple crumble, plum crumble. Fruit.

I'm starting to salivate but he refuses all their meals.

'Why don't you tell us something you *would* like,' one of them says, failing to hide her exasperation.

'Scrambled egg on toast – with smoked salmon. And meatballs,' he says.

They leave the menu on the table and go off, presumably back to their kitchen to get started on the meatballs and scrambled eggs. They must be wondering how they're going to persuade Matron to cough up for the smoked salmon, though. Adrian's sitting in his regular spot with the three wheelchair cushions around him on the bench, his notebook, today's *Daily Mirror* and a bottle of wine. I've brought his half-full bottle of Armagnac from the flat and we sit together outside in the blazing sun. I take out the various different bits and pieces of paper I've brought but he doesn't seem interested. It's really very hot, which means if we'd gone to Portugal we would have missed one of the best weeks of the summer.

'I've managed to set up a new account with Ladbrokes which is directly linked to my bank account,' Adrian tells me. 'I won a fiver and two lots of twenty quid yesterday afternoon.'

His mobile rings – it's Louise from Wandsworth Council.

'I've got this hospital bug, courtesy of St George's in Tooting, which was very nice of them…' he tells her.

His conversation is thick with sarcasm. I'm pleased to say he still sounds amusing. Today, more than any other since this nightmare began, I feel relaxed as we sit in the sun outside in these beautiful gardens, the afternoon drifting along in a haze of contentment. He looks and sounds so much better as the C.diff seems to be clearing up under the attack of several courses of antibiotics.

Aniela comes out and offers us tea and cake, which I readily accept. Adrian gives me a new list of things he wants me to bring him. His head's getting sunburnt where he has the beginnings of a bald patch so he wants a Panama hat. Jack and Ed have arranged to pop in to see him tonight so I'll give them a tape measure.

We talk about the future. In other words, the immediate future, when he leaves St Vincent's. Once the C.diff is gone, he will be able to move on. He's still considering Bournemouth, still rejecting my offers to move in with us.

'But Bournemouth is a long way away. I wouldn't be able to visit every day.'

'It's alright,' he says. 'I don't want to encroach on your family life.'

'But you're not,' I persist. 'I'm not working, except for a couple of hours on Wednesday afternoons. I've got time. The girls are growing up. They do their own thing. I don't mind.'

Sometimes he makes me feel unwanted and I wonder just how many women he's given this feeling to.

In the heat of this gorgeous English summer afternoon he moves on to the subject of his possessions he wants to give away. The dividing up of his goods and chattels…

During the eighties Adrian worked in Saudi Arabia, and from there visited much of the southern hemisphere – the Americas, Australia, New Zealand and the Far East. He has a watch he bought in Saudi which he values greatly. This is to go to Phil G. The picture which he made from a collage of old cigarette cards showing photos of the old players in long white shorts, such as Danny Blanchflower and…well, other footballers…is also for Phil G. He says he's already told Phil this is for him and I imagine how touched Phil must have been.

'It's lovely,' I say recalling the football card picture, which I've walked past so many times recently.

'Phil used to play football. In fact he was semi-professional, and he's always liked that picture,' Adrian says, as if he's trying to justify giving it to Phil.

'It's alright, Adrian. I didn't mean I wanted it for myself.'

'It's a nice picture. Most people admire it when they come to the flat. I made it myself.'

'I think it's nice too, and I'm sure it will mean a lot to Phil…'

He still seems to think I want this picture, which is not the case. Isn't this the way they do things in Saudi? If a guest admires something in your house you have to give it to them.

'You must of course give it to Phil.'

Adrian always wears a plain gold chain and this he wants to go to Bryony. He seems very fond of her and we talk about the prospect of her coming to visit him here since she has now moved out of London to Southend-on-Sea.

'If I was in Bournemouth then the train service would be better,' he says.

'But Frome is on the mainline from Paddington and easy to get to, plus I can collect anyone from the station.'

'I would like to go to Bournemouth,' he says. 'But not because I want to get away from you or your family.'

A different nurse appears with my tea and a piece of strangely damp Victoria sponge. Adrian tells her off for bringing tea for him as well as he hadn't ordered it.

'Well it wasn't *me* who asked what you wanted,' she understandably points out.

'No, I know,' Adrian agrees. 'It was Aniela.' By the way he says her name I wonder if she was the one who'd been rude to him.

Adrian points out a potted plant on the path and asks me what it is. I'm not sure. He says, 'Bryony would know. Her three main interests are plants, cooking and walking.'

Feeling rather lacking in the botanical department, I take all his things I brought inside to his room. Some shirts I ironed this morning, his other clothes, his wine bottles, and a box file with his will and Life Insurance Policies. Then I come back out to say goodbye.

'Don't forget Jack and Ed are coming tonight. Make sure they get your head measurement for the hat!'

'Okay.'

As I drive off he's standing by the table. He waves, holding one of his cotton handkerchiefs, and at this moment he is once again the person who is my brother and I feel tender love for him. On the journey home I mull over what he's been saying. Maybe Bournemouth would be good. The place is full of idyllic childhood memories for us, which is perhaps why he's drawn there. If he did move there I'd be happy to visit or even book into a hotel.

Maybe a holiday is on the cards after all.

Or maybe he feels the need to distance himself from me. Am I too pushy?

Probably not.

Tuesday 31st July 2007

Jack and Ed visited Adrian last night. By all accounts the head measuring for the Panama hat was a laugh. Today I go shopping in Bath with Fran. I manage to cash three of Adrian's ISAs – one without giving any identification – which under normal circumstances would be worrying. I buy Adrian a Panama hat in Marks and Spencer and all the other things he wants in Boots. Fran gets a few things, but I don't buy anything for myself. It's sale time and the shops are full of rubbish. We go straight to see Adrian on the way home. It's about six pm and he's in his room. I demonstrate the glove and apron procedure to Fran. Adrian is lying in bed, looking surprisingly short under the sheets, with both his feet in pristine white socks poking out at the end. He looks so much better since that day a week and a half ago when we first brought him here. This place must have done him some good.

'You've got a bit of colour in your cheeks today,' I remark handing him the Panama.

'I've been outside in the sun.' And, yes, the summer has now begun in earnest and I feel as if we've turned a corner. He's mellow and it's great to see him and give him the things he needs. He admires the hat and puts it on straight away.

'Does it suit me?'

'Yes! It really does! Ha! You look great!'

He takes it off and puts it on his bedside table.

'Bryony rang me this morning,' I tell him. 'She said she's coming on the eleventh. But she's a bit worried about the C.diff and how contagious it is.'

I couldn't reassure her on any of this, mainly because it is contagious, but is not a danger if one is healthy and young.

Adrian says the doctor visited him again to discuss pain control and this makes me wonder whether perhaps his mellowness is caused by increased medication. I'd suspected it may be due to increased intake of wine. He's asked for two more bottles, which means he's got through a lot.

'And thank Jack and Ed for coming.'

'They enjoyed it. They said they'll come again and take you out once you've got the all clear on the bug. Maybe you could go to the races together.'

Adrian is due to meet Olivia from Dorothy House Hospice tomorrow. He seems really positive now. Although I didn't print off the information about lung cancer and C.diff from the internet as he'd asked, I mention something now that I read on a website about lung cancer.

'Apparently they sometimes zap the tumour with laser beams to stop it getting any bigger.'

'I can feel it growing all the time,' he says and points to the top of his chest under his right arm. 'I can feel it here. It's fizzing, like Coke when the bottle's been shaken.'

'It might be worth giving the laser treatment a go,' I say.

'But the doc said the cancer was too far gone for treatment.'

Not for the first time I ask myself *why didn't he notice the signs of this illness before it was too late?*

As an after-thought he says, 'But you could ask the doctor about the laser treatment.' There's more than a hint of desperation here, but then these are desperate times. I'll ring the GP tomorrow.

In the evening Carol phones. She's calling on behalf of Welsh Phil and Stan from The Gardener's. Welsh Phil is coming to visit on Friday and Stan is coming on Saturday. This cheers me up, as I know it will lift Adrian's spirits and give me a break from visiting. Things are beginning to move along well. Carol says she thinks Adrian will be happier when he's in a routine. She probably knows him as well as any of us. And yes, I can see this. He has already established a kind of routine at St Vincent's. Sitting on the same bit of the same bench outside, with the same three black wheelchair pads arranged around the seat to cushion him from the hard wooden chair. The same tray of detritus on what has now become *his* table. The ever-present empty wine bottle lying on its side (to stop it falling over) in the middle of the tray.

Although I'm glad about the visits from the London gang, when I go to bed I fear all my little tasks are futile. Soon Adrian will be no more. I have my husband and four children but something irretrievable about my life will be gone forever. I recall the ending of Martin's last email: 'you're going to have to be brave.' I don't feel brave. Bravery doesn't come into it. I will buzz around doing things that need doing and even enjoy myself to a certain extent. Eventually, in some way or other, which none of us can foresee, everything will end, and I will be empty. That's not brave.

Hours later I fall asleep. For the first time I leave my phone switched on by my bed because if Adrian needs me I want to respond. I've always thought phone calls in the middle of the night are frightening. If there's a crisis I'd rather tackle it after eight hours' sleep.

Suddenly this kind of logic has gone out of the window. The light from my phone throws a blue glimmer on my bedside table.

Wednesday 1st August 2007

I wake early and can't get back to sleep, so as dawn breaks I walk down to the end of the garden. We have a long garden – just under an acre. By the house is the main lawn, which is flanked by trees, flower beds – well, weeds to be more precise – and a potting shed Ed converted into a music studio. Then there's the fishpond, beyond the fishpond is the orchard, and at the end of the orchard is a wild woody bit which is generally known as Down The Bottom.

Down The Bottom, or rather at the very end of Down The Bottom, close to the railway line that carries the quarry trains, is another more ramshackle shed which Ed built when he was eleven. This construction is put together with old bits of corrugated iron and sticks, and has been a den to all my children, as well as other people's.

This morning's sky is mauve, like freshly bruised skin. A rabbit scoots across the orchard heading for a breakfast of our neighbours' cabbages. As I walk across the damp over-long grass I detect a faint smell of cider from an old pile of last autumn's mulched up apples on the ground by the hedge. A smoke-stained milk bottle one of the boys used to launch rockets several bonfire nights ago is hidden amongst the buttercups by the fence. A branch cracks under my shoe sending a pheasant shuddering out of the undergrowth, hop-flying away from me. I always come down here to collect kindling in the winter but haven't been this far in months. Now the trees are lush and the paths overgrown with dandelions. Now I need some space to think – or to escape.

As a family we've always fantasised about what we might one day do with the land down here. I've always fancied a single storey building with a swimming pool where we could hold pool parties, writing events, guests could stay there, kids could live in there! The boys used to plan a go-kart track. Peter would probably prefer a driving range. Down The Bottom remains a jungle and I doubt any of these projects will ever come to fruition.

I walk further from the house towards the kids' den. As the girls were the last to use this, the walls and old pieces of furniture have been painted pink. There's an ancient pine table I bought in London – now entirely pink with the added embellishment of glitter on its legs, and an old bookcase, also Barbified.

I consider walking further, beyond our garden, but I'd have to climb over a hedge and negotiate the clumpiness of the field leading down to the shingle by the railway track. I think better of it. Running away might help clear the mind but I'd still have to come back. A bramble catches my ankle and a dark bubble of blood dribbles towards my shoe. I hobble back to the house in search of a plaster.

In the afternoon I arrive at St Vincent's after my teaching session at Center Parcs. Despite this morning's threatening sky, it's been sunny most of today. I've been swimming and my hair's drying through the car window in the heat of the sun.

I see Adrian as soon as I arrive. He's bent over, with head down, so thin, his neck seems elongated. When he sees me he looks surprised and happy. The Panama hat is on the table along with his usual stuff – tray, notepad, uneaten food, and tea things, glass of iced water and wine.

He'd texted me earlier to ask me to bring more wine. A bottle of red and a bottle of white. I have them with me – as well as the lottery ticket he wanted. He's slightly tanned and I think back again to the day we brought him here when he looked like death. Now, apart from being so thin, he's looking almost well. He's being more positive about St Vincent's too (although he still wants to move on) and says the staff are good.

'This is a beautiful place,' he concedes for the first time. 'But it's much too quiet here. There's no one around to talk to.'

I'm with him on this one. I mean, where is everyone? I've still hardly seen a living soul – apart from staff – since I've been coming here.

'Once you've got the all clear on the bug we can visit a few more places, and choose somewhere at our leisure.' After all, we did jump into St Vincent's without even visiting.

'I've seen the doc again,' he says. 'I asked for an increase in painkillers – and I've also asked for a second opinion.'

Everything seems different now. The sun is hot, a dazzling, blue-skied day in the middle of such a mediocre summer. Adrian looks better, the bug has been beaten, he's gone from wanting to die (he's said this to me more than once over the past few weeks) to wanting to live. Although this is positive and encouraging I also feel an element of desperation, like Steve McQueen who travelled to Mexico looking for alternative cures when he was dying of lung cancer.

Adrian goes on to tell me Olivia from Dorothy House has visited him today.

'She's a really nice lady. She asked me lots of questions about how I felt about things.'

Meanwhile, Adrian is planning his legacies and wants to talk about pensions. I don't want to talk about legacies and pensions, so instead I tell him about the laptop I've ordered which is due tomorrow. He's very enthusiastic. At this moment I feel as if I can fix him. Maybe just a little bit.

Thursday 2nd August 2007

S ummer was yesterday. Today it's raining. On waking I immediately think about Adrian stuck in his room again. I phone Dr Graham, the local GP. I'm not sure she can discuss Adrian's case with me – even though I am his next of kin – but I ask her whether chemo or laser treatment is an option after all.

'My brother has changed so much in the last day or so. He'd like a second opinion.'

'I can understand where he's coming from,' she says, 'but the cancer has probably spread too far. A second opinion, although always an option, may not offer any more hope.'

We arrange to meet tomorrow between one-thirty and two-thirty at St Vincent's.

Meanwhile, the man in the computer shop in Frome says there's a postal strike which means the SIM card hasn't arrived so the laptop I've ordered isn't ready. I feel like saying, 'But this is for someone who hasn't got time for postal strikes.'

I go straight on to St Vincent's. Adrian is clothed, lying on the bed.

'Peter came in to see me earlier. I'm just getting ready to put a bet on at Goodwood.' He has Goodwood on the telly. 'Look isn't it beautiful. The view, the house, the horses...'

He loves all things Goodwoodian. And I'd always thought Goodwood was a venue for motor racing. I decide not to share my ignorance. Or maybe it's both, horses and motors. But wouldn't the cars mess up the grass...No. I try to sound impressed but suspect I'm sounding unconvincing. It looks nice but it's just a piece of greenery as far as I can tell.

He's apologetic about putting bets on. Why, though?

He's propped up on a pile of pillows. I sit next to him in the armchair reading the paper and thinking how little we have in common. I've never visited a racecourse or even considered doing so, and yet for him horse racing is a fascinating and adored part of his life. Suddenly I feel uneasy. After all, he's much better now so my visit is less like visiting the sick. I'm visiting as I would have done in the past but with none of the usual things to do which would cushion our time together. I don't really know what to say about this horse racing stuff.

After a while he asks what the girls are up to. I tell him about their friend, Daisy, who has run away from home, but although he makes all the right noises, I can tell he's not really interested and doesn't remember Daisy anyway. In fact I am worried about Daisy. Maybe that sums up our different personalities. I'm more interested in people and he's more interested in…well, horses, historical buildings, Ancient Egyptian Mummies – and people too, I guess.

I've brought a pack of cards with me. Playing cards was one of our favourite pastimes when we were little. We spent hours during our holidays in Christchurch playing various card games. Throughout my childhood and into adolescence our family travelled the one hundred and twenty mile journey twice a year to the coast. London to Bournemouth, via the Hogs Back, before the M3 was even a twinkle in the eye of the A3. My grandparents lived in a bungalow in Christchurch, which used to be in Hampshire, but has now mysteriously relocated to Dorset. Grandma always greeted us with the offer of a bowl of Puffed Wheat which was served up with milk from the extra pint she'd ordered in honour of our arrival. We tucked into this delicious meal. Breakfast, not only at the wrong time of day, but served in pink floral soup bowls decorated with pictures of Chatsworth Castle. I have the one remaining bowl from Grandma's set on display in my kitchen dresser.

At Grandma's I slept in the spare bedroom with my parents.

From my bed I could see a monstrous wardrobe in the hall. Brown rigid suitcases containing dolls' limbs, heads and torsos balanced on top of this wardrobe. Before his retirement, Grandpa (an ex Lieutenant Colonel in the British Army) had owned a toy shop and dolls' hospital in Bournemouth. As a grandparent he was the best. He loved children and always made us laugh. When we introduced him to any of our friends he'd insist on calling them George.

My grandparents downsized from a four bedroom detached house in Radlett to this small bungalow near the coast. What it seems they didn't do was to get shot of any of the furniture from the Radlett house. The Walcott Avenue bungalow was rammed with tables, chairs and wardrobes. The living room was dominated by a dark mahogany dining table with six chairs. Given the room was about fifteen foot square, negotiating your way around meant squeezing between chairs and tables or clambering over sofas. To the side of the table was an upright piano. Behind and around the table, a brown leather three-piece suite was squashed against the walls. An ornate sideboard containing boxes of black and white photographs was jammed against the wall between one of these sofas. It was impossible to open the drawers of the sideboard without moving the sofa. And you couldn't walk around the table without climbing over the two-seater, or squeezing past the piano.

Grandma was a bulky, rather intimidating matriarch who walked with a stick. She always sat at the head of the table in a carver (which was the easiest chair to get to) and chain-smoked Consulate cigarettes, the tips of which she'd pierce with a needle that she kept pinned to the collar of her dress. This puncturing of the tips, she believed, would stop her getting cancer.

The television was straight ahead of her but hard to get to given the physical obstacles of the sideboard, the sofas and the other dining chairs. This was in the days before TV remotes. There were only two channels and Grandma preferred to stick to the imported cops and robbers series on ITV rather than soaking up the more sober offerings of the Beeb. However, televisions in those days often went wrong and if Grandma wanted to adjust the set she had a green comb she'd throw at the screen, which somehow seemed to do the trick.

Framed photographs hung from the picture rails showing my mother at the age of ten riding an elephant and other scenes from their years in Karachi. All their possessions had been shipped back to the UK at the end of the war. The most mesmerising for me being the black upright Steinway Grandpa played most evenings. He kept piles of old books of sheet music inside the piano stool. Every year when we got home I'd beg my parents for a piano and piano lessons. Eventually they relented, thus beginning my lifelong love affair with pianos.

One year when we were on holiday I took the sheet music of "We're a Couple of Swells" to bed with me. Instead of going to sleep I learnt all the words with the aid of a torch under the bedclothes. I can still recite the whole song:

We're a couple of sports. The pride of the tennis courts
In June, July and August we look cute when we're dressed in shorts...
Well, some of it.

Adrian always slept on a camp bed in our grandparents' bedroom until we got older when he insisted it wasn't fair because I always got to share with Mum and Dad. I therefore had to swap from time to time. Minus teeth and glasses, and in elaborate night attire, my grandparents seemed different, somewhat scary beings. They snored loudly, and kept a china pot under the bed – although the bathroom was less than a few steps away. Grandma made use of this pot in the middle of the night. It took me a while to work out what the tinkling sound was. Definitely not Grandpa practising his scales...

Apart from housing the family snapshots, the sideboard drawers were also home to games, two of which stick in my mind. One was a card game called Contraband which was based on smuggling spirits and luxury items such as jewellery, cameras and silk stockings.

The other was called Buccaneer, a board game also based on smuggling. The board represented the sea with home ports that you had to move your tiny plastic ships towards by throwing a dice. A tray placed in the middle of the board was the treasure island and contained tiny replicas of diamonds, rubies, pearls, bars of gold and barrels of rum – all the little pieces of pirates' goodies which had to be loaded onto the ships and moved around the board. Opponents' ships could be attacked and treasure or crew captured. I loved those little gems, but wonder in retrospect why my grandparents were so into games based on smuggling and alcohol.

Those childhood years now seem idyllic and yet at the time it felt as if we were still waiting for our lives to begin. They had begun, of course, and probably those were always going to be the best years of our lives. Strange, because if anyone had told me such a thing at the time I'd have been horrified.

I think maybe there's a moment when you slide your miniature plastic boat overflowing with illicit jewels, cameras and contraband booze, your innocent, still pure fingers moving your booty across a cardboard sea towards an invented desert island, that could be a perfect moment. Maybe the one moment we all strive to get back to for the rest of our lives. A moment so unworldly, when all we have to worry about is who will end up with the most boats on a fake island or whether Grandma will serve up stewed gooseberries for tea, and if so, how we might escape having to eat them.

In later years we moved on to more classic card games like Whist and Rummy, and a game called Oh Hell, although there was a period in between when Adrian wouldn't play with me when he thought he was cool and I wasn't.

To play games together now would be like coming full circle – back together – back to being children. Thrown together on a wet summer's afternoon, finding something amusing to pass the time.

I leave the cards on the shelf above the radiator without opening them, and when the racing is over I tell him about my recent contact with Benenden, who have put me in touch with a private consultancy. They will provide a full report on all the nursing homes in Bournemouth, Dorset, and near Frome. Adrian seems pleased with this.

He decides to go outside when I'm leaving as the rain has stopped. A couple of rays of sunshine manage to penetrate into the room and so he gets off the bed, standing precariously with the help of his walking stick, which was the other thing he brought with him, courtesy of St George's in Tooting.

He walks one step, then stops in pain. I help him carry out his carrier bag with all his paperwork about the flat and his finances, his jug of iced water, the *Daily Mirror* and his Panama hat. We call in the kitchen on the way to ask for his wine which they keep in the fridge for him.

He settles in his usual spot at the right hand end of the bench in the garden and I sit next to him. One of the nurses comes out.

'How are you today, Adrian? Recovered from being locked out?'

Adrian laughs. 'Ha, I thought I'd be spending the night under the stars.'

'No chance. One of us would have found you sooner or later!'

'I was dozing on my bench,' he tells me. 'I didn't hear the nurse locking the side door.'

It's wonderful to hear him joshing with one of the staff. I wonder if she will look at Adrian's corner of the bench and remember him when he's gone. Or do staff in places like this harden themselves to their charges dying? I suspect some of them will think about him. I hope so. We sit for a while, Adrian drinking his wine, me sipping a cup of tea the nurse brought me. As the afternoon draws on I think about all the things I should be doing at home.

'I'd better be getting off. I've got a pile of ironing and the dinner to cook,' I say. I pop to the loo and when I come back he's writing in the back of the notebook I got him.

'I'm glad you're making use of the notebook,' I say.

'Yes. I'm making a list of the bequests to all my friends. And…I'm making some notes. For my funeral. I've chosen some music…'

I stop preparing to go and sit down again. The music for his funeral. This is something I had wondered about but shied away from mentioning. I'd thought of "Fix You" by Coldplay and how the tears had streamed down my face that first night on my way back from Westbury in the car when it came on the CD player. But this song has more relevance to me than to Adrian. I doubt he even likes Coldplay.

He hands me a piece of paper and, although I'm curious to know what music he's chosen, I don't want to look at his notes and hand it back. There's a barrier between us preventing us from talking about what is really going on in his head. No doubt I'll find out sooner or later what pieces of music he's chosen.

'I've made a list of all the people I want at my funeral,' he goes on. Is he being brave or just realistic? The latter, I decide. Or maybe he has a lot of time to think. 'I'll add all the addresses when I get a chance,' he says, meaning he will do all he can to help me contact them when the time comes. I make a face – eyes closed, exasperated. What my expression really means is 'Oh, no. I can't cope with this…'

'It's alright, Ali. You don't have to do any of this if you don't want to…' He speaks the words so tolerantly, so like the old Adrian, but I fear he's misinterpreted my expression and has read it as 'Oh, no. Not more work for me.'

By the evening I feel sick and headachy – not exactly dizzy, but not right. Maybe I have caught C.diff bug after all? When I go to bed I fear I might collapse mentally and physically. I try to work out how long this has been going on. I envisage a scenario where I don't go tomorrow to the meeting with Dr Graham, because I simply can't take any more – a scenario where I leave Adrian to get on with things on his own. Some people might. Anyway, no one is indispensable. I decide not to go.

Friday 3rd August 2007

The meeting consists of Dr Graham, a student doctor whom the GP introduces and asks whether we mind him observing (we don't), Adrian, me and one of the St Vincent's nurses, (a scary one with a dark red dress and big hair.)

Dr Graham is quietly spoken. She doesn't acknowledge me, but then I don't put myself forward. The first topic of conversation is the C.diff. Dr Graham says clean swabs are no longer needed in order to give the all clear. In the parlance of the average Radio One presenter, I am gobsmacked. Haven't we been waiting for days – nay weeks – in order to get two or three clean swabs so Adrian can declare himself free of infection and get the hell out of here? I close my mouth and carry on listening.

Contrary to the information we've received from Matron, Dr Graham says the all clear is now dependent on symptoms and she is therefore officially giving Adrian the all clear. He's no longer a threat to mankind. Hooray. I can't believe it.

'So I can go out now? I've been like a prisoner here...' Adrian begins.

'This is not a prison!' Scary Red Nurse interjects.

'Well, it's pretty much like a prison from where I'm sitting,' Adrian replies.

All the infection paranoia is over. The GP's opinion is written in stone as far as the staff at St Vincent's are concerned. If she says he's cured of the C.diff then he is.

We go on to discuss possible treatments for cancer in the light of his improved general health. Dr Graham says Adrian will see an oncologist as an outpatient. He's chosen Salisbury Hospital rather than Bath for this. As I already know, he has a love of Salisbury – partly because it has a cathedral. He seems to dislike Bath, although I don't know why. I mention in passing a news item I heard yesterday about the RUH in Bath. Apparently they have a significant number of C.diff cases.

'Yes,' Dr Graham says, 'but Adrian only caught C.diff because he was on antibiotics for pneumonia.'

I remember reading this online. Patients usually contract C.diff when they are being treated with antibiotics for something else.

It's hot so Adrian and I sit out on the bench after they've gone. Nurse Janice comes out – she of the indelible pen fame – and I bravely ask for a cup of tea even though I know she won't bring one. Janice seems to have good banter going with Adrian, though. They are still laughing about him being locked out in the garden.

Before I leave, Adrian brings up the subject of his Life Insurance Policies again.

'I want everything sorted before I go. Have you paid off my credit card?'

'Yes.' I realise how worried about money he must have been before all this happened. He had virtually no income. I have paid the credit card but the rest of his paperwork is too exhausting to contemplate. Instead I promise to take him to look at the other nursing homes next week, though in my heart I don't feel I've got the energy. I say we'll view the one in Bournemouth and Sobel House. For now I just want to go back home and lie in my garden – which is what I do.

But first, I go online where an email is waiting for me to say three of my stories have been rejected by a woman's magazine, and I also have a letter turning me down from a new writing venture I'd applied for.

Blast. My writing career's well and truly in shreds.

Saturday 4th August 2007

This evening we're taking Adrian out for a meal to celebrate his new status as a non-contagious person. We're going to The George, a pub opposite the garage where I've been buying his newspapers and wine. The garage that sells everything: wine (choice of red, white or rosé); stamps; envelopes – in fact anything you'd get from a Post Office; lottery tickets; newspapers; magazines; sandwiches that come with a free cup of coffee. I am a fan of this garage. It even has big pumpy things outside in case anyone might want to put petrol in their car. I pop over to buy Adrian a lottery ticket (lucky dip) before we go into the pub.

We've all come. Myself, Peter, Emily and Fran, Ed, Jack and Willow. We eat masses of food. Even Adrian eats most of his fish and chips. This is amazing, since I haven't seen him eat anything for weeks. He talks a lot too but his voice feels the strain and when he's not talking and we're all chatting, exchanging anecdotes, I look across the table at him and feel immensely sad. Over the years we've been for many family meals, but this is the first time I've dined out with Adrian as a 'very sick person'.

People take on a new identity when they're sick. A disabled person or anyone who has changed in any way, and will not change back, takes on a new persona, whereas a pregnant woman or someone with a broken leg is not a 'sick person'. They are temporarily different. Adrian is remarkably unselfconscious about his new appearance, but after the meal I stand with him waiting for Peter to bring the car to the door. A man sitting outside is staring at Adrian. I won't have people treating my brother like a freak. I stare this man out until he gets the message and looks away.

In the car Adrian and I sit in the back with Em.

'I've really enjoyed tonight, guys,' he says. 'It's been great to escape *the prison.*'

Once we reach St Vincent's he kisses me on the cheek. He's allowed to kiss now. He gets out of the car unaided.

'Are you okay?' I ask. 'Do you want a hand up the steps?'

'No. I'm fine,' he says. 'I can manage.'

We wait in the car as he climbs the few steps up to the big glass doors. I feel anxious watching him trying to get into the lobby. He's never had to do this alone before. He doesn't know the procedure for getting in – in fact he's a lot more interested in the procedure for getting out. He doesn't realise you have to ring the bell. Em jumps out of the car, runs up the stairs and rings it. Eventually one of the night staff comes.

As we drive home in the dark Em's CD plays "I'll Stand by You," by Girls Aloud. Nobody's talking on the journey home. I shed a few silent tears in the darkness of the back of the car. We all go to bed full of food, and I toss and turn for what seems like hours with the Girls Aloud song going round and round in my head.

I'll stand by you
Won't let nobody hurt you, I'll stand by you
Take me in, into your darkest hour
And I'll never desert you, I'll stand by you

Sunday 5th August 2007

I awake in the early hours and lie in bed wondering yet again how I'm going to keep all this up. Stan from The Gardener's and John Commerford (who is another of the old Bromley gang) are coming to visit Adrian today. I think about Adrian's funeral list. I am by nature a party thrower, my brother has never organised and hosted a party in his life. Yet now he is organising this gathering of friends – and he won't be here to enjoy it.

By five, Adrian and John, who are coming for a late lunch, still haven't arrived at the house. They text to say they are lost and have gone into the Masons Arms, a pub on our side of Frome. I drive over to the Masons to meet them. It's good to see John. I haven't seen him for years. He's small built, with glasses, his hair totally white now. Engagingly bubbly he is good fun to be with. The last time I saw him, John Major had just become Prime Minister. As John had a look of John Major about him, he was being mistaken for the PM wherever he went. Like Major too, our John has an all-consuming love of cricket.

They follow me back home and we sit outside in the garden under the shade of the parasol. Adrian is relaxing in the sun with his Sunday newspaper, wearing his Panama hat. When the meal is served he eats quite a lot of the salad.

'This is great, Ali. Thanks for doing this meal for us.'

'I hardly did a thing. Jack and Willow prepared all the food. I just laid the table.'

'Ha! Jack and Willow. Thanks guys. Great meal.'

He's trying so hard, yet during most of the dinner I notice Adrian is solemn. He sits at the far end of the table, hardly joining in with the conversation, looking old and reminding me so much of Mum in her final months.

All the same, the occasion lifts my spirits. Adrian kisses me goodbye affectionately as he leaves, and when I wave the two of them off I feel satisfied with the day, thankful to John for taking over my role of carer, even if just for a few hours. John wants to come again, soon. Since Adrian is no longer contagious he's able to plan more outings. John suggests they go to the races, or a cricket match. I really hope he does come again.

In the evening I speak to Kyria who is now home. She says they had a good time in Portugal but missed us. We vow to holiday together another time. She mentions Madeleine McCann. She says there were no pictures of her around, although they were very near the resort she vanished from. Why aren't the police launching a big search for this child? Every parent in the country must be breathing a sigh of relief that they aren't the ones going through this particular nightmare. I know I do, though my girls are much older.

As they approach one hundred days since she vanished, how can anyone come to terms with losing a little one? Surely we all hold ours tighter in response to their anguish.

When I go to turn out the kitchen light before bed I notice Adrian's Panama hat on top of the television. He forgot to take it with him, so it sits in the kitchen all night. Next to Picasso's *Buste de Femme au Chapeau*.

Monday 6th August 2007

The Portuguese police found nothing when they dug up the garden of the number one suspect in the Madeleine McCann case, which must be a huge relief for her parents. The suspect is an ex-pat Brit and if he is innocent then he must have suffered. He looked lots thinner on TV last night than he did when he was first interviewed.

But back to my own drama. Today has been set aside for visiting Sobel House with Adrian to decide if this would be a suitable place for him. Sobel House is the nursing home with the added attraction of a bar and so is a strong contender. It's now the place Adrian is hanging his hopes on. However, when I ring him to arrange a time to go there, he says he's too tired after yesterday. Actually, I'm relieved by this because I feel exhausted too.

I ring Sobel House to rearrange for Thursday and then, over coffee, study my map of Dorset. For some reason I'd thought it was near Sturminster Newton, but in reality Sobel House is nearer Weymouth. Practically on the coast.

We might not be doing the Sobel House recce, but I don't want to leave Adrian without a visitor all day so I drive over there in the afternoon, arrive at St Vincent's and park in front of the house. Usually only a few cars are parked on the gravel, Matron's and some of the staff's. Today a black limousine is parked directly across the main door and a stretcher is positioned across the bottom step. A nasty thought crosses my mind. My feet crunch on the gravel as I hurry around to the gate to have a quick look at the side of the house where Adrian usually sits. I can't see anyone. I walk quickly back to the main entrance.

Both the front door and the inner door – which usually is only penetrable via bell ringing, knocking, phoning and the unlikely event one knows the entry code – are wide open. This I have never seen before. I make my way, past the car and the stretcher, and go inside, relishing my ease of entry. As I am about to walk into the main hall I pass two men in funereal suits who are carrying what I chillingly realise is a body bag. I don't want to appear nosy but I glance desperately at the bag for any sign of a human frame. Beneath the cloth I can see only the slightest outline. Someone small and frail. Another resident? One of the Unseen Ones?

I make my way down the little staircase and along the corridor to Adrian's room. I open the door, having dispensed with the glove, apron and antiseptic gel routine since the all clear on the C.diff front. The room is deserted. Lots more thoughts go through my mind in a very short space of time, not least the image of Adrian lying under the sheet on his bed the other day. He really did look very small then. My God. Could he have died, the undertakers alerted, and been carted out of St Vincent's within the space of a couple of hours? Could all these things have happened without my knowledge? I'm desperate to find him. I literally run to the back door leading to the terrace.

Adrian is sitting in his usual seat in the garden with his glass of wine and the *Daily Mirror* open at the racing page. He must have been in the loo when I first got here. I don't think I've ever been more relieved to see anyone in my life.

He's not alone. A shrivelled old lady is out there too in a wheelchair with a tray sporting today's *Daily Express*. As I walk towards them I check a bit closer to make sure the old lady's still breathing, the way I used to when the children were babies fast asleep in their cots. I see a flicker of life as her chest undulates slightly with a breath. At last, some sign of life here apart from ourselves and the staff. Although this poor soul is very thin, bent double and fast asleep, she's living, and possibly even showing an interest in current affairs.

Adrian greets me with a wave of his hand.

'Hi, Ali. Thanks for coming. It's good to see you.'

I keep quiet about my disconcerting brush with the body bag. Instead I give him back his hat, and get out the map of Dorset which shows exactly where Sobel House is in relation to Frome. He's still keen, especially as there's a historical site nearby which he thinks he's visited before.

How realistic all this is, we've yet to discover. Will Adrian be able to move to Sobel House, with its bar, its swimming pool and its proximity to historical sites? How often could I make the journey to Weymouth to visit him? We decide for today to take a trip out somewhere more local instead. Adrian wants to go into the town. He needs a haircut.

As we walk down the High Street I support him by his matchstick arm and we talk about the various possibilities to help him get around. I suggest a mobility scooter.

'Yeah, I'd like one of those. How much are they, though? They probably cost a fortune.' And yet again I think to myself, *but he's got money*. Plenty of the stuff, all tied up in shares and ISAs and loan notes, building society accounts, and secret internet sites.

'You *could* afford to buy one,' I remind him.

'Yeah, I suppose so.'

The first thing Adrian wants is an extra hole in his leather belt which is struggling to hold up his many-sizes-too-big chinos. We go into a shoe repair shop and Adrian asks the man behind the counter to put two holes in his belt.

'I've lost a bit of weight,' he says with a dry laugh. The man looks like he might be thinking a whole lot more than he's saying and takes the belt. When he's made a couple of holes he looks at Adrian again and says, 'no charge'. Adrian seems chuffed to get a freebie. He leaves his walking stick in the shop and I run back to retrieve it.

Next we find a hairdresser. Adrian greets all the women working in the shop cheerily, which is something I never do. I wonder if this is a characteristic of lonely people, or is he just more outgoing than I am? I leave him to get his hair cut while I go to the bank to move money to pay his bills. When I come back he's thanking the young girl of about nineteen who has just done his hair.

'That was great. Very relaxing. Thanks again.'

'She's nice, and she seemed friendly,' he says as we leave. 'And she's recommended a good place to have lunch. A French bistro over the road.'

The French bistro turns out to be a quirky deli selling unusual crockery as well as food. We sit inside rather than out on the pavement Parisian style as the day is beginning to cool. The décor is stylishly continental. The floors are wooden and the tables and chairs wrought iron. A small child is playing on the floor in a passageway leading, presumably, to the kitchen. We are the only customers. We peruse the menu. Adrian asks the very attractive young woman behind the counter whether they have any wine.

'What?' she says with a French accent. She looks confused.

She's French. This is a French restaurant. She must know what wine is. Still, Adrian's voice is croaky and she might not have understood him.

'*Du vin?*' I try. My A level French, after thirty-seven years' hibernation, swings into action. She points to a bottle of wine on a shelf behind her.

I ask about the *soup du jour* which is listed at the top of a menu on a blackboard. 'Could you tell me what the soup of the day is, please?'

She smiles, goes away to a room at the other end of the shop and returns with the answer.

'It's musher room.'

'Oh, mushroom. My favourite! Is it homemade?' I ask.

'What?'

'Homemade.' I make a stirring action with my hand. 'Made here. Not tinned...'

'What?'

'Tinned!' we say in unison. Adrian points at a tin of sardines to illustrate the word. The woman still looks confused.

'Is it homemade?' I try again.

'Or is it tinned?' Adrian joins in, still pointing at the sardines.

'Oh, no!' she replies.

'So it is tinned?' I say to clarify in my mind the status of the soup. 'Great! Heinz,' I mumble under my breath.

'I'll have the soup,' Adrian unexpectedly pipes up.

What the hell, I think to myself, and decide to go with the flow. 'Two mushroom soups, please.'

'Does the soup come with bread?' Adrian asks, I fear somewhat optimistically.

'What?'

'Bread,' he says. 'Does it come with bread?'

'*Avec du pain*?' I suggest.

'*Non!*'

'But I'd like some bread with mine,' Adrian persists.

'*Non.* We don't have the bread.'

'You don't have bread?' I ask. '*Pas du pain*?'

'*Non.*'

'What about toast?' I enquire somewhat illogically.

'I will ask,' she replies equally illogically, and disappears towards the back of the shop, past the small child who is still there playing with a plastic train.

She returns. '*Non.*'

'No bread,' I say.

'*Non.*'

'But there's a bread shop a few doors down. Couldn't you get some there?'

'*Non.* Too late.'

'Or the supermarket – there's a Tesco's near here.'

'*Non.* I cannot leave the shop and go to the Tesco!' she says glancing towards the child.

'Let's go somewhere else.' Adrian begins to stand up. I sense his frustration and try to gloss over my own disappointment. We've failed to do something as basic as enjoy lunch together in a café.

'You no want the musher room soup?' the woman asks, as if this is one of the bigger disappointments in her life.

'*Non...er, merci...beaucoup. Au revoir.*'

A restaurant *sans* food. Another phenomenon to add to Adrian's list of things lacking in Somerset – a nursing home with no ice or daily papers, a restaurant without bread.

Still feeling peckish we decide to try a hotel I've noticed near St Vincent's. The hotel is called Thurlstone Lodge (four star) and the building is similar in character and style to St Vincent's. The two houses were probably designed by the same architect, and would have been next door neighbours once. A hundred years ago one might have popped over on the horse to borrow a sack of sugar.

In the opulent library of Thurlstone Lodge Adrian orders a glass of Pinot Grigio whilst we study the menu. A waiter approaches with a pad and pen. We order soup. Soup! Will we never learn? We sit twiddling our thumbs only to be told twenty minutes later that the soup is off. In other words – no soup. *Pas de soup. Encore une fois.*

Adrian changes his order to cucumber sandwiches and I order a mustard ham sandwich on brown, which, when it arrives, is a ham sandwich on white. Oh well, at least one out of three ingredients is correct. Adrian eats his sandwiches and then explores the afternoon tea choices and enthusiastically orders scones. These arrive but are rock hard and burnt.

We complain about the scones, which Adrian has tried in

vain to nibble and because of our complaint he is awarded a second glass of wine for free. Result. Despite my feelings about his drinking, I'm relieved by this. I don't want him to be let down time and again in the county I've brought him to. The county I now own as mine.

I drop him back at St Vincent's. The men with their body bag are long since gone. Forgotten. I watch from the car as Adrian painfully climbs the five steps up to the front door looking like a skeleton dressed up in another man's clothes. He leaves the outer door open behind him and eventually, once I'm sure someone has let him in, I drive home.

Tuesday 7th August 2007

It's time for Adrian to move on. He bears no similarity to any of the other few inmates of St Vincent's I've seen, who all look the wrong side of ninety. Surely a nursing home is not for him. As he again turns down my offer to come to our house, I suggest Bradford-on-Avon as a possible place to rent a flat. Last night on the internet I found an idyllic-sounding ground-floor flat to rent there overlooking the canal. Bradford-on-Avon is on the agenda today.

When I arrive at St Vincent's Adrian is in bed.

'I feel really bad about that little nurse,' he says. 'I'm worried in case she thinks I've been rude to her. I don't want to upset her. But she brought me the same aspirins again even though I've told them I have to have the coated ones because of my stomach. This is what annoys me about this place. Because the prescription doesn't say coated aspirins they won't take any notice of what I say to them. They can't do anything here without consulting the fucking Department of Health and Tony Blair.'

I understand his frustration, but now he's snapped and upset Aniela. I'm sorry about this too as she is very sweet. Despite his anger, I can tell he's warming to her.

'I've asked one of the other nurses to ask her to come back so I can apologise to her. But she hasn't.'

In Bradford-on-Avon it's clear Adrian can't walk far but he's enchanted by the place and says he'd definitely like to live here.

'Peter brought me here for a drink in a Young's pub many years ago. That was really nice of him. I've never forgotten it.'

'It is a lovely place but I doubt there will be many one-bedroom flats in the centre of town.' Because of his lack of mobility he'd have to be near to the shops. Even then he'd need transport but I think he's coming round to the idea of a mobility scooter, despite the cost.

We stop at a bench on the riverside. He sits down while I carry on along the river bank in search of a restaurant for lunch. Adrian has his carrier bag full of bits of paper with him. He says he'll get on with his paperwork, which means filling in his application for Disability Living Allowance, as well as a list he's making up.

When I come back I realise with a mixture of curiosity and discomfort that this list is the one he mentioned before. The list of people I am to invite to his funeral. He's busy transferring their addresses and contact numbers from his address book to his list.

He bundles all this away and we amble slowly along the riverside to a shabby pub where we embark on yet another attempt to order refreshment. I ask for orange juice but they don't have any. He orders cold wine. The barman says someone has just gone to the Cash and Carry and will be back in half an hour with both wine and orange juice. Then they unexpectedly find a single stray bottle of Pinot Grigio. I plump for Orangina – but it's warm and so I ask for ice.

'We don't have any ice until the manager gets back from the Cash and Carry,' the barman says.

Is there perhaps a general shortage of ice in the West Country? An ice crisis? A frost famine? A glacial dearth? Not surprisingly, we are the only customers there.

'Another fucking place that doesn't have anything,' Adrian remarks once we are out of earshot of the barman.

Our food arrives and he eats half a sausage and a few chips but downs a pint of Special and a glass of the Pinot. Afterwards we drive to look at The Maltings which is the address of the riverside flat I'd seen on the internet. It looks promising. A newly built block with an attractive archway and lots of garages. But although the flat is described as 'ground floor', the garages are on the ground floor whilst the flats are built above the garages, so are at least twenty steps up. All the same, the location is stunning. Right next to the canal where all the houseboats are moored.

Having made the journey I want to get out of the car to take in the view over the canal. Adrian gets out too, but falls in a heap at the entrance to the garages before I can get round to his side of the car. He's crumpled like a marionette with broken strings, but still has hold of his walking stick and has managed to keep his Panama hat on. I want to help him up but I know he's too heavy for me to lift.

'I don't think this place would suit me,' he says from his position on the ground.

I begin to reassess the situation – once more. We are fooling ourselves. Adrian will not be able to live alone.

'I shouldn't have had that pint, I suppose,' he admits. Or was it the wine? He feels dizzy when he stands up which is why he's fallen in the first place. Another drop in blood pressure? We wait a few moments. He manages to get up with my support. We stand together. I hold him up by his arm as we look at the view that will be enjoyed by whoever eventually rents this flat. The canal, all the painted longboats, mysterious watery homes to the determinedly unconventional. The view is spectacular, the place lovely, and would be even better in sunshine. But the twenty or so steps mean this flat can hardly be classified as ground floor, and so we leave.

On the way back to St Vincent's we stop at the shops as Adrian wants some Milk of Magnesia. I park near a chemist and he says he'll get it. Not wanting to undermine his wishes I'm forced to watch as he staggers along, a pile of bones in sagging clothes, a cadaver in a Panama hat. He's gone for ages but returns minus the Milk of Magnesia. He's full of criticism for the girl who'd served him in the chemist.

'She doesn't know *anything*... Typical Somerset...'

I wonder if the girl could understand what he was asking for with his words swallowed up by his gravelly voice.

'I'll see if I can get some,' I say. So as not to humiliate him by going in the same shop, I try Superdrug instead. On my way back to the car I notice Aniela walking towards me. This is the first time I've seen her out of uniform. She really is a lovely girl, petite with long blonde hair and that distinctively eastern European dress sense that doesn't quite hit the mark. She sees me and although I want to say hello, she looks away. I don't blame her, but I feel sorry if she's feeling bad about what's happened with Adrian – and I'm still not sure what did happen.

Back at St Vincent's, I kiss Adrian goodbye and he staggers off with his plastic bag full of all his bits of paper, his application for Disability Living Allowance, his funeral guest list, and his Milk of Magnesia. How have I hardened myself to all this? I don't know – but somehow I have.

In the evening Adrian sends me a text: *Will need 1 of the girls 2 help me set up acer – never dun 1 b4. Red faced S.V*, which is a reference to the new laptop I left in his room today.

Wednesday 8th August 2007

The eighth day of the eighth month. I'm not going to see Adrian today. Olivia from Dorothy House is visiting this afternoon, and the kids are taking him out this evening.

Adrian rings me in the morning. 'St Vincent's haven't told Olivia about the all clear on the C.diff front. This means I won't be going with her to visit Dorothy House where I might've been able to join a group of other cancer patients. I'm really beginning to hate all the staff here. I'm sure they're trying to keep me here as long as possible. I reckon they need the money. Everything here's falling apart and everyone who works here is incompetent.'

'I suppose you could be right,' I say. 'Anyway, at least you're going out tonight. Jack and Ed will be collecting you at seven.'

I phone Olivia's office and confirm she is visiting later in the afternoon, but not taking him to Dorothy House. I email Jill Miller about the possibility of Adrian having a home massage, and she gets on the case straight away.

At nine I get a phone call from Jack from the pub.

'Mum? Adrian's still inside the pub with Ed and Willow but he's left a sort of nappy type thing lying on the floor of my car. I don't know what to do with it.'

'Well, I've always thought those things are kind of incontinence pads,' I tell him. 'Adrian was using them when he had the C.diff bug, but best not to mention it to him now. I should just leave it.'

'I didn't want to embarrass him,' Jack says.

'How's it going apart from that?' I ask.

'He isn't eating much but he's making the effort. In fact we ended up eating most of his leftovers!' he laughs.

I think nothing more of the nappy pad.

Jack drops Ed off at home before he and Willow go back to her house. Ed walks into the kitchen looking pale.

'Mum, I feel sick. I'm going to bed.'

'Drink some water,' I say running the tap for him. 'How was Adrian tonight?'

'After we'd finished the meal he told us he thinks he might have that hospital bug thing again.'

My heart sinks. Big time. I think of the nappy pad Jack mentioned. Surely this can't be happening. This is cruelty piled upon more cruelty. I despair, not only for my brother but also I'm now rather concerned for my two sons and Willow who reportedly had been eating his leftovers.

'He went to the toilet a couple of times when we were in the pub. He was in there for a while,' Ed says before heading up for bed.

I feel desolate for Adrian. Not only is he going to feel ill again, he's going to be a prisoner in St Vincent's. How can we ever get him out of there?

Jack rings me later confirming what Ed said about Adrian's visits to the loo.

'Adrian definitely said he had the bug again.'

I pray he's wrong.

I go up to Ed's room and ask him what he had to eat.

'Lobster,' he says.

'No wonder you're feeling ill. Lobster can be a bit dodgy,' I'm mightily relieved to say.

Later I sit on the bed with Emily before bedtime. Adrian has sent me a text, written yesterday. The text says, '*Ta 4 tday. Herd ad 4 scarecrow exhbn nr ere. Mite b fun! A.*'

When I first read this I thought 'how nice!' An exhibition of scarecrows! I'm so pleased he's planning more things we can do together. I text him back and say *'that sounds different'* but then I want to say more. I want to ask him about the bug and to think of a way to ask in a text whether he's got diarrhoea again. But I can't even spell the word, and when I try it in predictive text it comes out as 'diarrhod'. Anyway it seems the wrong kind of question to put in a text. Emily suggests I ask how he's feeling, but I decide not – I don't like saying one thing when really I mean another. I turn my phone off, say goodnight to the girls and go downstairs to catch a bit of *The Pumpkin Eater*, an old black and white film about a woman who keeps having more and more babies. I first saw it years ago – before I had any...

get up earlyish in case we decide to visit Sobel House. Yes, we are still clinging on to the Sobel House card. Since independent living in Bradford-on-Avon is a no no as far as Adrian is concerned, Sobel House has now become the lifeline he's reaching for. A very important lifeline. If we can get him in there, everything will be alright...

I eat breakfast before ringing Adrian, but he's already sent me a text: '*Got bug back. All off...*'

I think of replying with the single word 'shit' but then think better of it.

I eat my Crunchie Nut Cornflakes and All-Bran. I *will* build up some strength from somewhere and then I'll phone him. I'll go over and sort out the laptop for him. He'll need it more than ever if he's going to be incarcerated in that room again.

Before leaving the house I ring St Vincent's to enquire about the refund of the fees I've paid but have since learnt Wandsworth Council is going to reimburse. I get a nurse called Fiona, who is very chatty, but I think one of the main culprits in the Failure to Deliver Brigade. She tells me Adrian will not be able to go out with me now he has the bug again, nor will he be able to come to my house, etc. etc... Okay, I'd worked that one out myself.

'I think it would help matters in general if, when Adrian asks for something, it was forthcoming and he didn't have to wait ages as this is very frustrating for him,' I say.

'I realise this is not your brother's fault, but often we have a great deal to do and don't do things as quickly as we might.'

'But this is an expensive nursing home and he should be able to expect good service.'

'Yes,' she says. 'But it's not always possible to go to a patient each time they call as we are short staffed.'

'Then surely some of the residents' fees should be spent on employing enough staff to look after them.' The line goes quiet. 'Hello, are you still there?'

'Err, yes. I see what you mean...'

'And if he's getting more antagonistic towards the place then it makes things more difficult for me,' I point out. 'Do you understand what I'm saying?'

'Yes,' Fiona says, and I leave it at that.

I arrive at St Vincent's just after two in the afternoon. Even though it's a hot day, there's no sign of Adrian in the garden – just the crumpled up figure of the woman (or, on second thoughts, is it a man?) who wears a purple hat and was here the other day asleep in front of the *Daily Express*. I've heard the nurses call this person Doctor Jenkins, so no extra clues as to the poor soul's gender. With a little more scrutiny I decide she is indeed a 'she'. A she, nonetheless, who happens to have a penchant for dressing in men's clothes.

I go back into the house, down the corridor to Adrian's room. Outside I don the apron and gloves, a fresh supply of which I note is on display outside his door. Back to the old routine. He's lying in a heap, foetus style again, and the room smells bad – a mixture of the stuffy rancid paint smell that's never faded, with a faint backdrop of poo. I give him a little radio I've just bought. I know, I know, I keep bringing more and more gadgets – although the laptop remains in the briefcase where I left it two days ago. I'm almost embarrassed to tell him I've brought yet another offering. As if any of these things will make him better.

Two nurses arrive in the room. One of the older women and a girl called Gift.

'They won't leave me alone,' Adrian complains,

understandably not wanting lots of people in his room fussing around him.

'She want to be left in peace,' Gift says. I've noticed her around before. She's young with fine, beautifully chiselled African features – the sweetest of faces. Sometimes her English is muddled.

'He,' I correct her.

'Oh yes, he. I sorry! Did I say she?'

Adrian doesn't seem up for company and as I want to eat my sandwich outside I go out to his old table and start my picnic lunch. As I eat, however, although I'm alone, I can *feel* the energy coming from Matron whose office is directly behind me. I sense her coming out before I see her. Suddenly she's standing in front of me, blocking the sun.

'I'm extremely sorry to hear your brother is again suffering with C.diff,' she says.

'Yes, it's so depressing,' I hear myself say, momentarily dropping my guard.

'Yes, and it's extremely difficult for the staff here. Last night it took two nurses to clear up the mess which was all over the bed and the carpets. This was at two in the morning.'

I hadn't realised quite how awful this illness was. How humiliating for Adrian – how horrible for him.

'Then they had to Vax the carpets and even wash their own shoes.'

Fuck off, I think to myself. *This is your job and you're getting paid for it.*

'Of course, the drinking hasn't helped,' Matron continues. 'The fact that he's been drinking undermines the antibiotics which eradicated the C.diff in the first place. But then of course he is *dying*, and who knows what you or I would do under those circumstances.'

'I can't imagine how I would react,' I say, feeling myself seduced into a heart-to-heart with someone so strangely heartless. 'And I think he's been drinking heavily for some time. I'm surprised I didn't notice he had a problem years ago. Although I don't like to think of him being classified as an alcoholic.'

'Oh, but he *is*,' Matron says. 'The hospital report clearly states he is an alcoholic.'

'Maybe. I know the medical definition of an alcoholic is quite low down the scale,' I say recalling my conversation with Verity Jones. 'You don't necessarily have to drink a lot to be classified as an alcoholic in the world of medicine. To be perfectly honest, I think I've only seen him drunk once in my life.' (I'm thinking back to a year ago when he came to Somerset for the anniversary of our mother's funeral. The time he told me he'd joined a dating agency.)

'Oh, no! You wouldn't have. Alcoholics don't get drunk!'

I decide to change the subject. Although the funding has been approved by Wandsworth Council and should be in the coffers of St Vincent's I still haven't seen any sign of the three thousand pounds plus I've spent on the fees and is due to be refunded.

'Why is this?' I ask.

'As soon as we get it, it will be refunded to you...' Blah, blah, blah...

I go back into Adrian's room. The curtains are closed. The smell is vile. I open the packaging surrounding the new radio – one of those hermetically sealed double-glazed jobbies the manufacturers really don't want anyone to get into.

'Whoever made this blasted thing didn't want anyone to actually open it!' I observe as I hack my way in with an ice pick (okay, a pair of nail scissors). I know he will join in with this sentiment – i.e. the world is a ridiculously absurd place and everything is stacked against us.

'Yeah, yeah,' he says with a mirthless laugh.

'The smell of paint in here is making me feel a bit sick. Would you like me to come back later?'

I leave the room and bump into Gift again in the main hallway. She's receiving Adrian's new batch of antibiotics from a pharmacist delivery woman. Yet another course of antibiotics. How many more can his body cope with?

I say goodbye to Gift in passing and she touches my arm.

'Take care,' she says.

Her gentle words catch me unawares. *Take care*. I have to turn away from her in order to hold back my tears.

I drive home too fast. The sky is perfect blue but with *Simpsons* clouds. At home I try to relax and find some energy for returning to St Vincent's later, as I'd said I would do. *Richard and Judy* is on TV and features a conversation with a man who lost both legs in a fire. He sits on the *Richard and Judy* sofa with a gruesome prosthetic leg showing – why isn't he wearing trousers over the false leg? His other leg, which is covered, is half removed. The man claims that losing both his legs is the best thing that ever happened to him. As his life was before, he'd probably have spent the rest of his days in a boring job in a warehouse. But now he's just written a book (he doesn't seem the type) and is a stunt double in films requiring characters with no legs.

Next Richard and Judy turn to the subject of the missing child, Madeleine McCann. The finger is being pointed at the parents as day 100 since her disappearance approaches. The Portuguese police are now suggesting Madeleine may have been murdered inside the apartment. Why on earth would these parents murder their little girl? The simple answer is, they wouldn't. You only have to look at them to know they aren't murderers. And why would *anyone* kill her inside the apartment and then carry her body away? Those parents are suffering hell already without being accused of murder. The world is sick. I feel so tired but can't nap. Jack rings and asks me to come to The Bell in Buckland Dinham tonight for a drink.

'I might come, but I've promised to go and see Adrian later on,' I tell him.

I don't get moving until after eight so by the time I get back to St Vincent's dusk is falling.

Just as I pull up in the car park my mobile rings. It's Phil G. He's spoken to Adrian and is worried. 'Adrian said *"I can't do this"* and ended the call.'

'I've just arrived and I'm about to go in and see him,' I say.

'I think I might come down tonight,' Phil says. While I'm sitting in the car outside the main entrance of St Vincent's, Gift comes out and waves. Again I'm choked by this small act of humanity from this beautiful girl. This act of friendship. But it's late. I'm tired. I break down whilst still on the phone to Phil. 'I'll phone you back when I've seen him,' I whisper between sobs.

'Are you alright, Ali?' he says. I feel as close to this man I hardly know as I do to anyone right now. He always calls me 'Ali', even though this is my pet name.

I blow my nose, wipe my eyes and go into St Vincent's. Adrian is lying on his back, looking bad.

'I just want to die,' he says turning away from me. 'And I'm sick of all the people in here making a fuss all the time.'

Is this his way of maintaining some sort of macho dignity?

'Do you want me to stay?' I ask.

'Yes, ten minutes,' is his reply. I sit down and watch the television even though the screen is half hidden by his bed. He's on the History Channel – still soaking up information about a world he's soon to depart. Queen Victoria's chubby round face smiles out at us. What's it like to be dead, Vic? I'd like to ask her. Or to live on after death in the lives of thousands in the guise of an East End pub in a soap opera? Or as an important figure in history for people like Simon Schama, who is presenting this programme? Adrian speaks without turning round to face me.

'I'm not very good at talking...' he begins. I wonder if he's about to say something like a statement of his affection for me – love maybe? How many times recently have I felt the need for a show of affection from him. Yet when it comes to the crunch and he seems to be putting something into words, I don't pursue it. I brush off this beginning of a conversation by saying 'oh, that's alright,' because I fear I'll break down. The moment is lost. His words lost as well. I'm too tired for this and whatever he was about to say fizzles out.

I touch him tenderly on the arm with rubber-gloved hands as if he were my child. How often Em and Fran say 'love you!' Those two words come so easily at the end of every phone call, every text. *Love you. Love you Mummy. Ly.* And here we are, two adults who have known each other all our lives and neither of us is capable of saying those words. I feel tears coming again – so many during the course of this very long day. I manage to compose myself before speaking.

'Phil rang me,' I say.

'Which one?' Adrian asks.

'Gullifer.'

'What did he say?'

'He just wondered how you were because you ended the call when he was speaking to you.'

We sit in silence for a moment.

'What are the others doing?' Adrian asks eventually, meaning Peter and Jack. 'Playing golf?'

'They have been but they're in the pub now. They're in The Bell at Buckland.' I know Adrian likes to hear about pubs. 'And the girls are at a friend's house. I'm going to get them soon.'

I leave, sensing he wants to be alone.

Phil G rings at ten-thirty on the land line. He's rung Carol too. I think he's worried about me.

Carol texts to say she'll leave her phone on all night. I've told Phil not to rush down here, but to have a good night's rest. He can ring me tomorrow.

I switch my mobile off and if the house phone rings during the night I hope I don't hear it.

Friday 10th August 2007

Thank goodness, there are no messages on either phone. After breakfast I ring Matron. Adrian is a bit better but still had incontinent diarrhoea during the night. She seems to enjoy describing the mess all over the carpet (again) rather than focusing on her patient's feelings.

I spend the morning walking the dog and lying in the garden in the build-up to going to St Vincent's. I arrive at two-thirty and go in the side entrance, which means I don't have to wait for the door to be opened by a member of staff. I've recently discovered this unorthodox method of entry that means I don't sign in either, thus flaunting the fire regs. Very naughty.

Dr Jenkins, the only other visible living resident of St Vincent's, is slumped in her wheelchair under a parasol. I wonder what she was like in her day. Presumably a very intelligent woman.

Adrian's in his room. I put the gloves and pinny on. I'm reminded of Peter's last visit when he said they only had a box of size small gloves. The thought of him squeezing his big man hands into these tiny gloves makes me smile.

Adrian looks better and is propped up in bed. His voice is clearer, less strained perhaps because he hasn't been talking so much for the last couple of days. I tidy up a bit and Gift comes in offering tea. The tea arrives with the now predictable offering of wet cake. I suck my way through yet another slice of damp Victoria sponge.

Then I try to get the two gadgets going. The radio and the laptop. Adrian is frustrated with both. He used to be an expert at IT. He set up my first computer for me. But now he seems even less techy than me. I decide to take them home so one of the children can sort them out. Adrian's angry – everything's 'fucking useless'.

I sit down beside him. 'Matron said if you drink alcohol the work of the antibiotics is undermined, which is why the C.diff keeps coming back.'

'I won't drink again,' he says. 'Anyway just thinking of alcohol makes me feel sick.'

He needs the loo while I'm there. He's been given a commode to use at night which has the words 'Mrs White' written on the side. Was it she I passed in the hallway dressed in a body bag two days ago, I wonder? And where are Miss Scarlet, Rev. Green and Colonel Mustard? Anyway the commode doesn't look especially clean but when I arrived I put my handbag on it without realising what it was. I have a good rub at my bag with the disinfectant gel while Adrian is out of the room.

When he comes back from the bathroom we get on to the inevitable and unending topic of his will. In his new version he wants to increase the legacies to some of his friends and to include some of their children. I suggest we make his new version legal otherwise it will mean nothing. He has his address book and a piece of paper from his notebook. He's sober and tetchy. Laboriously, he copies the beneficiaries' postcodes down before handing it to me.

I look at the back and recognise this as being the same piece of paper he used to list the details of his funeral. I had decided not to look at this but can't help noticing the first piece of music. It's the old Pink Floyd favourite *Dark Side of The Moon*.

I feel bleak. Bleak at the thought of having to stand and listen to Pink Floyd on what will be one of the most horrible days of my life. Bleak because my brother is still stuck in the seventies and has chosen this far-off music to explain his life. I look further down his list. His other choice is Minnie Riperton – "Midnight at the Oasis". Another seventies song. There are a few other choices for his wake plus the Beatles "Let It Be" and

"A Day In The Life", then something by Bobby Darin called "Beyond the Sea". I already feel heartbroken in anticipation of listening to this music. But I must put these details to the back of my mind and concentrate on what he needs now.

'Oh, Ali. I'd like you to take over my affairs now. And I'd like some chocolate. And a dressing gown. And would you mind taking all the will stuff to be updated? Thanks.'

I feel overloaded and a bit distant. I still haven't done anything about his claim for Disability Living Allowance or the other thing he wanted me to apply for – can't even remember what it was.

Before I go Adrian tells me Bryony has cancelled her visit tomorrow because of the C.diff.

He gets up to go to the loo again. 'It's fatal,' he calls to me from his en-suite – a place I have not yet ventured into.

'Oh, you mean you're thinking about Bryony's boyfriend's mum?' I ask, knowing such a person exists and that Bryony is worried about carrying the infection back home.

'No. I was thinking about me,' he says.

'Oh.'

The bathroom wall is still between us and I wonder why he's saying this now. Has he only just realised C.diff can be fatal? My reaction is inadequate, to say the least. But I'm shocked at his scant understanding of the condition that has taken over his life.

I get ready to go home, equipped with all Adrian's stuff I've got to sort out.

I pop into Asda to see if they have a black towelling dressing gown. They do have a small-sized towelling men's dressing gown but it's mud colour. Well, shit colour to be precise. 'Light Diarrhoea' would be a fitting description. I give the dressing gown a miss and just get him a folder to tidy up his bits of paper, and some lounging pj. pants, size 'extra small'.

By the evening I have a headache. Phil G rings to say he's

coming on Sunday. He says Adrian would like to go to the races. I suggest Wincanton, which is reasonably near.

'I really do want to take him. Even if I have to push him in a chair...' He means wheelchair and of course wheelchair is one of those words we all like to avoid using. In fact wheelchairs are one of those things we all like to avoid using.

In the evening I feel the tension and the enormity of all this in my marriage. When I came in tonight everyone was sitting around the dining table eating a McDonald's. They'd got me a cheeseburger Happy Meal which is cold. From the point of view of the rest of the family it must seem as if I've disappeared off their planet. I haven't done much around the house in weeks and now I keep getting phone calls from a man called Phil.

'Will you be there when I come down?' Phil asked me.

'No, I doubt it,' I told him. 'I think I might have a day off.'

Saturday 11th August 2007

A heatwave has finally arrived here, and in Portugal, Madeleine McCann has been missing for one hundred days. This is a real landmark for her poor parents and speculation in the papers about what may have happened to her dominates every tabloid, every broadsheet and all the news programmes.

Outside the sky is pure blue. I take the radio I bought for Adrian back to the shop, as it only seems to tune into Radio Wiltshire, and get a refund. I take the laptop back because it doesn't connect to the internet. But I'm in a hurry. Today is the day of the visitors. Both Bryony (who has obviously changed her mind about the threat of infection) and Carol are coming to Somerset.

I meet Carol at Westbury station. It's strange seeing someone after a while when you've been talking a lot on the phone. We kiss and it's good to have a woman with me who is involved in Adrian's plight. I feel for her because she's about to have a difficult emotional experience.

As we're driving along Carol has a call from Bryony. I momentarily wonder whether these two are friends, or weren't they at one time rivals for Adrian's affections? He'd courted them both at different times in his life without offering either the security of marriage, children, a shared home. But the past seems irrelevant now.

Bryony tells Carol she's seen Adrian, has been greatly upset and decided to leave early. Now she's walking back to the station. Maybe she wanted to be gone before Carol arrived. Are they chums or not? Adrian met Bryony at a Spanish evening class in London, whereas Carol was from the Cheltenham years. Bryony turns down my offer of a lift. It seems she wants to walk to clear her head.

As we approach St Vincent's I spot a woman with reddish hair, slim, in a black top and leggings walking in the opposite direction. She's carrying a shoulder bag, the sort you might take on a long journey.

'Is *that* Bryony?' I ask Carol. The last time I met her I was pregnant with my girls.

'I don't know.' Carol hasn't seen her for years either – or has maybe never seen her? Why would she? I don't ask.

We drive past the woman in black. It's too late to stop but I think it is Bryony. The way she's walking, her whole demeanour is of someone striding purposefully away from something horrible. I'm sure it's her. After all, there's no one else around the area of St Vincent's Nursing Home, except for the staff and I don't recognise this woman as one of them. As we drive down the sweeping circular road leading to St Vincent's, Carol talks enthusiastically about the things she's seen on the train. The green fields, woodlands, cattle and sheep. She gasps as she spots a group of horses grazing around the land at the far end of the garden.

Then leave London, Carol, is what I feel like saying. There's a whole world out here. Trees, horses, fresh air, double your living space for the same money. Still, I suppose she has to stay in London for her work.

As I park the car we exchange train travel anecdotes and have a good laugh. Carol has had some hilarious mix up over seat numbers on her way down. The calm before the storm...

We go into St Vincent's and I show her the protocol for signing in, the gloves, the apron, the hand gel, and last but not least, the escape route to the garden. In the hall we pass Aniela and she is, I'm delighted to see, very smiley and friendly. Maybe she and Adrian have made up. She tells us he hadn't eaten much for lunch but had taken his antibiotics. I hope Adrian has been nice to her. It would be worth his while to at least try – you get more out of people when you try – but then I think of his situation and how frustrating it must be to ask for a pillow and be brought a pill. I guess he has to take this frustration out on somebody. Before we go into Adrian's bedroom I tell Carol about the aromatherapy oils and other kit I've left in his room, secretly hoping she may offer to use them on him.

'Is it okay to kiss him?' she asks.

'No. Probably not,' I advise her. 'Probably best not to take any risks.'

We enter the bedroom. Inside Adrian is propped up on a mountain of pillows watching the horse racing. I give him his folder and the lounging pj. pants, for which he seems very grateful. I ask him what Bryony was wearing and although he's vague about this, I think the person we saw was her. He's sure she was upset, though. I leave Carol, saying I might look for Bryony and pick her up as I have to go in the direction of the bus stop anyway.

But this isn't true. As I approach the junction I realise my normal route home is to the left, the opposite way from the bus stop. I make a snap decision. I don't know Bryony very well but if I was her I'd probably want to be alone with my thoughts. And she clearly wants to walk. Adrian said one of the nurses had offered her a lift. So I turn to the left, wondering whether I'd have been a better person if I'd tried to catch up with her and help her.

But *I've* coped on my own – time after time. I've driven away from St Vincent's choked with tears. I've driven and cried at the same time. I wouldn't have wanted anyone trying to help me then.

By the time I reach the roundabout on the outskirts of Frome, I'm already thinking about other things. The laptop. I must collect Adrian's laptop.

In Frome I go for some retail therapy in Coco's and Spirit, the two most expensive dress shops in town. In Spirit I buy a sundress in their sale.

'Why did you buy that?' Peter asks when I get home.

'I don't know,' I reply. But I do know I'll be glad of it if we eventually get away on holiday.

Sunday 12th August 2007

I settle in the garden with the Sunday papers which greet me with the headlines that a cure has been found for cancer. The article explains how all cancer sufferers will be cured within a few days, no matter how far the disease has progressed and whichever organs are affected. A new special kind of 'zapper' has been developed to destroy all tumours. After this simple, painless treatment, the victims will then eat until they put on all the weight they've lost, returning to the way they used to be. This amazing breakthrough means hope for everyone. A cure for heart problems and alcoholism has been found too.

The paper is full of columns devoted to the financial and other implications of these breakthroughs. The number of pensioners will go through the roof. Undertakers will go out of business. Solicitors will be bankrupt with no wills to sort out. The world will be in chaos...

...But my brother will live. No need to listen to *Dark Side of The Moon* and cry. No Minnie Riperton. No Bobby Darin. We'll party instead – with him there.

Oh...and Madeleine McCann's still not found either.

Monday 13th August 2007

My mission today is to change Adrian's will. While I'm in town I call into my solicitor's office. Quite understandably her secretary says they could only change the will in the presence of my brother. They could do a domiciliary visit (cost, over two hundred pounds – isn't everything, involving a brief?) but in view of the C.diff they aren't keen. In fact the more I explain the situation, the more it seems they wouldn't touch the job with the proverbial bargepole. I can see their point of view. The will can't be changed unless Adrian is present. He can't get to them, and they won't go to him.

'If your brother came in here with *your* will and asked us to change it then I'm sure you wouldn't want us to alter anything without your permission,' the receptionist explains. I understand what she's saying. All I'm trying to do is find a way to change the will for him. In the end she suggests I get in touch with the people who drew up the original will. Now why didn't I think of that?

I drive over to see Adrian and meet Matron in the hallway. I immediately ask about my refund. She babbles on about Wandsworth and some problem with the finance officer at St Vincent's.

'It should be with you tomorrow,' she affirms. *Does* St Vincent's have a cash flow problem? I've noticed the owner of the home has been there a few times recently, her top of the range BMW eclipsing the rest of the cars in the car park. Has she come to look into the finances? She certainly seems to be doing alright for herself.

'How is he?' I ask before taking my leave of Matron. After all, Adrian's wellbeing is what this is all about.

'He looks very weak today, but I wasn't here over the weekend and I haven't caught up with everything yet.'

As I approach the room I feel a sense of doom and gloom. It's a dull, cloudy day, which normally means Adrian's spirits will be dull and cloudy too. He's sitting upright in bed, corpse like, watching TV. I've brought him a black towelling dressing gown from Marks and Spencer which is exactly what he'd asked for. He doesn't seem to register what it is but I hang it on the door anyway.

I notice someone has unpacked the aromatherapy kit I got from Center Parcs and laid it out on the mantelpiece and radiator. I ask him if anyone has used them on him.

'No,' he says.

'Would you like me to give you a massage with the oils?' I ask him.

'Yes,' he says without hesitation.

I take away the pillows stacked up behind him and help him lie down flat. I rub the oils into my rubber-gloved hand and begin. For years my children have been giving me vouchers for Elaine's beauty shop in Frome every birthday, Christmas and Mother's Day. I try to repeat the technique of Sally, my favourite masseuse, starting with his back, rubbing deep into his skin. His skin is loose and pliable and moves with my fingers. Like someone who has dieted too much, there now seems more skin than body. Then I use the brush on his arms and legs. I can tell he's really enjoying this. I am too. I'd been afraid I might feel awkward but I'm finding the experience relaxing. I remember the bits I really like myself – the hands, feet and head. I feel odd massaging his chest with its curly, wiry stitching – a straight scar down from his heart. The instructions in the aromatherapy booklet said you should 'massage towards the heart'. I keep this in mind, focusing all the time on his heart, moving towards its centre. Although surely this is for men. Women don't get massaged on the chest.

When I rub the skin on his head it turns pink.

'Your skin's going pink!'

'Oh, it doesn't matter. It doesn't matter,' he says as if he doesn't want anything to cause me to stop.

Afterwards I ask if he wants the pillows plumped up again.

'No. I just want to lie here in a warm glow.'

Just then Scary Red Nurse from last week's meeting arrives to check on Adrian.

'You're looking better,' she says. She and I have a little chat about massages and she's nice (of course). Adrian lies there relaxing in his warm glow. This feels like the most important and useful thing I have done so far.

When Scary Red has gone I get out the laptop and manage to get an internet connection for an instant – only to lose it again.

Back home, when I tell the rest of the family over dinner (ready-made lasagne with oven chips and frozen peas) about Adrian's massage, I sense they all think it's a bit weird – me massaging my brother. But who else would do it? With the bug back there's no way I could pay someone to go in there. I couldn't ask anyone else to do something so intimate when he has a contagious illness. And when I tell them all about the laptop I realise (courtesy of Ed) that I have to keep the battery charged in order for it to work. There's no point in even pretending I knew that. Duh, duh and double duh.

At night I can't sleep and so I get up and iron at least fifty T-shirts from my ever growing ironing pile.

E d rings me from work.

'Mum, I don't feel well. I think I've caught the bug thing from Adrian.'

Lots of horrible thoughts crowd my mind. I was aware Jack and Willow were cross Adrian didn't tell them the C.diff was back until *after* they'd eaten his leftover burger and touched his mobile. Willow is a nanny and is currently in charge of a new born baby, so this is especially relevant to her.

'No, Ed. I'm sure you're okay,' I say, but I ring the doctor's surgery. A nurse tells me they will leave a sample pot for me at the reception. Before I go to St Vincent's I make a diversion to the Health Centre to collect the pot. The rain is back and although it's the middle of August, it feels more like October. At St Vincent's I run into Matron in the hall and she gives me the cheque for the refund of Adrian's fees.

'How is he today?' I ask, slipping the cheque into my handbag.

'I've got a huge report to complete because the inspectors are coming,' she replies, indicating a big wad of papers and folders under her arm.

What sort of answer is that? Like I'm interested in her fucking report. Is she looking for sympathy or just covering up her lack of interest in her patients' welfare? She obviously hasn't got a clue how Adrian is.

I carry on to his room and find him propped up on pillows again, watching *Sky News* as usual. His Panama hat hangs on the back of the door, a reminder of the few days of summer and his last tantalising days of freedom – now gone.

I try unsuccessfully to connect the laptop before getting the oils ready for the massage. Aniela comes in with a pill.

'You going to give massage?' she asks me and then taps me on the shoulder as she leaves. 'I would like one too! Back sore,' she adds, rubbing her side.

This time Adrian turns the sound off on the TV. After the massage I leave, like a doctor who has done their job – administered their therapy. I'm becoming less and less emotional. I suppose practical help is a good substitute for sentiment. And Adrian's stopped talking about money or his affairs. He just asks about the family and occasionally comments on the news.

'There's going to be trouble in Pakistan.' And 'this government's education policy is a mess.' He even asks me what I've been doing today and I have to think. Oh yes, I've written a critique that's been waiting on my desk for weeks. *Art Lovers of Harlech.* A funny story that was entered in the short story competition about a Welsh public school boy.

Wednesday 15th August 2007

It's raining all morning. Even the dog doesn't want to go out. My day for teaching at Center Parcs again and one of the punters, a lady from Byfleet, asks me for my autograph. It would seem churlish to refuse but I feel ridiculous giving it to her. Every time I sit in Luciano's Restaurant with a group of holidaymakers who've signed up to my creative writing class, I think back to a young Irish man who came along in May. He had the bluest eyes and the blackest hair, real Irish good looks. He was on holiday with his wife and two little boys, both under five. During the chat we always have before beginning the class, he talked about his wife who was dying of cancer and would be dead by October.

I remember how shocked I was when he said this. My heart went out to this young man and his family. I remember thinking on the hop and changing the exercise I'd planned. The exercise was to begin with students writing a list of things that make them cry, followed by a list of things that make them laugh. This was based on my most recently published story, *Things That Make Me Cry*, which was about the song "Stand By Me" by Ben E. King (which does always make me cry) and a shopping trip to Trowbridge with Emily (which was funny).

How different I am today from the person who was shocked by the Irish man's revelation. Now a similar nightmare is part of my everyday life.

After Center Parcs I head westwards to visit Adrian. He's propped up, cadaver-like, in the bed again and sounds unusually groggy.

'Sorry, Ali, I've just woken up. Sorry if I'm a bit sleepy.'

234

I wonder what drugs he's on but I don't think he knows so I don't bother asking. Is this the effect of the morphine?

'I think I'm going mad,' he says. 'I've been a bad boy.' He has adopted these funny little phrases I wouldn't have associated with him before. Like 'tootsies' for feet and 'bye-byes' for sleep. It's quite sweet. But the going mad is worrying.

'I don't think I'll ever get out of here,' he says.

'Of course you will!' I say, inwardly cringing at my own hollow sounding words. 'Of course you will – you said the same about St George's and you got out of there!'

We sit quietly for a moment or two. 'Does it help when people visit?' I ask.

'Yes,' he says. 'Peter popped in earlier.'

Maybe I should increase my visits. A day is a long time in a place like this. Perhaps I should come in the evenings as well. But giving up my evenings – and for how long? The more strain on me, the more I'm going to be wishing for this all to be over… and the only way for this all to be over is…

I massage him, but have to leave by four-thirty. This is the third massage I've done. He moans with pleasure and I give him an extra five minutes on his feet. Fran did mine last night and I made a mental note to spend longer on Adrian's feet as it's so delicious. In a way the rubber gloves help, as I'm not sure how I'd be about massaging feet without them.

As I massage we talk. I tell him about today's Center Parcs group. One of them, a man from the Isle of Wight, said he knew Maurice Dix who was at university with me in the seventies. The same man also revealed in one of the writing exercises that he was once stuck for over four hours in a packed tube train just after the Paddington bombings, strap-hanging in a big overcoat. I tell Adrian all this, although normally I don't think he's interested in small talk. The massaging situation seems to open up the door for chit-chat.

He says something about India and Pakistan but I haven't

seen the news. He's convinced they're about to blow each other up.

Adrian thanks me, asks me to buy him some chocolate rolls and I leave.

At home Peter tells me about his visit to St Vincent's this afternoon.

'I sat with him for about three hours.'

But Adrian had made this sound like a short visit. *Peter popped in.* Is he aware of what's going on? Before leaving Peter says he went to look for a nurse – and found Scary Red Nurse.

'I asked her how long it will be before the C.diff clears up. She said it could take six months but they haven't told Adrian this because it's too depressing. I'd like to take Adrian to the Beerfest in Buckland Dinham this weekend. But if it takes six months to get the all clear then that's not likely to happen.'

Great. I wish he hadn't told me either. Now I know why I don't cross examine the staff about medical things.

'What did you talk about for all those hours?'

'We talk and then have silences. I fell asleep a few times. His room's so hot.'

'It's good you can sit together and not have to talk all the time,' I say remembering something my mother said about Adrian and Bryony when they were a couple. They were good together because they weren't uncomfortable with silences. I think she was right. A good relationship does mean you don't have to talk all the time.

'This C.diff thing is such a bloody nuisance, though. If it wasn't for this illness Adrian could spend his last days or weeks or months or whatever doing things like going to the races – or the Buckland Dinham Beerfest. He would've enjoyed going to the Beerfest.'

'Yes,' I agree. 'And of course you would only be going to the Beerfest to support him…'

'Of course.'

'He says he thinks he's going mad incarcerated in that room.'

'I'm not surprised.'

I'm tortured by the decisions I made which have led to my brother's current situation. That afternoon when we collected him from Putney and brought him here. The random choice of nursing home. Not listening to the woman we met in the local pub who was so insistent St Vincent's wasn't right for him. On that first evening we should have collected his things and brought him home with us. And yet he'd refused my offers to come home so many times. Although I'd never even heard of C.diff then I don't know how I'd have coped with cleaning up diarrhoea at three in the morning.

The pub we visited on that first night is now closed down. My God. Did we play any part in its demise? It had probably been there for centuries. Did they hear about the man suffering from a hospital superbug who'd been drinking there? Or maybe it was closed down by the Department of Health just for being dirty.

After dinner Welsh Phil phones. 'I've been trying to talk to Adrian but he sounds groggy and it's really hard to hear what he's saying. I suppose he might answer a text message but I don't do texting. I've never done texting and I'd like to know how he is because Carol and I are hoping to visit him at the weekend, see?'

'You could both stay here if you want,' I suggest as I know the local B&Bs can be expensive.

'Oh, I don't know about that. I mean, I don't want to create more work for you.'

Having guests for the weekend uses up a different kind of energy. 'No, you're more than welcome to stay here...'

'Oh well, I'm not sure – I'll have to check with Carol...'

'There is another problem,' I tell Phil as a different thought comes to mind, 'I really don't like to think of this from Adrian's point of view. Us all together having a good time while he's stuck in there.'

'Oh. Quite so. Yes. I do understand. Oh no. No, it would be a bit unfortunate. Yes I can see what you mean...'

I think about Welsh Phil and now understand why he's one of the beneficiaries in Adrian's will. He is a totally genuine and thoroughly nice, unpretentious man who is going out of his way to help his old drinking buddy. He's probably missing Adrian a lot.

I remember one Saturday night at the beginning of the year when I was visiting Adrian in London. We were walking down the road towards East Putney station on our way to meet Kyria for a drink when Phil phoned him on his mobile to make arrangements for their regular Saturday night drink. I remember feeling touched when I heard Adrian say 'no I can't make it tonight, my sister's here and I'm going out with her.'

But why did Adrian let Welsh Phil down so glibly and at such short notice when they always drank together on a Saturday night? Maybe theirs was a flexible arrangement, but even so I think of him on that particular Saturday night in January, alone. Hey, he could have come along with us. I think Adrian likes to compartmentalise friends, which is probably why he's not a party-thrower.

Ten pm. I get a text from Adrian.

'Pls get Cad Swiss rolls. Think I'm going mad. A.'

What more can I do to help him? Apart from stocking up on chocolate cakes. If I visited more what would we do? Could we play games together, after all? Could we peel away the past forty-five years and sit together playing Old Maid, Oh Hell, Snap, Chase the Ace, Happy Families?

The pack of cards I bought him is still on top of the radiator, unopened.

'Don't you get tired of going to see Adrian all the time?' Emily asks. We're in the study where I'm doing some writing.

'Yes and no,' I say, wondering whether in fact it is she who's tired of me going to see Adrian all the time.

'It's something different, and in a way it's nice because I haven't really seen him on a regular basis for years.' And, yes, in a way it *is* nice. Although nice seems the wrong word, in view of the circumstances. But recently I have been enjoying the practicalities of trying to help him. Although of course I know Adrian is having the shittiest of times.

Fran is desperate to have her belly pierced, and, as an early birthday present, I have agreed. Or rather, I apparently said 'yes' at some point when I was distracted by something else. After lunch we drive to Trowbridge to find a shop Fran has found online. It's in a back street, a small, garishly painted emporium with two fat, greasy men, who look more suited to carving slices off a doner kebab, standing by the door. They remind me of pimps outside a Soho peep show.

No way will I allow my baby into the clutches of these two. I say as much to Fran, so emphatically she doesn't protest. We go back to the car and change direction for St Vincent's.

Adrian is sitting in the same position I left him in last night. But he's feeling better and is now focusing on moving. Olivia from Dorothy House has been to see him and this has cheered him up immensely.

'She's a really nice lady. We had a long talk. She asked me

how I was feeling. And when I asked if I was in quarantine she said "no." She doesn't even bother with the gloves and apron.'

This is interesting. Olivia seems to carry a lot of clout and Adrian is saying she's not worried about the contagious nature of the C.diff. Or at least she's not worried for her own safety, although I do recall she wouldn't take him to Dorothy House to meet with the other cancer patients. Her laid-back attitude makes me feel hysterically lightweight with my fanatical adherence to hygiene regulations.

Apparently Olivia is coming again for a meeting with a doctor (and social worker?) next Wednesday and Adrian wants the focus of this meeting to be getting him out of St Vincent's. He's still convinced the staff want to keep him there and I think this may be true. When Peter was here yesterday a nurse told him they have three empty beds out of twenty-eight. Each empty bed presumably represents a loss of three grand per month.

St Vincent's definitely has financial issues. This morning Adrian said he asked Scary Red Nurse if he could wash his hair in the shower and she said 'no'. This bugs me. Firstly, because he felt the need to ask permission to do something as basic as washing his hair; secondly, she's treating him like a ninety-year-old; and thirdly, it could mean the shower is broken, which at the rates we're paying is preposterous. Adrian is still talking about moving into his own bed-sit or flat. But I know in my heart this is impossible. Apart from anything else, from the point of view of a prospective landlord, who would let a place to him if they met him? Unless they were very compassionate, they'd see him as a dying man who'd only stay for a short term tenancy. Anyway, he could fall over / wouldn't eat / take medication etc. It would be a disaster in the making.

Yet again I suggest he comes to live with us. 'We'd like you to. I've checked with everyone and they're all in total agreement.' These words trip off my tongue so lightly, as they have on so many other occasions. I don't even register that they aren't true. In fact I haven't mentioned it to the others for months.

For the first time since I initially suggested this in June, he says 'Yes'.

I do a double take. *Yes.* He's said yes to moving in with us. I can hardly believe what I've just heard.

I'm shocked, pleased but more than a little apprehensive.

'Yes? Oh, okay! That's brilliant news.'

This has got to be a positive step forward. By moving Adrian in with us we don't have to worry about what we can and cannot do in relation to the C.diff. Olivia's attitude to infection has made me less worried about my family catching it. And I won't have so much driving each day. All the same, I have to stop to get everything straight in my head before we finally put this plan into action.

'Okay,' I repeat slowly. 'So, what about the diarrhoea?' I recall Matron's stories of seas of the stuff in the middle of the night.

'I've got control over it now. This last course of antibiotics have kicked in,' he says dismissively. Nevertheless there is a bucket of water in the middle of the room, which makes me wonder.

'So,' I carry on, 'what exactly are they doing for you here?' There's surely nothing they're providing that I can't provide at home.

'Dishing out pills and serving up inedible food,' he says.

Ah. I can do both of those things.

'Why don't you check with Olivia whether it's safe for the family to be in contact with the C.diff bug, and then I'll get the study ready for you.'

'Okay, Ali. Thanks…'

Gift arrives with a salts drink to counteract the effects of the diarrhoea and help build Adrian up. She's being very stern with him but he tells her to leave the drink on the table. After she's gone he says he needs to eat.

'I looked in the mirror today. I think I look really gaunt.'

Has he only just noticed? He's skeletal. His eyes are tiny and dull, his teeth, brown tombstones. His nose a fleshless bone.

'And I'm getting lazy. I'll get up tomorrow.'

'When I come over next I'll get one of the wheelchairs and take you out into the grounds if you like.'

'Yes, that would be good.'

'Would you like me to give you a massage today?'

'Yes!'

I give him a long massage. Adrian asks lots of questions about the girls, Ed, Jack, Peter. What they are all doing, what I've been doing. Is this so I'll forget the time and keep the massage going longer? We chat about him coming to live with us, the nutty neighbours, his friends...

I'm scared at the prospect of taking on full care of my brother, but it seems the right thing to do. The only thing to do. After all, if he was my husband or child I'd have had him home immediately, no matter what was wrong with him. I can't bear to think of him ending his days in a place he hates.

On my way home, as I drive along the dual carriageway, rain lashes down. I can hardly see, but then as I come out of Frome and round the hill bend, the sky stretches out before me with a panorama of white peaked meringue clouds.

Over dinner I bring up the subject of Adrian moving in.

'I've asked Adrian again about coming to live with us and he's actually said yes! I told him everyone has said it's okay, and although I know you are all okay with him coming, I just wanted to run it past everyone – just to be sure no one has any objections...'

'No, it's alright with me,' Ed says as he squirts a small lake of tomato sauce onto his chips. 'As long as he doesn't eat all the sauce.'

'Of course it's fine,' Peter says. 'The sooner he's out of St Vincent's the better.'

Jack and the girls mumble agreement. So the decision is final.

At night I have a dream. Adrian's lying on his bed in St Vincent's and he's dead.

I have to get him out of that place and home with us before it's too late. I just have to.

HOME

HOME

Friday 17th August 2007

'I think you're being incredibly generous, letting your brother move in with you,' Crysse says.

'I feel a bit scared but I wouldn't say I was being generous. Anyone else would do the same in the circumstances.'

'That's exactly what all generous people would say.' Crysse and I are eating soup in Nano's Wine Bar after our Friday morning Body Basics workout. Crysse always sees good in other people.

After lunch I trudge up the hill to the computing shop where I bought Adrian's laptop. I've been back there so often I'm beginning to feel embarrassed just opening the door. I walk in, intent on cancelling the contract with Vodafone but Jeff, who owns the shop, insists he knows someone who's using this 'up and down the country' and managing to get online without any problem.

I hand him the laptop and he proceeds to sign onto the internet straight away.

'It looks as if you've done a few things you shouldn't have,' he says examining the screen. I shrug, once more feeling technologically inept. Jeff tunes into Five Live, the station Adrian so desperately wants to listen to.

I'm distracted by another customer. He's one of the McGann brothers. I've noticed him in Frome before – brother of the more famous actors, Paul and Joe. So, I'm in a computer shop and I'm excited by the fact I'm with someone who is the brother of two people who are reasonably famous. Yikes. I'm turning into my mother.

Whenever we went up to London for the day Mum would spend half her time staring into taxis. She assumed only famous people took taxis so it was worth her while having a good squint inside the windows of the many black cabs cruising around.

I have a photograph of myself and my mum on one of these trips, standing in Trafalgar Square. I am ten and have a pigeon on my head. It's school holidays – Easter probably, going by our raincoats. Mum used to put one day aside from her regime of washing, hanging laundry out to dry, ironing, and trudging four miles to the nearest shops with her shopping trolley, to spend with us. For one day of the school holidays we were reluctantly persuaded to swap our bikes, friends and secret dens for the sooty smell and prickly seats of the second class carriage on the Charing Cross line. A day up in London.

From Hayes, the train would rattle its way through increasingly less suburban stations as we approached the city. We'd hurtle past back gardens with lines full of washing billowing in the wind, deserted stations and then great concrete chimneys belching smoke, with big hoardings bearing familiar brand names like Jacob's Cream Crackers, or Brooke Bond Tea. Just remembering these trips I begin to feel warm and cosy. Sitting next to the window, I'd let my bare legs swing, catching the flow of hot air from beneath the seat, my brown school lace-ups dangling above the cigarette-butt strewn floor.

The first thing Mum did as soon as we were settled in our seats was to take a nail file from her handbag and file her nails into points. This nail-filing was an integral part of our London trips. Not only was it a statement about Mum's lack of time to look after herself properly, but also an affirmation that each clanking rail on the track we passed over, each station we whizzed through, and each house that flashed by, was bringing her closer to her past. Closer to the beautiful young woman I never knew who worked in a big factory that made soup. A young woman who wore nylons with seams at the back, and the wobbly high heels I used for dressing up.

Just before London Bridge Mum would point out, with her

newly shaped nails, the Heinz factory where she worked as a secretary before she got married. I pretended not to be impressed whilst Adrian hung out of the window to get a better view. On the pavement outside Charing Cross we passed rows of empty taxis as we made our way towards Lyons Corner House, where we lunched on Welsh rarebit or congealed beans on toast which we chose from brightly lit hot plates covered by plastic windows. Mum's tray was crowded with plates, cups of tea and pieces of cutlery that slid about as we searched for somewhere to sit. Then the three of us would huddle together at a Formica table surrounded by the delicious Lyons Corner House atmosphere that was a mixture of heat, condensation, steamy food smells from the kitchen and cigarette smoke. The food tasted wonderful, especially after my regular diet of school dinners and Mum's boiled fish.

After lunch we'd make our way on foot to our destination, sometimes the National Gallery, maybe The Mall, Piccadilly Circus or Trafalgar Square (home of the photogenic pigeons). This was the part of the day where Mum really came into her own. As a child my worst nightmare was to stand out in a crowd or attract attention to myself in any way whatsoever, which is why I cringed every time Mum peered into the window of each passing taxi, lacking only the assistance of a telescope or a pair of opera glasses in her quest for the sight of a 'famous person'.

'That looks like that fellow David Whitfield in the back of that taxi!' She'd point at the shadow of an unidentifiable figure squashed in the back seat of a cab, his face hidden by a trilby. I looked down at my feet, praying all passers-by would think I was alone, and nothing to do with this deluded woman. If the Queen, Prince Philip and the entire cast of the *Billy Cotton Band Show* had waved and called me from the top of a number eleven bus I would have continued my in-depth study of my school brogues.

'Isn't that Arthur Askey on the other side of the road? Look,

Ali! No, over there, quick, you're going to miss him. Too late –
he's gone into Lilywhites.' For Arthur Askey insert Charlie
Drake, David Nixon, David Jacobs, Diana Dors or whoever…

Adrian joined in with her enthusiasm and even I couldn't
resist a peek from the corner of my eye. I did once catch sight
of a short man with glasses disappearing through a shop door.
But to Mum, every short man with glasses was Arthur Askey,
just as every fat man with a handlebar moustache was Jimmy
Edwards, every other married couple was Pearl Carr and Teddy
Johnson and every tall dark-haired man, Cary Grant. 'Cary
Grant was born in England, you know. He could be back visiting
a sick relative or something.'

At home Mum kept a signed photograph of a matinée idol
called Robert Taylor in her side of the wardrobe behind a pair
of silver evening slippers that I'd never seen her wear. In
deference to my father's rather jealous nature the photo
remained hidden. But I'd seen it – and read the inscription *To
Betty with love.*

Despite my disdain for Mum's celeb spotting, as the years
passed I realised with a mild amount of horror that I'd inherited
the star-spotting gene. By the time I was sixteen I'd make the
same dusty train journey up to London, by then with a giggly
school friend in tow. We'd visit the same Lyons Corner House,
which had miraculously transformed into a bright, airy
restaurant where customers perched on tall bar stools around
high circular tables decorated with yellow plastic tulips.
(Although still serving the same congealed beans on toast and
over-cooked Welsh rarebit.)

One summer, around the time of the film of *The Railway
Children*, the actress Jenny Agutter was sitting at the table next
to mine.

'She's tiny!' I reported back to Mum as soon as I got home.

'I do wish I'd been with you.' And wish was all she could do
since my trips on the Charing Cross line were by then essentially

an opportunity to smoke as many Embassy Blues as possible in forty minutes, and to lure any dishy boys into our compartment with our pink lipstick and hipster mini-skirts. The last thing I needed was my mother cramping my style.

But once a star-spotter, always a star-spotter, and as the years rolled by I continued to enthral Mum with the odd, but genuine, sighting. As I passed through my twenties, thirties and beyond, there was Bill Wyman from the Rolling Stones outside his flat, and I had his autograph to prove it; Nerys Hughes, from *The Liver Birds* who I met in the communal changing rooms at Miss Selfridge and who told me how lucky I was to be so thin, whilst all I could think of was how lucky *she* was to be so famous; Nurse Gladys Emmanuel from *Open All Hours* who I met in a queue for the loo at a charity ball; and one of the policemen from *The Bill* who lived in a flat over the road from me. Mum loved all the anecdotes. 'You have such an exciting life!' she'd say. She was older too, of course. The Arthur Askeys and Jimmy Edwards of this world were by that time no doubt starring on that great stage in the sky. And Mum didn't get out much any more.

But like most children I didn't tell her everything. I thought better of recounting the time I met the American rock group Canned Heat at a concert when they were waiting to go on stage, or how their roadie tried to persuade me to go away with him and join the tour. Although I did mention to her a few years later that I'd had a face-to-face encounter with Van Morrison in Bath.

'Van who?' she asked, her rheumy eyes looking into the distance. 'Do I know him? Your father used to have a Morris van. I don't suppose you remember. You were only little.'

Mum kept her signed photograph of Robert Taylor in her wardrobe right up until the end, although she no longer needed to hide it after Dad died. And she still kept her eyes peeled for stars when she went anywhere on holiday – even though it took her a while to recall their names. After a cruise she went on with

Adrian, she returned tanned, a bit shaky, but full of her old excitement.

'Do you know, there was a fellow on that cruise and I'm sure he was that actor in *Emmerdale*...you know the one. Except in real life he looks completely different...'

I resisted the temptation to point out that if he didn't look like the actor in *Emmerdale* then he probably wasn't. But then who was I to argue?

'You got his autograph, though?' I asked.

'Oh yes, Ali, of course.'

'Then I expect it was him.'

'Oh yes, it was definitely him. He does look a lot different on TV though...'

So my mother had come home with the autograph of a random holidaymaker.

The McGann man is quite short which makes me wonder if his brothers, who look big on screen, are below normal height too. Seeing him also reminds me of the little girl still missing. Madeleine McCann. Her parents are on the front page of today's *Daily Express* with the headline 'Only minutes away from finding Madeleine'. Will they find her, though? Her parents' lives must be torture. According to the papers both Madeleine and her twin siblings were conceived by IVF. Are they now implying the McCanns weren't meant to have children? Why can't the press leave them alone?

I arrive at St Vincent's and eat my lunch in the car, feeling the need for a bit of space before I go in.

In the room, what's left of my dear brother lies propped up in bed watching an old sitcom starring Rodney from *Only Fools* with the sound switched off. As I walk in he says, 'I feel crap. I woke up full of the joys of spring. But then started to feel crap. I think what you said was right. You know, when you said the way I feel depends on the weather.'

It's another rainy day.

A plate of tasteless-looking fish (of the packet variety) with a smattering of unappetising chips and peas is abandoned on his bedside table. He's obviously taken a few mouthfuls then given up. Next to the dinner plate is a bowl of congealed spotted dick and custard. This also looks as if he may have taken a couple of mouthfuls, but is the kind of pudding even I as a fan of school-type dinners would have left on the plate and tried to cover up with my spoon.

Adrian is quieter of late. He's started to talk more in a whisper, only occasionally allowing his voice to go really high and louder when he's pleased about something. I sit down and together we work out the date he'd have to leave here in order to save Wandsworth Borough Council paying the next set of (non-refundable) fees to St Vincent's. He must be out by the twenty-third.

'So, you've got to be out by next Thursday.'

'But the doctor isn't coming till Wednesday,' he says, procrastinating. Before he became ill, Adrian had been planning for the past ten years to move to Salisbury. Procrastination is his middle name. Actually, it's Nigel.

'That's okay. You could still leave by Thursday.'

'But it could take me a couple of days to pack up.'

'What? You're kidding. I could get you out of here in one hour.' Lock, stock and four crates of wine. 'I took the laptop in again, and the guy in the shop managed to get online.'

I get it out and do get online, but then I can't get onto the Five Live website or hear it. The connection fails. I press lots of buttons and swivel various bits of wire. Nothing.

After I've finished murdering the laptop I ask if he'd like to go out in the wheelchair as planned, hoping he'll say 'no' as I'm feeling knackered. But he says 'yes'. I'm in awe of his strength to carry on.

In the hallway outside Adrian's room I come face to face with Matron. Who better to ask for a wheelchair?

'I was wondering if it would be okay to take Adrian into the garden in a wheelchair.'

Matron looks uncertain. 'Well, we don't actually *have* any wheelchairs.'

My face must show what I'm thinking. That there are at least fifteen identical fucking wheelchairs parked in a row by the back door. Adrian's been using the cushions from them as padding against the hard wooden benches for weeks.

She continues. 'The ones we *do* have, which you might have noticed by the back door, all belong to individual residents.'

Ah, yes, of course. All those hundreds of *individual residents* milling about all over the place…why didn't I think of them?

'I suppose you could use one if you disinfect the seat thoroughly afterwards,' she concedes.

Sure thing. Just pass me the Dettol.

I help Adrian with the now painful process of getting dressed and lift him into the wheelchair. He's still heavy, despite his lack of flesh. I push him round the garden and we stop and I sit on one of the benches outside his bedroom. He has his legs crossed, so he doesn't look like a real wheelchair user. We talk about Carol and Welsh Phil coming tomorrow. I've suggested they book into The George Hotel in Frome.

'Carol says The George doesn't have any vacancies this weekend,' he says.

I'm tempted to take over these arrangements but I'm sure the three of them can organise this without me. Except I know the area better and so it's much easier for me. I decide to leave it to them though, unless they ask for help.

It's cold in the garden (mid-August still seems more like October) and Adrian has a pain in his back. I suggest another massage and his voice goes up an octave in the way it does when he's pleased.

While I'm massaging his back he asks me about Body Basics (which is where I've been this morning for a workout) and what everyone in the family is doing. It's nice to feel he's interested in my life. For so many years when my children were small he'd seemed indifferent. On another wavelength. But did I ever try to engage with his career, his travels? He's never asked much about my writing, although I've always had a secret fantasy I'd find a stash of women's magazines containing stories I'd written hidden away in a drawer in his flat.

As I move onto his arms, wrists and fingers a new nurse comes in. She's middle-aged with chestnut brown hair and bright pink lipstick. Her name tag identifies her as Angie. I haven't met her before and wonder what she thinks seeing us together. A brother and sister in such an intimate situation could seem strange. But then I dismiss this thought. Who cares what she thinks? If she's chosen this job then she should understand about caring for others.

Angie potters about the room and tells me she lives in Frome. She also tells me Adrian's shower isn't working and she'll report this. No wonder Scary Red Nurse said he couldn't wash his hair in the shower.

'The lifts here aren't working either,' Angie says.

'I think I heard one of the nurses talking about the lifts. How long have they been out of order?'

'I'm new here but I've heard they've been out of action for the last six weeks.'

'Wow, six weeks is a long time to be stuck upstairs.'

Angie laughs. 'Yes, it certainly is.'

No wonder there are never any residents around. Maybe the people upstairs (the unseen ones) are trapped on the first floor. What on earth would happen if a fire broke out? But then, you're not supposed to use lifts in a fire, are you?

Adrian asks for some banana and cream and Angie brings it. Clearly she's not been properly trained yet, and therefore isn't fully conversant with the 'wait three hours before you do anything' *modus operandi*.

As I massage around his back and the sides of his lungs Adrian groans with relief.

'When you massage me there it stops the weird fizzing sensation under my right arm – the Coca Cola fizz. It's strange this should be under my right arm when the doctors at St George's said the cancer was in my left lung.'

I carry on with the massage, unable to explain this anomaly.

Adrian speaks again. 'She's been very good to me,' he says quietly. Momentarily I think he said '*You've* been very good to me'. I feel so uplifted and encouraged, then realise he's talking about Carol who's coming tomorrow.

'She's stood by me for years.' I suppose she has. Also he has a card on his bedside table from Bryony, which he hasn't opened. I'm not sure why. Maybe he's keeping it for later, or can't summon the energy.

Angie carries on pottering, all the while asking me questions as if Adrian isn't here.

'I thought he was asleep. I wasn't talking over him,' she says when I defer to Adrian in answering one of her questions. Oh well, at least she was quick with the bananas and cream.

When I leave Adrian thanks me but doesn't make eye contact and, since I recently pointed out St Vincent's isn't exactly on our doorstop, he's started telling me to be careful driving home. On the way home I call into The Ship at Oldford. Jack is there. I wonder how all this is affecting the other people in my family? Jack has always been fond of Adrian. I think I'll try to spend some time with him. But not tomorrow as he's going to a wedding.

Saturday 18th August 2007

A cold, grey, rainy day. I pity the couple getting married. Who would have anticipated such murky conditions when planning a summer wedding? Today is my day off and I start by writing a critique I've been waiting and waiting to do…oh, well at least the author will possibly presume I've been on holiday. Before I can finish the crit, Fran drags me off to Glastonbury to get her belly pierced.

Against my better judgement I find myself sitting in a tattooist and piercings shop in the middle of Hippyland while my fourteen-year-old daughter lies on a couch about to be pierced by three trainees under the aegis of a short elderly man who, if his website is anything to go by, clearly feels the need to assure any potential customers that he is 'scrupulously clean and sterile'.

Fran has wanted her belly pierced for a long time and has relentlessly searched online for someone who is a) nearby, b) not too expensive, and c) acceptable to yours truly. Apparently I agreed to this piercer when my head was probably elsewhere, and now have to stick to my word and let Fran have a hole inserted into the creamy white, virgin skin of her belly. The short man shows me the needle in its scrupulously clean and sterile wrapper and, nodding his head, awaits my approval. I can hardly bear to look, but nod back, and mumble something to give him the go ahead. I wait in the reception area while the deed is done.

Minutes later Fran emerges with a beautiful pink belly bar under a plaster on her beautifully flat stomach. After I've paid the bill we go on to Haskins to choose a new bed for her since hers collapsed when she and Daisy were jumping on it. Daisy, the girls' friend who had run away, has now returned home and celebrated with a visit to our house where they used Fran's bed as a trampoline.

While we're in the shop I phone Peter to check on the size of Fran's old bed, and he asks if I'm getting a bed for Adrian.

'No, not yet,' I say, although I have noticed an orthopaedic one in the corner. But I've also noticed Haskins have a two to seven week delivery time.

In the evening over our weekly takeaway curry, a text arrives on my phone from Adrian saying Carol and Phil have been to visit him today and they '*supp the prop*'. I wonder what this means, but decide they 'support the proposition' i.e. for Adrian to move in with us. I'm gradually learning how to interpret his text speak.

'Adrian is still wavering over coming here. I thought he'd made up his mind but he's obviously seeking other people's opinions,' I say as we clear away our curry plates. Peter suddenly becomes serious.

'I'm going to *tell* him what he's got to do. Get the hell out of that nursing home and move in here, without any more messing about.' Peter scrapes his leftovers into the bin. 'He can't make decisions for himself any more.'

After loading the dishwasher, I flop in front of the television. While I'm watching Leona Lewis screeching her heart out on *The X Factor,* Peter phones Adrian without telling me.

'It's all sorted,' he says coming into the living room. 'I've told Adrian. He's moving in here as soon as possible.'

This is so out of character for Peter to interfere and put his foot down. I delete Leona and scuttle off to the study to look online for orthopaedic beds with memory foam.

When I log on I see I've had an email from Jackie Tomey who is one of the few friends I've ever had who is a committed Christian. Jackie and I worked together in the early eighties at Hammersmith and West London College. She saw the light at a Billy Graham gathering in the sixties. Jackie already knows about my brother's illness as we have corresponded earlier in the year.

'*I do hope you still have him with you,*' her email says. *And that you are able to give each other all the love and comfort you have for each other…my love and prayers are with you all.*'

Gulp. Someone is praying for us. And these aren't just empty words – she really will be praying, if I know Jackie.

Sunday 19th August 2007

Another day off from visiting Adrian. I'd intended to clean the house and get the study ready but end up going to the shops to look for a bed for him instead. Having begun last month with the idea of borrowing one from Margaret, I'm now at the other end of the scale with an electronically operated, memory foam and integrated massaging mattress. A snip at only one-and-a-half grand. They have one in Helibeds in Trowbridge.

When I get home Phil G phones. He says Adrian sounds much better since deciding to move in with us, and he's working towards a day out at Wincanton Races with him.

I get an email from Hazel, an old school friend who's just back from the States, and I realise Margaret is back from her holidays too. I suspect they will both be wondering whether Adrian is still alive. But no – they will realise he is, because I'd have let them know if anything had happened.

In bed at night I try to imagine life without him. It seems empty and horrible. He hasn't been highly significant in my life over the past few years and yet somehow here we are now as close as when we were kids. I'm tangled up in his life.

All the different information I have about C.diff is confusing. Having been certain Adrian couldn't possibly leave St Vincent's, or move here or anywhere else whilst still infected, I'm now beginning to wonder if this is true. I'm certainly not going to let it get in the way of his move to our house. Ed's symptoms didn't materialise – thank goodness. Maybe I've felt a bit dodgy a couple of times but not for long.

I recall Adrian saying Olivia didn't bother with the gloves and apron. The most vulnerable are the very young, very old or weak. No one in our family comes into that category. Surely if we are careful we are not in any danger of becoming ill. Anyway, sod it. He's leaving St Vincent's no matter how many bugs he's got, and moving back into the real world. I'm going to tell Matron this tomorrow.

Monday 20th August 2007

If the First Great Western Railway staff are the offspring of Lucifer, the employees of Dorothy House are most certainly the opposite. These people are angels. During a telephone conversation with them this morning I'm informed by someone called Breeze – Breeze, even her name is ethereal – that a bed, an armchair, a commode and daily visits from a care worker will be provided if Adrian is living with us.

A bed. But I spent all yesterday searching for a bed…time wasted when I could have been cleaning the study. Breeze also says I have to register Adrian with our GP as soon as possible. We decide Adrian will move in with us this Thursday.

Breeze says she used to be a bowel nurse and she recommends 'neat bugs' to eliminate C.diff. At last, someone with a specific interest in bowels and who has some knowledge and experience of C.diff and, furthermore, has some positive suggestions (apart from antibiotics) to combat it.

I drive into Frome and trawl all shops likely to stock neat bugs. Who on earth would sell such a thing? What are they anyway? I have an image in my mind of a large pot containing something resembling the maggots the boys used for fishing bait. I try Boots, Lloyds and some small chemists on the outskirts of town. All say they don't have neat bugs. I visit the health shop and a shop selling nuts and live yoghurt. Both give me similarly negative replies. The fishing shop appears to have closed down so I'm not tempted to make a complete fool of myself there. But no one can help and I'm getting some pretty funny looks from the shop assistants to boot. I decide to check online when I get home. Will there be a neat bug website? Probably – there's one for just about everything else.

As I have some old clothes in my car I take the bags to the Dorothy House charity shop which is a bit of an extra walk up the hill from Help The Aged but this is where I donate my things now.

I arrive at St Vincent's in the late morning and go straight into Matron's room for a talk. I tell her Adrian will be leaving on Thursday.

She smiles, nods, draws breath, and says, 'What about the C.diff?'

'He told me it's cleared up again. After the last course of antibiotics.'

'You do know the C.diff virus stays in the system for at least three months after the symptoms have gone...'

'I thought C.diff was a bacteria, not a virus.'

'Oh yes, bacteria, I meant...'

'Yes, and if it comes back we will be very careful.'

'What about the baby?'

'There is no baby.'

'Oh, I thought you said there was a baby living with you in the house...'

'No. Jack's girlfriend is a nanny and a family she works for has a new baby.'

'Oh. I thought you said there was a baby living in your house.'

'No,' I repeat. 'No baby.'

She goes on to explain that Dorothy House are not entitled to receive the funding we've been awarded from Wandsworth Council for Adrian's care.

'That's not really anything to do with me,' I say.

'What time will he be leaving on Thursday?' she asks

'We'll fit in with you.'

'Not early, though, I expect,' she says. 'Adrian doesn't get up early.'

'No, I expect he doesn't.' Let's face it, there's not a lot to get up for.

'But we don't mind when he goes.' I thank her for all she's done for us and make my way to his room.

Adrian is sitting on the bed dressed in a shirt and looking much happier. He feels cured (again) of the C.diff and I realise, not for the first time, that it's the bug making him seem so ill – not the cancer. The cancer just gives him pain. He's full of positive plans, which is great. I tell him about Thursday. The big day. He says he can't wait.

'I told them here I'm leaving – and there's nothing they can do about it. I said, "My people will be coming to get me on Thursday".'

His people. That's us.

'But don't get too excited,' I warn him. 'It's only our house, after all.'

It's now the 20th of August and Adrian's been in the West Country for thirty-one days. A whole month. According to Dr Weeks-Rather-Than-Months from St George's, shouldn't he be dead by now? Jill Miller sent me an email saying I'm amazing for taking my brother into my home. But yet again I think, wouldn't anyone do the same under these circumstances? Nevertheless, I feel as if we are at the end of the road. I doubt there will be any more stops after this.

Adrian tells me he wants to go out and explore the locality with Welsh Phil once he gets to our house. He's sure there must be some interesting history around these parts. The first thing that comes to mind is our connection with famous nursery rhymes.

'The hill Jack and Jill supposedly fell down is in Kilmersdon, which is one of the villages on the way to Bath.'

'Not a good start,' he quips.

'And Little Jack Horner lived in a cottage in Mells…'

'I'd like to go up to London again too. I can't remember whether I've ever been to Westminster Abbey. I may have been as a child, but certainly not as an adult.'

'I think we went there with the school,' I recall. 'I seem to remember being struck by Poets' Corner. I'm sure Chaucer and Dickens are buried there.'

'Probably. And I've never been to Newcastle either,' he says after a moment's thought.

'No. Neither have I. Although I've been through it on a train when I went to Dundee to meet Peter's family years ago…'

'I haven't been to Newcastle…I've never been there,' he repeats, looking down at his hands. For the first time he sounds desperate as the realisation hits him. Things not done are now lost for ever. Suddenly I feel very sad he's thinking like this. I wonder what I'd want to see if the roles were reversed. Probably nothing, except the faces of my four children and my husband.

The words of the Roger McGough poem go through my head again as I carry out the now routine massage. *Let me die a youngman's death. Not a clean and inbetween the sheets…* Not that the sheets here are particularly clean.

As I leave, Angie thanks me twice on the way out for helping her by putting a bucket in his room.

Well, she did ask me to put the bucket in his room, and, to be honest, it wasn't much trouble.

In the evening I get on with clearing out the study. The Picasso has been propped up in the kitchen for the past five weeks. I hold it up against the wall where Adrian's bed will be (when I eventually get one) and it looks good – it looks spectacular. Thank goodness I didn't take it to St Vincent's. It would have been so out of place amongst what Emily and Fran call the granny furniture there.

Tuesday 21st August 2007

Already Thursday is two days away and I still don't have a bed for Adrian. But I've been making arrangements for the big day all morning. The phone rings. It's the Health Centre.

'Mrs Clink? I'm returning your call about a request for a bed for your brother. I'm sorry to let you down, but we only supply beds to patients who are either bed-bound or only have a few days left to live.'

'But I was told by Dorothy House I'd be eligible for a free bed.'

'Then, I'm sorry but the information you were given is incorrect. We've contacted St Vincent's and they've assured us Mr Tilbrook is not bed-bound. Nor has he been given a terminal diagnosis with only days to live.'

'But Dorothy House made it clear...'

'Perhaps you should ring them back. I'm sorry, Mrs Clink, but we cannot provide a bed in this case.'

Now I have to re-focus on buying a bed myself – and quick.

I ring Dorothy House first to tell them what the Health Centre said.

'Mrs Clink, the information you've been given by the Health Centre is wrong,' the secretary tells me. 'A bed and any other equipment your brother might need whilst he's living with you will be provided by the District Nurse. I'll organise a home visit for you immediately. One of the District Nurses will then come to your house for an assessment and to arrange delivery of a bed by Thursday.'

Ugh! Who is right?

I arrange cover for my Center Parcs writing group tomorrow. Adrian's new Frome GP rings to say she's worried because she's away for ten days from Thursday. Anxiety bores into my heart as she speaks. This weekend is a Bank Holiday. However, she does reserve us an appointment with another doctor for Friday morning. I can either go alone, or with Adrian, or cancel if we don't need it.

In the afternoon I take the girls with me to Asda. The bill comes to two hundred and sixty-two pounds. They have put loads of make-up and stuff in their trolley and I have a mixture of fattening food for Adrian and my usual slimming stuff to keep me down to the nine and a half stone I struggled to reach during my dieting phase in May.

I drop the girls off at their friend's house with a few bags full of the shopping and drive on to St Vincent's.

Dorothy House have asked me to establish exactly what St Vincent's *do* for Adrian. As far as I know they just give pills. I stop a nurse in the corridor and ask her.

'I'm temp here,' she says. 'I jus' been brought in to help out. Sorry my English is not good. I do not know the answer to your question, but I will ask Matron when she come back.'

I noticed Matron's Vauxhall Corsa in its usual spot in the car park when I arrived, but I don't mention this.

There are no gloves outside Adrian's room. I look for the nurse again.

'Cheer up,' she says when I find her taking sheets out of a linen cupboard. 'You look so down. Come on – cheer up! You shouldn't look so sad.'

I hate it when people talk to me like this. I've got a headache and anyway what's my face got to do with her?

'I'm a bit tired,' I say, trying to be smiley nevertheless.

'Then would you like a cup of tea?'

'Wonderful.' I say, but I pass on the soggy cake.

In the room Adrian is sitting up, dressed. He's still wearing the pj. trousers I bought him, which pleases me.

'Hi, Ali,' he says. 'How's the plans going for my release?' He has an intense glare.

'I've had a few problems with the bed,' I confess. 'But whatever happens Thursday will be the day you escape.'

'Yeah. D-day. Bed or no bed.'

'Exactly. If we don't get the bed sorted in time then we'll just have to push you upstairs to Jack's room.'

'Sounds good to me.'

'There is just one more thing, though,' I tell him. 'Olivia won't be your key worker once you've moved in with us because you won't be in her geographical patch any longer.'

Adrian doesn't answer but his expression says more than words could. How many more set-backs can a man handle?

'Maybe I could ask her if she'll stick with you?'

'Yes, Ali. Would you mind?'

I give him a massage and he asks lots of questions about the family. I tell him about Abbie, Emily and Fran's friend, who has just come back from a holiday in Sting's house in Italy where she met Elton John and Pierce Brosnan who were both staying there too. How cool is that? Although Abbie didn't seem to find the experience particularly special.

'Elton John was there – I passed him in the hall and he said hello or something, and someone called Pierce something was there too who used to play James Bond…I didn't take much notice of them to be perfectly honest…'

'I'd love to do something like that! I was so envious when she told me. And the way she just brushed it off as if they weren't interesting.'

'I've never been bothered by celebrities,' Adrian says. (Uh, he *so* is! After all he is my mother's son.) 'But I did once go to John Cleese's house.'

As I rub my hands up and down the loose skin on his back, he tells me his John Cleese story.

'It was about ten years ago. When I was going out with a girl called Hilary. She got invited to John Cleese's house to a dinner party and I went with her. There were lots of people there and I didn't get to talk to him. I was hoping Connie Booth would be there but of course he'd divorced her years before. I'm not sure who he was married to at that time but he had a woman with him. He had a lot of problems I think. I had a book he'd written with his psychiatrist – *Life and How to Survive It*. I only read half of it. I'm pretty sure it didn't provide the answers to any of life's unanswerable questions.'

'What was his house like?'

'Nice. From what I remember. He's a very wealthy guy.'

'Wow. You're so lucky. I don't think I've ever met anyone famous. Certainly never been invited to a dinner party at a famous person's house. Although I did once go to a party in a London flat that belonged to Roy Jenkins but only because a friend of mine knew his son. I still remember the room we were in with walls covered in bookcases from floor to ceiling. I saw the Queen once in a car in Hammersmith but I can't think of anyone famous I've *met*. Only writers like Fay Weldon and Helen Dunmore.' Lost in thought, I rub my hands down the backs of his arms. 'Oh, and I once saw Gail from *Coronation Street* outside Marks and Spencer in Hammersmith.'

'Who's she? I don't watch *Coronation Street*.'

'Oh, and Rowan Atkinson in a shopping mall in Hammersmith. Jimmy Nail was in The Rutland once and David Hemmings was outside The Blue Anchor. In fact one of the actors from *The Bill*, Simon Rouse, lived opposite us. I knew him before he was famous. But you definitely take the celeb meeting trophy with your John Cleese encounter.'

He laughs. 'Not sure about that. He certainly wasn't as funny as he is on screen. Thanks for the massage, Ali,' he says, pulling the sheet back over him. 'I'm a bit worried about my eyes. They seem a bit up and down. This morning they were blurred and I couldn't read the paper. But I can see okay now. I hope it's not glaucoma or something.' He taps the side of the bed. 'Nothing serious. Touch wood.'

Oddly, although at the same time reassuringly, Adrian seems to be thinking of himself as a well man now the C.diff has gone again.

'Maybe you should have an eye test.' I say these words lightly but deep down I fear what might lie ahead. Blindness could result from cancer in the brain. But he had a brain scan in St George's and the result was negative. If the cancer spreads to the brain, it could damage the optic nerve, I suppose. But what do I know? I'm only guessing.

Wednesday 22nd August 2007

The study is now spotless. I had no idea I was sharing my work space with so much dust, so many spiders and useless pieces of paper. Only the computer desk and two bookcases remain.

Like most weekdays I'm alone for most of today. The girls are out most of the day usually at a friend's house, not returning till early evening. Peter, Jack and Ed are all working long hours. I've hardly spoken to anyone all day and I'm beginning to wonder what's happened to the bed.

Time is slipping away. It's only a matter of hours until the Big Day, but all I've done to prepare is wash things. My washing line sags beneath rows of towels, sheets and clothes. The downstairs loo is unrecognisably sanitary. I have a bed-sized space in my newly clean study. But no bed. I phone the social worker at Dorothy House.

'There's been a meeting about your brother's needs,' she says.

'He's coming to my house tomorrow and I'm feeling stressed. Especially as the bed hasn't arrived.'

'Don't worry. The bed will come and there will be lots of support on offer. But you do realise you may have to stay up all night with him sometimes. How do you feel about this aspect of his care?'

'I have four children, so being kept up at night isn't alien to me,' I tell her. But am I ready to stay up all night with an adult – in a non-drunken-party-type situation? I'm uneasy about the night time duties, but don't share my misgivings with the social worker. I don't want anything to get in the way of the Big Day. She asks me, for the second time, if I've found out from St Vincent's what they specifically are doing for Adrian.

271

'No I haven't mentioned this to the matron yet,' I confess. 'I saw her yesterday and had to ask her for Adrian's food which hadn't been forthcoming. Engaging her in conversation about my brother once in a day is enough for me. I find her quite intimidating, I'm afraid.' I feel like a wimp, but regrettably this is true.

Louise from Wandsworth Council has been trying to get hold of me. I've several missed calls from her on my phone. Adrian rings me to say she's rung him too.

'I know she's the one holding the purse strings for Wandsworth but she had a real go at me when I told her I'm leaving here tomorrow. I couldn't believe what she was saying. Telling me I should stay here. How the hell can someone like her tell me where I can and cannot live? It's ludicrous.'

'I'm not entirely surprised,' I say. 'I had a feeling she might take this attitude. Although, I agree, it is absurd.'

Adrian's voice is even more croaky than usual. 'I said to this Louise woman, "Look, love. I'm dying. I'm not spending the last days of my life living somewhere I don't want to be." That shut her up...' He's too upset to carry on.

'Would you like me to talk to her? She's got no reason to react like this, especially as I left her a voicemail on Monday giving her prior warning that you were leaving St Vincent's.'

'Yes, can you talk to her?'

Later I ring Louise. She didn't get my voicemail.

'Louise, I think you've upset my brother. But I don't understand why, as I made sure his leaving date would be on the last day we've paid for, so Wandsworth didn't have to fork out for the whole of the next month.'

'It's very sweet of you to worry about the multi-million pound Borough of Wandsworth,' she says without the merest hint of sarcasm.

So she is on our side after all.

'It's all fine. Wandsworth will help with funding after Adrian has moved in with you if you need any nursing support.'

I tell her a bit about St Vincent's to reinforce our justification for moving on. About the broken lifts, the masses of olds stranded upstairs, defective showers, help buttons that don't make any noise – the inmates could be calling for help all night and no one would know. The inedible food. I have first-hand experience of the wet cake. Louise sounds shocked.

'You love your brother?' she says gently, abruptly changing the mood of the conversation. She's softly spoken with a South African accent. Her remark is somewhere between a statement of fact and a question. Unexpectedly, I'm lost for words. Her attitude is so much at odds with what I was expecting. Either she's been thinking this over between talking to Adrian and talking to me, or he'd misinterpreted what she said. I suspect the former and gather myself together.

'Yes,' I squeak.

Adrian rings again, but in a much more cheerful frame of mind. He's had a visit from Olivia and a doctor from Dorothy House.

'The doctor examined me and listened to my chest. He told me I'm not about to drop dead in three days' time! This doc seems to be saying the cancer isn't as bad as I've been led to believe.'

'Wow. That is really good news.'

I feel sucked in by this new turn of events. But hasn't this doctor *seen* Adrian? Why is he so skeletal? Or is his weight loss due to the C.diff? And how can this doctor contradict what the others at St George's said, when they were the ones who saw all the scans, X-rays and results of the biopsies? I'm desperate to believe him but at the same time I'm sceptical. And if I'm honest, I feel mild panic about the length of time I'll be giving up my study. Of course I want him to survive, but my preparations are for a short-term set-up. And yet how can I even *think* about all this in terms of a *room*?

Because I'm desperate to get away on holiday. Because I long and need to get back to my own work. Because I need to slot back again into my own family. What a mad hotchpotch of conflicting emotions.

'Phil G came to see me again,' Adrian says. 'I want to go up to London with him. Phil's arranging everything. He'll meet me off the train at Paddington.'

'That's great. A really good plan. I think it would do you good,' I say, even though I'm sure this could never happen. I remember what Matron said about Adrian having an unrealistic grasp of what he could and couldn't do and I know in my heart he couldn't even board a train on his own.

'Yeah. I really want to go back to my flat. You know, I've lived there for twenty-two years. I didn't have a chance to sort things out properly when I left. You know, when you and Peter came up.'

'Yes, of course, I understand. You need to go back.'

'Hey, Ali, and another thing. Phil was saying we've had our first customers for the London Walks business. So, looks like the biz is taking off after all.' He's referring to an off-shoot of their original business plan which consists of corporate walks around London, followed by pub quizzes.

'This is really exciting. Our first customers. Though apparently they're members of the Royal National Institute for the Blind, so I'm not sure how much of it they will be able to see. Phil wants me to make up all the questions for the quiz they'll do at the end of the walk.'

'How brilliant,' I say, although at the same time wondering whether the visually impaired are their ideal inaugural clientele. 'Brilliant,' I say again. 'A new beginning.'

Thursday 23rd August 2007

My alarm goes off at six-thirty. A British Telecom engineer is coming to mend our phone extension ready for when Adrian arrives. The phone in the living room hasn't been working for over a year, everyone has been using the extension in the study. But now we'll need to use the living room one again to give Adrian privacy.

At nine a man rings regarding the delivery of a commode. I give him directions to our house.

This is it. The events of this strange day have begun.

The day we've chosen for the big move turns out to be one of the hottest and sunniest this summer. All morning I wait for delivery of the bed, putting the girls on dog-walking duty for the third day in a row. At midday a commode arrives but the man from Medequip who delivers all the equipment in a big van assures me there has been no order for a bed.

'What? I can't believe it.' I sound embarrassingly like Victor Meldew. The Medequip man is apologetic but keen to get on with his other deliveries.

I ring the District Nurses.

'There was never going to be a bed. Your brother doesn't qualify. You have to be bed-bound with only a few days to live in order to qualify, and we've contacted St Vincent's and they say he's up and fully mobile. This means he doesn't qualify. *And* we've told you this already.'

'Yes,' I say, 'but I talked to the social worker at Dorothy House and got the impression she was organising a bed for us via another route.'

'There is no *other route*,' the District Nurse informs me emphatically.

In mounting desperation and with one eye on the clock I phone Dorothy House.

The social worker, Gill, says, 'They should supply a bed because Adrian has a continuing care package.'

I'm truly panicking now because it's gone half-two and I still haven't collected him and I still haven't got a bed. There's no way he'd make it up the stairs in our house, my suggestion to push him up was facetious, and no, we don't have a Stannah Stairlift. Could I get one installed in the next couple of hours? No.

Meanwhile, Adrian has texted me to say I should pick him up by five because of 'male help' being gone after then. I phone him and say I'm coming, but the bed isn't.

'Sod the bed,' he says. 'Just get me out of here.'

I can see why he's so impatient, but I don't want to sod the bed. I think about Helibeds in Trowbridge and their irritating advert on the telly. *Order at lunchtime and deliver by bedtime.*

Could half-past-two be considered lunchtime? In the world of Helibeds maybe not. I log onto their website. The orthopaedic bed I saw in the Trowbridge branch is on sale for three hundred pounds less online than in their shop. But delivery is four weeks. So much for their order by lunchtime promise and their picture of a cartoon bed with helicopter blades on top.

I go on eBay. Someone has an identical bed but there's a bid for 99p on it. How does eBay work? I wish I'd fathomed this out before now. I manage to get myself an ID number and a password and decide to email the seller, who, I notice, is also doing a roaring trade in jigsaw puzzles. One of her jigsaw purchasers has pasted the following comment – 'I can't wait to make it up!' I express my interest in buying her bed and offer one hundred pounds if we can collect tonight, which might just be possible as she lives in Wootton Bassett.

The phone rings. It's the District Nurse. A bed *is* coming. What are they trying to do to me?

'I do apologise but we didn't know Adrian had a continuing care package.' Does this mean Wandsworth are still picking up the tab for any help we get? I don't ask. I'm so relieved. I log off from eBay and cry a few tears before preparing myself for the next round.

Peter rings offering to leave work early and collect Adrian.

'That would be a great help. Then I can wait at home for the bed.'

An hour later I glance out of the window and see two figures walking down the front path. Peter and Adrian. Adrian, swaying a bit and holding onto Peter's arm. The late afternoon sun is still fierce in the sky. Adrian looks almost dapper in his Panama hat.

My heart moves in my chest.

He's made it.

He settles in the garden with a glass of wine and a wide smile. Ten minutes later the bed arrives. Literally a hospital bed – probably circa 1920. I'm thinking even further back – the Boer War. Florence Nightingale. The Black Death. I resist the urge to burst into the fifties pop song "Any Old Iron". Two men carry its components into the study and assemble it. The thing looks unmanageable – but, they put it together. I thank them, take a deep breath, swallow hard, blink away another tear and join Adrian in the garden.

We sit at the table under the parasol soaking up the heat of the early evening sun. Adrian is busy texting both Phils and Carol.

'Ali, how do you spell *yippee*. Is it one p or two?'

'I think it's two, Adrian,' I tell him, but it doesn't really matter. He's home.

Yippee indeed. (It is two.)

We have dinner with Jack and Willow. Roast lamb. Adrian only has meat and potato and leaves most of his, but he does have strawberries with cream for afters. It's so wonderful to see him here, no longer a prisoner in St Colditz. His new bedroom in the study is cosy and warm – even if the bed is like something from a documentary on the History Channel.

Eventually I leave him downstairs and turn in for the night. The study is directly underneath our bedroom, which means I can hear him from our bed. He's mumbling and making a lot of grunting noises. I nudge Peter awake.

'Can you hear Adrian? He's talking.'

'He's probably on his mobile.'

'No. I don't think so. It doesn't sound like he's talking on the phone. And anyway it's a bit late to be phoning people.'

'Do you want me to go down and check he's okay?'

'No, it's alright. I'll go.'

Peter has to be up early for work tomorrow. I drag myself out of bed and go down to the study. Adrian is lying in the dark in the Any Old Iron bed with the portable commode at his side.

'Are you okay?'

'Yes.'

'Only I thought I could hear you talking.'

'No.'

'Goodnight then.'

'Goodnight, Ali. And thanks.'

I go back to bed, but as I drift off to sleep I can still hear him talking.

Friday 24th August 2007

Adrian and I sit in the garden in the searing heat, waiting for an assessment visit from the District Nurse. Inside, the house has been taken over by Darren the electrician (without doubt the shyest person on the planet) who is working on the lighting and heating for our new bathroom, and Helen, my newly-appointed ironing lady, who is…well, ironing. I'm about to make a mid-morning coffee for everyone.

'Ali, do you think you could get me a glass of wine?' Adrian asks. 'I'd rather have wine than a coffee.'

'I don't think drinking wine in the morning is a very good idea.' I know it seems pointless to encourage him to give up drinking on health grounds at this stage in his life, but his drinking is possibly linked to the continual return of the C.diff.

'I don't want you to fall over,' I add, as if this is the reason I'm refusing him the wine.

He looks disappointed. I'm hurt, I'm embarrassed. I don't want to turn into the reincarnation of Matron, especially after he's put so much faith into coming here. Yet, at the same time, I know I'm right.

The District Nurse arrives and joins us in the garden. She fills in a form and answers a few questions I have about the pills I have to administer, about the possibility of getting a better bed, a wheelchair, an armchair, and a step up to the house since our house is quite hard to climb up to if you have any disability. I remember Mum finding it a big haul up to the French windows.

I'm having to administer Adrian's medication. Three times a day I'm to work out from the assorted boxes a cocktail of different coloured pills, pink, yellow, green and the ubiquitous white. I don't know what they're all for, although one box is clearly morphine. Some I suspect are anti-depressants, some diazepam, and maybe water tablets. I've been putting them into a small cup and then handing them to Adrian with some water. When I asked him what they were he seemed to have no idea. Again this reminds me of Mum and the times when I had to give her the pills she took at various intervals during each day. I hated it for some reason, even though whenever this happened it usually meant we were on holiday somewhere hot. I'm hating it now – it's so fiddly and I'm afraid I'm going to miss something out. I double check the number each time, terrified of giving him the wrong dosage. As I struggle with the minutiae of this job, a little bit of me wonders why can't he do it? But now I'm the carer and dishing out pills is part of my job.

I feel tired in the morning and as the day progresses my exhaustion increases. But in view of Adrian's new-found freedom and release from the dreaded St Vincent's it's important we go out. Just because we can. After lunch I help him into my car.

'Do you know, I don't feel depressed. In fact, I feel inexplicably quite happy,' he says once settled in the passenger seat. 'Not despondent in the way I thought I would.'

I say something feeble, like 'good', and put the car into gear, as ever, wondering why I can only come out with trite answers like this when I feel like saying 'Yes, I'm so glad. I'm enjoying being with you too. I'm enjoying all this sociability with your friends, and you.'

But no, I just say 'good'.

I take him to Orchardleigh Golf Club for lunch, struggling to help him out of the car. Although I've parked practically in the flowerbeds, so as to be as near the clubhouse as possible, he finds it a mammoth task to walk along the path to the entrance.

While I go inside to order, he sits outside on a hard wooden bench and I ask the restaurant manager, who I know from the short story competition lunch, if he can find me a cushion for my brother who isn't well. Instead of a cushion, he brings out a big, soft, comfy armchair. As he places the chair down next to Adrian I notice that same air of shock, sorrow, fear and deference the man in the shoe repair shop displayed when Adrian took his belt in to be altered. Some people are less good at hiding their emotions than others. I ask Adrian what he'd like to drink with his meal.

'A glass of white wine. Or have I got to have tea and scones?' he says, an oblique reference to my refusal of the vino earlier. Oh dear. I hate telling people what to do. I order him the smallest measure of Sauvignon, nevertheless.

After we've eaten we drive down to the church. St Mary's at Orchardleigh dates from the middle of the twelfth century, was restored in the late 1800s, and is the only island church in the country. It sits on a small piece of land (the churchyard) which is surrounded by a moat. This church is one of my favourite places in the world.

The church has no electricity and services are conducted by candlelight which makes it a romantic venue for weddings. Half of the island is banked by a lake that glimmers with silver sunlight in summer and is home to superior looking swans and ducks who crash land on the water. I've never encountered another human being when I've been here. It feels like the closest anyone could get to God without actually ascending to Heaven. The Orchardleigh church is one of the sites on the cross-England ley line of St Michael/Mary where it's believed spirituality is intensified. The suffix 'leigh' is a form of the word 'ley'.

Slowly Adrian manages to cross the bridge over the moat and stands with his weight on the walking stick beneath the shelter of a yew tree. There's a bench in the churchyard by the lake.

'We could sit down over there,' I suggest.

'I'll stay here. I don't think I can make it any further,' he says. He's quite steady, even though he's had two glasses of wine.

I'm keen to tell him about the poet, Sir Henry Newbolt, whose ashes are buried here, just a few feet from where Adrian is standing.

'Newbolt met his wife on a train. She was the daughter of the Duckworth family who lived in Orchardleigh House. There's lots of graves over on the other side of the churchyard belonging to the Duckworth family and their servants. There's a monument too, commemorating a dog that belonged to Sir Thomas Champneys.

'A dog?'

'Yes, the dog was called Fidele and Newbolt wrote a poem about him. Newbolt was the Poet Laureate – a very successful and well-known poet. He wrote the words of the first ever broadcast to the nation of a king for George V. I researched him for a project I did a few years ago for an event in the Frome Festival.'

A plaque beside the tree reads:

'In memory of/ HENRY JOHN NEWBOLT/ poet/ Knight/ Companion of Honour/ 1862-1938/ and his wife MARGARET EDINA/ 1867-1960./ "Death is a gate, and holds no room within: Pass – to the road beyond."'

I was always fascinated by the story of *Fidele's Grassy Tomb* which is the poem by Newbolt relating the story of Sir Thomas Champneys, whose dog, Fidele, saved his life. Champneys ordered his faithful companion to be buried with him when he died. They were buried together, but when the Bishop found out he was horrified and demanded the dog be dug up as an animal had no soul and therefore couldn't be buried in consecrated ground. The Sexton pretended to remove the dog's bones, but took the law into his own hands and left them where they were. Later when the church was renovated they discovered the dog's remains still buried with those of its master.

I look over at Adrian willing him to be as fascinated by this place as I was by the time stones outside the hospital.

'That's really interesting,' he says quietly. 'I'm surprised you haven't brought me here before.'

'I suppose at Christmas we're always too busy. But you're right we should have come before. It's so close.'

The sun is shimmering across the water as we stand amongst the ancient bones. By the church door I notice a plaque on the wall relating to the story of Fidele, which I read out to him, to substantiate what I've just told him.

THE ADJOINING MONUMENT, FORMERLY IN THE PARK, COMMEMORATES AZOR, A FAITHFUL DOG OF SIR THOMAS S. CHAMPNEYS, WHICH DIED IN 1796. AZOR'S DEVOTION TO HIS MASTER, WHOSE DEATH AND BURIAL IN THE FAMILY VAULT HERE HE IS SAID TO HAVE SHARED, INSPIRED SIR HENRY NEWBOLT'S BALLAD 'FIDELE'S GRASSY TOMB' WHICH HAS BROUGHT ORCHARDLEIGH LOCAL LITERARY RENOWN. THE MONUMENT WAS RE-ERECTED BY LULLINGTON AND ORCHARDLEIGH P.C.C. IN 1989 FOR ITS PRESERVATION AND IN THANKSGIVING FOR THE LIFE OF ARTHUR DUCKWORTH OF ORCHARDLEIGH, 1901 – 1986.

'The church is used a lot for candle lit weddings. Tamsin Outhwaite got married here last year.' I'm so keen to impress him I'm resorting to the fame of an ex-*Eastenders* star. 'And Noel Gallagher was one of the guests...' Finally I feel he is impressed, maybe even captivated by the magic of this churchyard, a place that never fails to enchant me.

By the time I get home I'm worn out. This is more tiring than the days when I was lugging two babies around. The amount of physical support Adrian needs to do anything is totally draining. I have to help him into and out of the car, in and out of the back door. I have to support him in virtually every step he takes. Carol is coming tomorrow and I'm looking forward to her visit very much. However, she has had a problem changing her ticket as she's decided to stay with us overnight on the Saturday. It seems changing is going to involve extra cost.

'You could offer to pay for her,' I suggest when Adrian tells me about this, knowing he wouldn't have thought of doing this even though he's made a bequest to her in his will. He agrees and texts her.

In the evening, as tiredness attacks and gnaws away, I worry about what I have done. What *have* I done? Adrian is living here, which is different from the many times he's stayed before. For a start, he's in my study. The room I love, the room I write in. My *room of one's own*. Yes, I would rather have him here than in St Vincent's – but I'm terrified I might wish his time away so I can have my space back.

But this is just a fleeting worry. Later I feel better and Adrian and I sit in the kitchen looking at the new programme for the Merlin Theatre in Frome. He notices a play by Alan Ayckbourn coming up. But it's in November. What can I say? 'Let's go together.' That's what I'd like to be able to say. And no doubt we're both thinking the same thing. *Let's go if you're still here… and able to go.*

This has happened a few times recently, like last night when Peter, Adrian and I were watching television. Suddenly every programme seemed to have some mention of death. Previously innocuous comments like 'Oh, I thought he was dead!' 'He bores me to death,' 'I'll kill you…' All these phrases, either from one of us or spoken by an actor on the television, now make me feel uncomfortable.

We watch the ten o'clock news. Other people are suffering as well as us. Madeleine McCann is still missing, her mother still accused of murder. An eleven-year-old boy has been shot dead in a pub car park. As we listen to the news Adrian seems angry about everything. Also another shooting. This time in Letchworth, the sleepy garden city where he went to school.

At night I leave him in bed with his book. When I'm upstairs I can hear him talking to himself again. Maybe this is something to do with the drugs he's taking.

Saturday 25th August 2007

I wake in the early hours with stomach cramps and loose stools – have I caught C.diff after all? I'm woken again at seven forty-five by the phone ringing downstairs. I don't like early phone calls and, although I don't manage to get to the phone in time to answer it, I do a quick mental roll-call of who is here and who is not. All the kids are home so I know the most important people in my life are safe. It rings again before I have a chance to do 1471. It's Lizzie, Adrian's new care worker, who is lost and needs directions to the house.

Lizzie arrives, a small bundle of nervous energy, chewing gum, smelling of fags and eager to help. I am again amazed by the NHS / Dorothy House / or whoever arranged this for us (free of charge).

Lizzie washes Adrian, cleans out the urine bottle he's been using at night, and wipes some wee from the study floor. Someone will be coming to do this every morning, she tells me – including tomorrow, which is Bank Holiday Sunday. Wow.

I will need to be up by eight to let this someone in – not so wow. But we agree it will be good for Adrian to get up early for his wash.

Mid-morning I drive him to Westbury to collect Carol from the station. I park outside the main entrance leaving him in the car to wait for her whilst I take Billy for a walk. It's a hot sultry morning – the kind of morning that makes you feel good to be alive. I've noticed a river skirting the road leading to the station many times before, but have never walked there. Why would I? Usually when I'm here it's in order to catch a train. There are little jetties all the way along the towpath and men fishing in individual spots between trees. I drag Billy along, anxious in case he disturbs the fishermen, or indeed the fish.

A few minutes after I return to the car, Carol's train arrives. Adrian is in the front seat and she sits in the back, chatting to Adrian, continually leaning forward to talk to him. She is so bubbly and I realise I am hopeless at this kind of thing. Lizzie too has the gift of the gab. Chattering on, filling the silences, eliminating the embarrassment of the situation she's dealing with. Carol's the same. She's so attentive and full of chit-chat, talking about the most routine things non-stop. Once again I understand why Adrian is so fond of her. We stop for lunch in the now blazing sun at The Bell in Buckland Dinham. Peter joins us and then we lounge in the garden at home for the rest of the afternoon with newspapers and conversation.

Just the most perfect day.

I'm still feeling a bit off colour so, rather than cook for everyone, we decide to have an Indian takeaway. I go to the Indian and when I come out loaded with a box full of everyone's choices, I suddenly imagine myself running off and not turning up with the curry. I even divert to the Cheese and Grain to see who's playing there tonight. It's the Peatbog Faeries, according to a poster on the door. What's to stop me abandoning the curry, going into the Cheese and Grain and spending the evening jigging to the Peatbog Faeries? I try to imagine how everyone at home would react if I simply didn't come back…

…But I do come back…and I feel much better after the meal with so many people, Peter, Adrian, Carol, Jack, Willow and Ed, although Emily and Fran are staying the night at a friend's house so Carol can use their room.

It's a mellow, companionable evening. After a few drinks Peter mentions the fact that he's had to iron his own clothes recently. I look over at Adrian hoping he doesn't interpret this as a dig at him. He seems oblivious, but Peter's remark triggers a light-hearted debate about men, women and housework. Adrian doesn't join in and is quiet for most of the meal which makes me think more and more of Mum at the end of her life, when she stopped joining in. Carol and I keep trying to encourage him to eat but although he'd seemed keen on the curry idea, he leaves most of his on the plate.

Sunday 26th August 2007

I drag myself out of bed at quarter-to-eight to be ready to let little Lizzie in. I finish last night's washing up while I wait for her, but she doesn't turn up till ten-thirty by which time I'd presumed she'd changed her plans.

She comes buzzing in, efficiently hurried, chewing hard on the gum, and signs in over the phone. She has to use our house phone to do this as proof she's here. Then Busy Lizzie gets on and does her stuff.

'I was here at seven-twenty,' she says as she walks past me carrying a bottle of urine. 'But you must all have been asleep.' At twenty past seven on a Bank Holiday Sunday she's surprised no one heard her knocking?

After she's gone Adrian falls asleep. Just before midday while I'm loading the washing machine a loud bang followed by the sound of breaking glass punctuates the Sunday morning silence. I rush outside expecting to see cars flung all over the hedgerows, but the road's as empty as it always is at the weekend. I walk round the house looking for signs of breakage, but all the windows are intact – nothing seems different. I go back inside. The noise came from the study side of the house and has woken Adrian up with a jolt.

'Jesus, what was that?' he says. 'It nearly gave me a heart attack.'

'I don't know what it was. I'll have a look upstairs – it sounded like glass breaking.'

Upstairs everything seems fine. I search the garden once more but can see no sign of anything that might have made such a clatter. It's only when I go back into the study to tell Adrian I have no idea what it could have been that I notice a blank space on the wall where the Picasso had hung. The picture, which is big and must have been too heavy for the hook holding it up, has slid down the wall by the side of his bed. The frame and the picture itself are completely unharmed but the glass has shattered.

Adrian is upset because this is *the* Picasso, the *Buste de Femme au Chapeau*. She's well and truly bust now. His favourite picture, but at least he can see the funny side. 'That picture could have killed me,' he says with a laugh.

Peter and I take Carol and Adrian to the Golf Club (again) for lunch and are offered free meals all round as there is a competition going on. Adrian is stronger than he was just two days ago when he'd had such difficulty getting up the slight incline leading to the clubhouse. Now he manages the slope on Carol's arm.

Carol helps him with everything. She's such a sweetie and so vibrant, still chatting all the time. She's unpacked for him and found homes for all his socks and underwear in the study, which was something I didn't have any energy for on Thursday. At the Golf Club the sun boils above us, Adrian has a sticky flan and cream but when he stands he's like a child who's put on his dad's clothes, and tried to pull them all together with a belt at the waist. At least he eats the flan – good fattening grub. When I leave to take Carol back to Westbury, Adrian and Carol bid each other goodbye, but although they kiss, I notice he doesn't turn around to watch her go...

On the journey to Westbury she chats all the way, unfazed when we are stuck behind a defunct Mr Whippy ice cream van doing twenty miles per hour. We get to Westbury just in time for her to catch the London train – she says she'll visit again in a couple of weeks' time. We all keep making these plans but is she wondering in the back of her mind, as I am, whether this will be?

When I get home Adrian is in the garden doing the crossword. If it wasn't for his voice and his skeletal appearance, this could be just like old times. In the evening we go to McDonald's for a takeaway to please the girls, who are now back home. But Adrian seems grumpy and only nibbles at the edges of his burger. I soon realise he's feeling sick.

Phil Gullifer phones to tell Adrian about a drama on TV tonight starring Martin Clunes, so we plan to watch it. It's called *The Man Who Lost His Head* and I like the sound of it but then realise Peter is settled in the living room watching *Sharpe* which looks like it might go on for some hours. Peter decamps with some reluctance to the less comfortable chairs of the kitchen to watch *Sharpe* in there and Adrian obviously feels bad, and *de trop*.

'I don't want to cause any trouble here,' he says.

'It's okay,' I say. I realise Adrian may not understand the subtle dynamics of a family of six people, not to mention the dynamics of myself and the man I've lived with for thirty years. We have unwritten rules about television viewing. New dramas starring Martin Clunes score higher than old re-runs of *Sharpe*, which have been on a million times, last for ever, and are not exactly what could be called female friendly – except that Sean Bean is attractive-ish – if you're partial to a red-coat with a Leeds accent.

However, as Adrian and I sit together on the sofa watching what turns out to be a love story set in Africa, I wonder whether he'd prefer to be watching *Sharpe* in the kitchen with Peter.

'This is a bit slow,' he says at least twice.

But I enjoy the story. I like the way Martin Clunes and the girl, who is his love interest, both see the blood red sun from opposite sides of the world and then end up together. And the way Martin Clunes' fiancée says of one of their prospective guests (when trying to organise her wedding reception), 'but if I put him on that table, then every man on the table will have a moustache.' There are some nice supernatural touches as well

291

as some good minor characters like the policeman who wants to get Martin Clunes away from the island so he can have the girl for himself.

When Emily rings for me to pick her up, I tell her I'll come when this has finished – even though I'd intended to leave and miss the ending. I stay and watch it to the end. Lovely. Thanks to Phil G for recommending it. Not sure Adrian would agree, though.

Adrian finishes the day with a large brandy. How much has he drunk today? I haven't been counting...

Monday 27th August 2007

Adrian's carer today is Jean from Beckington. She's less buzzy than Lizzie. Less thin. Less highly strung. In less of a rush. After making his bed she sits down for a coffee with us in the kitchen. I decide to ask if the service could include the cleaning of the downstairs toilet which Adrian is using. She says 'yes'. As we sit chatting Adrian says he feels sick and looks very miserable.

'I'm feeling rough,' he says. 'I've taken an anti-nausea pill but I think I might need more than one. I'm going back to bed.'

'That's ok,' I say. 'We can go to Lullington another afternoon.'

We'd planned to go to Lullington, a village on the other side of Orchardleigh, which is full of up-market cottages, most of which have been renovated by rich Londoners. Adrian was going to sit in the car while I took Billy for a walk. Instead he adjourns to the study.

As Jean leaves I manage to have a talk with her in private as I walk with her to her car.

'Surely if you drink alcohol when you're taking morphine you're going to feel sick?' I say. 'Doesn't morphine cause nausea? I think my brother is an alcoholic but I've never really seen him drunk, except maybe once or twice.'

'Alcoholics don't get drunk,' she echoes Matron's words of a couple of weeks ago. I'm still not convinced this is true, though. She says Syd, the nurse from Dorothy House, might be the one to talk to Adrian about the dangers of mixing pills and booze. When Jean has gone I sit in the kitchen waiting to take him out but he's asleep. And the sun has gone in anyway.

At the weekend Carol said Adrian must be very strong to continually fight off the C.diff.

'Maybe he'll live on and on despite the London doctor's gloomy forecast. I'll never forget those words that doctor used,' I said to her. 'Weeks rather than months.'

'But that was *weeks* ago, and will soon be months ago,' Carol pointed out.

So where does that leave us now? Where does that leave Adrian? Surely the medical profession isn't always right?

I pray the London doctor was wrong.

Tonight over a dinner of roast chicken and apple crumble, which Adrian has chosen and eats well, he tells us about the new-build flat Carol has bought in east London.

'One of her friends rather spookily told her she would never live there. This reminded me of something that happened to me in The Gardener's. There was a strange guy in there. No one knew who he was. When he left the pub he singled me out, although there were a lot of us in there. He said "you are the most spiritual and religious person in this room".'

Everyone gasps. 'How did you react?' I ask him.

'At the time I laughed. But his remark stayed with me. Funny that I should think of it now.'

We all agree these kind of random remarks, made by people who may well be slightly unhinged, do have a big impact. I tell the story of a similarly bizarre encounter at a jumble sale in Kensington in the seventies.

'As I rummaged through the jumble I was suddenly aware of a man beside me who was wearing a brown blanket over his head. He was dressed as a woman but had a full beard and was a large, masculine man. He looked so disturbing I was shocked when I caught sight of him. For a moment we locked eyes as he peered at me from beneath the blanket.

'"You're evil," he said to me.'

Everyone shudders and laughs.

I have been thinking about Adrian in relation to spirituality and religion. I can see him being spiritual – even more so lately. Though not particularly religious. There is a difference, I think. And I can feel him moving away from us. Moving away from life. After dinner Adrian and I watch *University Challenge* together, but as the evening progresses everything changes. At about ten o'clock I'm upstairs about to have a shower when I hear him calling me from the downstairs loo. I come down. His pants are in a mess and the room smells horrible. The C.diff has returned – with a vengeance. I clean him up and he shivers with cold since he has hardly any clothes on and then eventually I manage to settle him in bed with instructions to ring my mobile in the night if necessary.

At four-thirty my mobile rings and I stagger out of bed to find him in a mess again. Diarrhoea is everywhere. There's a fat bluebottle buzzing round the kitchen that's probably had a leg in something juicy and I can't seem to swat the blasted thing. After I've cleaned the floor (and Adrian) I go back to bed, tired and hopeless, feeling so sorry for him. He takes a few steps forward and then a hundred faltering steps back. He looks destroyed, but, unbelievably, ready to face the C.diff challenge again.

'We'll have to get onto the docs in the morning and get more antibiotics,' he said when I'd got him back into bed. He's up for the fight again. Where's there's life there's hope, they say. How extraordinarily true.

Tuesday 28th August 2007

Today turns out to be a long, miserable day. It reminds me of long, miserable days spent at home on my own with babies. With each of my kids I seemed to have at least one day like this. The kind of day when the baby's only slept for an hour the night before and cries all day with colic.

Lizzie arrives and cleans up. She tells me I must call the doctor because of the return of the C.diff and because Adrian has conjunctivitis in his right eye. Do I need to be told when to call a doctor? It seems I do, but with so many things wrong it's hard to know when we need help and when we don't. Have things got worse?

Yes, things have definitely got worse.

I phone the surgery to arrange a doctor's visit. Then I wait. She'll come between eleven-thirty and two-thirty apparently. I carry on waiting until two twenty-five when the dog is fastening his own lead around his collar and eating his way through the back door. I ring the surgery again.

'The visit was cancelled because you had a visit from a District Nurse,' the voice on the other end of the phone tells me.

'No, we haven't had a visit from a District Nurse. At least, not today,' I reply. 'And I've been waiting in all day. I need to take my dog out.'

'Well, I can offer you a visit by six-thirty pm. You can take your dog out for half an hour as the doctor won't be coming straight away.'

Oh, cheers! I'll go and share that piece of encouraging news with Billy who is now sulking on the sofa.

When I get back from the dog walk, Olivia from Dorothy

House arrives. We chat together over a cup of tea before she goes into the study to see Adrian. As nice as I'd imagined from Adrian's description, she is personable and quick to laugh. She talks about a group at Dorothy House which Adrian could join. The thought of him joining a group of fellow cancer sufferers seems depressing, yet I wonder what Adrian's take on this would be. I don't see him as a group-joiner. But this is academic since he can't meet with them now he has C.diff again.

She mentions the 'neat bugs' once more. I never did manage to find a website selling them. I tell her I'll go on the internet to look for them later. She also says that when she first met Adrian he made a point of making it clear to her he was a graduate and said everyone at St Vincent's was talking to him as if he was a five-year-old.

'Well, he certainly did seem to have a problem with the staff there, but I think he was a lot younger than most of the other residents. It wasn't really the right place for him.'

'Listen, I think Adrian is a lot younger than most of the *staff* at St Vincent's!' she says. From hearing her talk I can tell Adrian has touched her, and that's why she's come to see him, despite the fact he's no longer on her patch. He likes her too and don't we usually like people who seem to like us? Maybe he makes her laugh.

I relax as we chatter whilst waiting for the doctor. Suddenly I hear myself asking her the sixty-four thousand dollar question.

'How long do you think he's got?'

'Well, he won't be collecting his pension when he's eighty,' she says. 'But I can't make any other predictions.'

Olivia makes me feel as if he could fight this. As if we all can. These nurses who work with cancer patients are truly amazing people. They have something extra tagged on to their souls the rest of us just don't have. A little bit of God. She leaves me and goes into the study.

By the time Olivia comes back into the living room after she's spoken to Adrian her mascara looks smudged. She's been crying. How can people like this who must be dealing with cancer patients all day and every day afford to be so easily moved? Maybe Adrian is a bit special to her. I'd like to believe he is.

She tells me Syd, who is to be her replacement, will come tomorrow.

'Everyone loves Syd,' she tells me. How many times have I heard this recently? Although his name makes him sound like someone who might be selling second-hand Jags I'm feeling I already like him too, despite not having met him.

While Olivia is here I take the opportunity to ask more questions. Like, why is Adrian's voice so hoarse?

'The tumour in the lung sometimes touches the voice box,' she says. 'Which is why his voice is affected.'

I feel shocked by this revelation. The explanation as to why Adrian's voice is so weak seems obviously graphic and at the same time unsettling. I'm about to ask whether this will get worse, when the locum GP arrives.

The GP is small, youngish – probably in her thirties – with a strong Teutonic accent and two Mary Poppins sized bags. Billy barks at the bags for a moment before trying to have sex with the larger one. After looking in on Adrian she joins us in the living room with the news that she will prescribe the usual antibiotics. Olivia and I have just been discussing the antibiotics. It seems as soon as Adrian comes off them the C.diff recurs.

'I've heard drinking alcohol makes patients more vulnerable,' I say.

'Possibly,' Olivia says. The doctor is too busy writing out the prescription to join in this debate. As a mother of four who's had my fair share of drugs prescribed for various throat infections etc., I suggest a liquid form of the antibiotics might help Adrian since the pills he's been taking are so big, he refers to them as horse pills. The GP reluctantly agrees to this and writes out a new script for a liquid antibiotic. Her bedside manner is unengaging and she is completely overshadowed by Olivia's easy, people-friendly demeanour. After handing me the prescription she totters off with her two carpet bags. What on earth does she have in them? Definitely a rubber plant, a tape measure and an expanding hat stand.

When Olivia has also left I head off to Sainsbury's where the pharmacist informs me they don't have the liquid form of antibiotics so I can't have them.

'Okay, I'll have them in pill form, then.'

'I'm not allowed to dispense anything unless it's written on the prescription,' she says. 'And I can't get anyone on the phone now as the surgery is closed.'

She's young. It's gone seven. Once again, *computer says no.*

'But surely the pills contain exactly the same ingredients as the liquid.'

'Yes, but the patient may not be able to swallow anything but liquid.'

'But that's not the case here. It was my suggestion to try a liquid. The GP wanted to prescribe the usual pills, but I suggested liquid to make it easier for my brother, who is the patient, to swallow them. He needs them tonight. Have you heard of the hospital superbug, C.diff? Well, he has C.diff and he needs antibiotics urgently.'

'I'm sorry but I'd be breaking the law if I dispensed something not on a prescription.'

I do my other shopping while she prepares the eye drops for his conjunctivitis. I need lots of antibacterial sprays, disinfectants and air purifiers to make sure the bacteria isn't passed on to any of us. Although my symptoms of the other morning have gone, I want to be careful. But as I look around Sainsbury's for all these things I'm boiling up inside. I cruise around the aisles preparing my speech for the pharmacist when I go back to collect the eye drops.

'Look, these antibiotics are for my brother who has terminal cancer as well as a potentially fatal superbug which he contracted in an NHS hospital. If he doesn't get the drugs tonight, it might mean life or death for him. I understand your rules but you must know the liquid is the same as the pills and ok 'computer says no' but have a heart, use your initiative, use your brain, what is this country coming to? I blame the Labour government...'

When I get back to her counter the same woman pharmacist is standing waiting for me with the eye drops and a packet of antibiotic pills in her hand. She hands them to me before I can speak.

'I'll be taking full responsibility for dispensing something not written on a prescription,' she says. 'And I'll let the surgery know first thing tomorrow morning what I've done.'

I swallow my planned tirade, hold in a sob that's about to bubble up and burst, only managing a barely audible 'thank you' before heaving onwards with my trolley full of disinfectants, sprays and rubber gloves towards the queue at the checkout.

Back home I juggle the tasks of cooking spaghetti bolognaise and cleaning up another commode-full of liquid poo. Stressed, and baulking at the smell (the study is off the kitchen) I phone the out of hours nurse to see if I can get some extra help with the cleaning up in the evenings. However, they don't offer this kind of service.

Before I go to bed I tell Adrian something Olivia said today. Apparently the doctor who visited him at St Vincent's said the lung cancer didn't appear to have spread. I had noticed in Adrian's *Daily Mirror* racing diary against Wednesday 22nd August he'd written *3.15 Dr Higgs* with a tick beside his name and the words *Good Guy*.

Adrian then surprises me by saying, 'Do you think it's all a mistake and it's just benign?'

I'm cut. This is a far cry from his original 'I'm stoic' whatever-will-be-will-be attitude way back in June.

'No,' I answer. Quite harshly, in fact. Too harshly. 'No,' I repeat, softening the word. 'Because we know it's spread to the liver and kidneys.'

'Oh, yes,' he concedes, looking down at his crossword.

In bed Peter is softly snoring beside me. As I drift off to sleep I try to imagine whether there's anything I could say to Adrian to help him if we came to the point where he was actually dying. *Wait for us. I'll see you when I get there. I might not be so far behind. I'll see you on the dark side of the moon?* If I said something like this maybe it would help him feel better, not so alone. And wouldn't it be true in a way? We're all going to die one day. The only difference for Adrian is he's been told it will be sooner rather than later.

Just before midnight, Emily calls me. She's been watching a film in her room and went downstairs for a cup of tea. I go down to find Adrian sitting at the kitchen table with excrement down his new white tennis shoes, the ones he bought with his winnings on the horses when he went AWOL from St George's. It's all down his new dressing gown too. He's obviously been to the toilet but not realised the state he's in. This is tough. I don't want to humiliate him, but I have to point out to him what's happened in order to help him clean up.

'Sorry about this, Ali,' he says as I help him to the bathroom where he nearly passes out with cold as I wash his body...

We have reached an all-time low. The smell is foul. The situation is so humiliating for him and repulsive for me, which is why we need the help of an outsider. Everyone I've spoken to in the caring agencies has told me I'll need all the practical help I can get, thus ensuring my relationship with my brother is not jeopardised. I now see what they mean. We have crossed a new boundary.

Once he's cleaned up I settle Adrian into his bed. I tell him again to ring me on my mobile if he needs me in the night. I keep my phone switched on next to my bed every night now.

Wednesday 29th August 2007

The first thing I do is check my phone. Adrian hasn't rung me during the night, which is encouraging – I hope. But what I don't realise is that this is going to be another one of those really horrible, rock bottom days.

In this morning's post is a letter from a literary agent rejecting an excerpt from my novel which I submitted in January. Why did he have to pick today to send it back?

Then I receive a phone call from Bristol University telling me I'm not accepted onto a course called The Writers' Room which I'd been looking forward to as a lifeline back to civilization in October.

Thirdly, the weather has changed again. It's no longer hot enough to lie or even sit out in the garden.

And number four. Adrian looks like a dying man.

He says he feels awful. I can hear him talking to his friends on his mobile. He's putting Phil G off from visiting and yet he does manage to write a letter to Welsh Phil with a list of things he wants him to bring when he comes to visit.

Apart from taking Billy out for an hour, I wait in all day for the delivery from Medequip who are meant to be bringing some extra bits and pieces to make life easier for Adrian. Eventually they arrive – horrendous looking implements: a raised toilet seat to fix on our downstairs loo, a wheelchair (Adrian doesn't even flinch when this is brought into the house) and an electric reclining chair with a safety cut-out mechanism in case a small child should get trapped underneath. I can see its potential danger when I try it out. A dog could also be squashed if it was in the wrong place at the wrong time. Especially a little white fluffy dog by the name of Billy.

However, the ramp we requested which would enable Adrian to get back into the house unaided, if we were out for example, is not there. And we still have the Any Old Iron bed.

Later, as I struggle through the Disabled Living Allowance form – yes, I still haven't managed to fill this in – the fiction editor from a woman's magazine phones. Hurray – she wants to buy my latest short story, *Daphne Higgenbottom's Holiday*. This piece of good news cancels out the two earlier rejections and makes me feel my writing career is back on track. The magazine have asked for a few words to be changed in the last paragraph so I read the ending to Adrian and we set to work to come up with a better last line. However, I don't think he understands how this works. He asks if I now have to write the story.

'No, I wrote it months ago,' I explain. 'Then I sent it to the editor, and now she wants to buy it.'

Adrian did once edit one of my stories – a comedy about a woman whose husband was addicted to gambling on the horses. He added some good authentic horse racing details.

While I'm trying to get the ending of the *Daphne Higgenbottom* story right Adrian keeps asking me for things like an envelope and stamp for his letter to Welsh Phil. But I'm busy. Can't he see I've got a life too? It must be very frustrating for him not being able to get little things like this for himself, but I'm so elated to have sold a story I just want to get on with the alterations. Eventually he offers a few suggestions for the ending, which I use.

Later in the evening, the poo smell pervades the cooking again. Chilli con carne doesn't lend itself to the concurrent smell of diarrhoea but, although we have been allocated extra cleaning help, no one will come until tomorrow. I'm getting used to the pong, but even tough little Lizzie said the smell made her feel sick.

The whole family gathers for dinner. Jack and Ed are at home and the girls are also in. It could be like a big happy dinner party. But it's not. Adrian doesn't eat anything and goes straight back into the study to lie down. I try to persuade him to have a pro-biotic drink since an article in today's paper suggests they're good for people suffering with C.diff. He says he doesn't like them but tries to force it down.

Half an hour later he comes out of the study from his bed and sits in the adjustable chair which I've positioned in front of the kitchen television at his request. He says he'll have it moved into the living room later. I look at him in the chair. He's like a ninety-year-old, a bag of bones. He hasn't shaved. He watches a bit of the football. John Commerford rings me on the house phone to say he's worried because he's not getting any answers from Adrian to his text messages. John wants to visit this weekend. He sounds so bright and cheerful. Such a contrast to the mood here. He says he's watching the cricket in floodlight at his ex-wife's house. Actually, he always seems to be at his ex-wife's house. He then becomes solemn. I've noticed he does this sometimes and this reminds me he's now a grown man and not the teenage John I knew years ago in West Wickham.

'I do think you're being awfully kind taking Adrian in,' he says. I feel a bit emotional when he says this, but yet again I think, anyone else would surely do exactly what I am doing under the circumstances. And John has a twin sister. I'm convinced he'd do the same for her.

Every time someone tells me how great I'm being, I find it hard to accept the compliment. When Mum was ill, I didn't take her in, though she'd have loved to live here. Dementia presents a different set of emotions and problems, and when it came to the crunch, I let her down. The *old* Mum I would have taken in at the drop of a hat and thoroughly enjoyed her company. But not the Mum at the end of her life who wandered outside on her own looking for her passport in the bushes, or thought we were on a ship sailing to India in the 1930s. I found the change in her difficult to cope with. I could have emptied the study out for my mum and got her a bed, but I didn't – and I clearly remember thinking at the time that if I did bring her home then I'd probably end up being the one losing the plot.

The choice was either her or me, and in the end I chose me.

∗

Thursday 30th August 2007

Busy Lizzie arrives, does her job and leaves before I even wake. When I come downstairs Adrian is in bed looking, and clearly feeling, dreadful. I just don't know what to do to help him, so I empty the commode, which I am getting used to, even though the smell is like nothing I've ever smelled before. A mixture somewhere between sweet and foul. I spray the air, the furniture and any surfaces I can find with my new disinfectant, at the same time pottering around wiping door handles and tables. But all the time I'm worried about Adrian. Eventually I call the doctor again. As Adrian's a 'gold star' patient I don't have to give a reason for requesting a home visit.

I wait and wait. The GP, Dr Hill, arrives in the afternoon, a bespectacled youngish, curly-haired giant with a gentle bedside manner. He looks at Adrian and orders a blood test from the District Nurses – which makes me think – where the hell are the District Nurses anyway?

As we walk from the study through the kitchen and into the living room the doctor asks me who owns this house. 'I do,' I say wondering why he wants to know.

'So where does your brother live?'

'In London. But he's staying with us.'

'So you're looking after him?'

'Yes.'

'You're very kind.'

'Not really…'

'Well, I don't think either of my sisters would take me in and look after me!' The doctor laughs and I seriously doubt his sisters would turn their backs on this man in a million years. Then he crouches at the coffee table in the living room to write something out and I ask him for information on C.diff. How dangerous is it really for us living here with someone who has the infection?

'I've seen a lot of it,' he says. He's reassuringly confident and down to earth. For the first time all day, or in fact for days, I feel protected from everything going on around me. I'm heartily relieved the diminutive locum with the Mary Poppins accessories wasn't on duty today. Dr Hill asks who else is living here.

'Apart from myself and my husband, there's my oldest son, Jack and his girlfriend, Willow. Then there's my other son, Ed and my twin daughters. So all in all seven people when everyone's at home.'

'You've got quite a house full.'

'Yes. I suppose it is. And eight now Adrian is here.'

'Goodness. You have got your hands full. But no – in answer to your question, none of you are in any danger of contracting C.diff. So long as you are all healthy, you're not at risk. It's the elderly and the very young or those already ill who are at risk of catching it.'

So we could have had him here weeks ago. Damn.

'But I've heard it's fatal – or can be. In what way can it be fatal?' I ask.

'Dehydration is always a danger when a patient has persistent diarrhoea,' he says. 'And there's also a likelihood he could have renal failure.'

Up until the 1960s when they discovered the simple cure of drinking salt water, diarrhoea was a killer. Which is why Adrian is prescribed sachets of Dioralyte.

After the doctor has gone I whizz off to Sainsbury's again, this time for creams and extra soft pillows, drinking straws, a lottery ticket and other things for Adrian. Yes, he still wants a lottery ticket for Saturday night. That's my boy.

In the early evening when I get back from Sainsbury's I'm relieved to see Adrian has perked up. Phil G phones him on his mobile but he doesn't want to take the call and doesn't pick up. Afterwards Phil rings me on the house phone and I tell him I think Adrian will be better tomorrow night and perhaps he should ring then. Phil says he'll come down. He's prepared to come any time. Now. Whenever. When we've finished talking I realise, possibly for the first time, what a huge loss this will be for Phil G too if Adrian dies. His friend, buddy, business partner, he's losing so much. As much, if not more, than I am. They see each other, or at least communicate, on a daily basis. They share a love of horse racing, crosswords, pub quizzes, boozy trips on river boats. They've created a business together. I sit in the study with Adrian after talking to Phil and we chat about things. He asks me about the Ian McEwan book, *Saturday*, which is in bookcase. It's about a brain surgeon.

This reminds Adrian of a man he used to see in The Gardener's who was also a surgeon, somewhat of a loner, who Adrian noticed was shaking a great deal as if he had something seriously wrong with him.

'Then, years later when I was at some business course in a pub in Parsons Green, I started thinking about this man for no reason at all. He just popped into my head out of the blue. Later when I left the pub and walked round the corner I came face to face with him. I couldn't believe it. He wasn't shaking any more. I mean, before he looked like he had Parkinson's or something. Very strange.'

This story on reflection raises several questions. One, what had Adrian been *drinking* in the pub at Parsons Green? Two, why would a business course be held in a pub? Three, could he perhaps have seen the man without realising it beforehand and this was what made him come subconsciously into Adrian's mind? And four, if he wasn't displaying the same excessive shaking then maybe this wasn't the same man.

However. Whatever. We talk on about this kind of supernatural intuition and in fact I think I believe in it more than he does. I then tell Adrian about the morning when Mum died. She was in hospital at the time, and I woke at five-thirty, which I later discovered was the time she passed away.

'My whole body was in pain, everything, even my gums were throbbing,' I recall. Adrian's response is to say he too has had problems with his gums... So I guess he's not really on the same wavelength. I've always believed in this kind of transference of feeling, though. I saw a TV programme once about mothers whose children had been in serious accidents. All of them experienced physical and mental sensations at the time their children were injured, even though they'd been nowhere near them and had no idea what was happening to them. I don't believe in ghosts, but I do believe in a kind of transference of pain or strong emotion between people who are very close.

During the night when I'm in bed I hear Adrian mumbling again. I consider going downstairs to see if he's alright but I'm so sleepy and I don't want to wake Peter and everyone else in the house. Exhaustion takes over and I drift off, recalling his mumbling the first night he was here – when I did go down to see if he was alright. On that occasion he seemed to be just talking to himself. But he had been drinking then, and is not drinking now. Anyway I have my phone switched on in case he needs me...

Friday 31st August 2007

I wake at eight-fifty to the sound of drilling. Darren, the shy electrician, is working on the new bathroom lights. When I go downstairs I realise Lizzie is here too, because I can hear her voice in the study.

I open the study doors. Adrian is sitting on the floor with Lizzie crouched beside him. He's slumped against my desk, dressed only in underpants. Being only small, and with the radiator turned up high, the room is swelteringly hot.

'What's happened?' I ask as a string of thoughts speed through my mind.

'It's alright,' Lizzie says. 'I've already rung for help.'

'Oh, my God, what happened? How long have you been there, Adrian?' I recall the mumbling noises I heard in the night.

'I fell over while I was trying to reach the commode and then I couldn't get up. I couldn't reach my phone. That was about four hours ago.'

'Oh no.' I bite my thumbnail. 'Oh, no.' I feel absolutely terrible. Totally responsible. I didn't come down when I heard him mumbling in the night, and obviously Peter and Ed didn't look in on him before they went to work, either. They must have been in a hurry and left without having breakfast. And Jack is staying over at Willow's. But has he really only been there for four hours? Surely it was more than four hours ago when I heard him talking. I can't work this out. I doubt he can help me. However long it's been I can't bear to think of him stranded on the floor like this. There isn't even any carpet – the floor is oak and the rug is in the wash.

But life goes on. Whoever Lizzie called hasn't arrived so I enlist Darren's help to lift Adrian back into the bed. Poor Darren. He can't be more than nineteen. His face reddens. He looks shocked. Shell shocked – but he helps quietly and so obligingly, bringing his own gentle presence into this strange scenario. How bizarre this must seem to him, coming as he has from the outside, normal world into our somewhat abnormal one. Adrian groans with relief as he is reunited with his bed.

Mid-morning a District Nurse, Judith, arrives. I haven't met her before. She's suntanned and more glamorous than the one who came a week ago. Judith tells us she's just back from Greece, but has returned to chaos. I tell her that none of the District Nurses have turned up to help us. Even though the GP ordered a blood test yesterday nothing has been done. Judith seems unimpressed by the way things in her department haven't been happening in her absence.

One of the first things she asks me is whether I've been giving Adrian Imodium Plus, the over-the-counter bog standard cure for holiday diarrhoea. My answer is 'no' and yet a full packet of Imodium Plus resides in my medicine cabinet and has done all summer.

I feel like kicking myself. I could scream. I could have been giving him Imodium. And to make matters worse, I had thought of trying it, but decided it was too ordinary to deal with this seemingly extraordinary illness.

Judith rings Dorothy House to arrange an overnight sitter. She seems angry at the lack of support we've had. Eventually Judith and Lizzie leave and Adrian and I are alone. He is now out of bed and sitting, or rather lolling, in the adjustable chair.

I'd promised myself a visit to Body Basics this morning for a workout, but have to accept I won't make it. I have to help him onto the commode again before he's even had a chance to get himself comfortable in the chair. He is in pain, agony. Desperate.

'I just can't be bothered any more,' he says as I lower him onto the commode.

I try to chivvy him along, the way Lizzie does. Try to imitate the kind of upbeat chattiness she's so good at.

But I'm not Lizzie.

'I'm going to die,' he says.

'No, you're not,' I reply.

He sits on the commode for a few minutes after which I help him back to the adjustable chair and mix up a sachet of Imodium Plus.

'I must have been a very, very bad person,' Adrian says.

I can't think of a fitting answer to this. *Of course you haven't. Don't be so silly.* Every reply sounds trite. He must know he hasn't. He's a good man. A lovely man.

'Shall I put the television on?' is all I can think of as an answer.

'Yes,' he says and I switch the kitchen television on. Fuck. Why does today have to be the tenth anniversary of the death of Princess Diana? All the channels seem to be showing live broadcasts of her memorial service. The kitchen television doesn't have a digi box or any other channels than the main four. On BBC One the commentary is following A-list royals as they climb the steps to the chapel where the service is taking place. I'm half watching. Wills and Harry are there. Some women. Possibly Beatrice and Eugenie looking awkward in peculiar hats shaped like flying saucers which have accidentally landed on and become affixed to their foreheads. In fact, not dissimilar to the hat worn by Picasso's *Femme au Chapeau*.

I don't know what to do, so I spray one of the antibacterial sprays I bought in Sainsbury's around the study and in the general direction of the commode. I know it's mad, but I've got into a habit of doing this when I'm not sure what else to do. I spray around the study door handle and the kitchen table near where Adrian is sitting.

'What are you doing all that cleaning for? Are you afraid? You keep running away,' he says.

I can't tolerate people being rude to me, and yes, to be perfectly honest, I am afraid. Why would I not be? But I still won't accept rudeness. I hold my anger in, sit down near him at the kitchen table, touch his hand.

'Can you move me into the living room onto the leather sofa,' he asks after a few minutes.

As we have a slippery leather sofa (which no one likes sitting on) and a squishy faux suede sofa, which could look as if it might be leather, I ask him which one he means.

'There's only *one* leather sofa,' he snaps.

'Don't be rude to me,' I say clearly and leave the room to get the sofa ready.

When I come back into the kitchen he says, 'I'm sorry. I didn't mean to be rude to you.' I'm holding back on tears, affection, fear and exhaustion.

'That's alright,' I say.

All this against a backdrop of the memorial service for the death of Diana. One of the Dimblebys or some other voice-over drones on. There can't be many people less interested in the memory of Princess Diana, and the charade accompanying her death, than my brother. This is so not his thing – or mine either. Although I admit to enjoying watching all the royals and celebrities arriving. I help him transfer from the chair he's in to the wheelchair, wheel him into the living room and, with Darren's help, lift him onto the leather sofa.

'Can you close the curtains and I want to face away from the television.'

'Shall I turn the television on?'

'Yes, if you want. But I don't want to watch it.'

'Would you like me to sit with you?'

'Yes.'

By now I'm feeling tearful. I put the living room television on, and like Prince Harry and all the gang in the chapel I rein my emotions in. Outside the chapel where the service is taking place a camera scans bystanders (one of whom when interviewed admits to having left home at four in the morning in order to be there) who are sobbing aloud over a woman they didn't even know, most likely never met, probably never even heard speak more than a few sentences, and who died ten years ago. Another lady in the crowd is interviewed. She says she travelled overnight from Manchester to listen to this service from outside the church – a service which isn't even being relayed on monitors. She has two young boys with her. She's dragged her children along to support her, she tells the interviewer. Why would anyone do such a thing?

During all this, I'm here supporting my brother, or trying to.

'Ali,' he whispers. 'I'd like to thank you for everything you've done for me now – in case I pop off.'

'You're not going to pop off!'

'You will carry out my wishes, won't you?'

I know what he means. He wants to be sure I'll organise and carry out the alterations to his will. I try to reassure him I will do everything he's asked, at the same time feeling slightly miffed that he feels the need to double check.

'Everything's in the green and white folder. All the instructions for the music I want played. And I'd like you to thank all my friends as well...' His voice is weak. His eyes unfocused. I can feel him drifting away.

'Don't worry. I'll do all the things you've asked.'

I get up and go into the kitchen to phone Peter at work because I simply don't know what else to do.

'You're doing everything you can,' Peter says. 'And he's not worse, is he? Maybe you should call the doctor again just for reassurance. All you can really do is to make him as comfortable as possible...' As ever, Peter makes a critical situation seem less so. I take a chair from the kitchen and carry it into the living room placing it next to the leather sofa.

I'm sitting next to Adrian. I'm here now, sitting next to him, watching the duvet I've placed over him, moving ever so slightly up, and then ever so slightly down. I'm wondering why exactly he was so insistent about going into the living room. Was it to avoid having to lie again on that horrible iron hospital bed? Is he thinking ahead, making sure he's not in the way when the new bed (which has been promised by the District Nurse following the disastrous night on the floor) arrives? For a change of scene? To be out of the study?

To die?

Maybe he doesn't want to be in the study after last night. If only I'd come down when I heard him mumbling. I continue to keep an eye on the duvet as it rises and falls. Up a few millimetres, then down.

Eventually there's a knock at the front door. The new bed has arrived, delivered by the man from Medequip who has a pony-tail, shaky hands and cigarette breath. The same man who has so helpfully delivered all the accessories relating to the terminally ill. He sets the bed up in the study then demonstrates to me the way the mattress pumps up.

'You must make sure you let all the air out when you've finished with it,' he says. 'It must have all the air let out of it if you don't need it any more.'

'Why would I do that?' I ask.

'If you don't *need* it any more, you have to deflate it.'

I still don't get what he means.

The Medequip man stares at me patiently. Clearly he is loath to state the bleeding obvious, which is that when Adrian dies I won't need the bed any more, and then I must unplug it to let the air out.

Eventually the penny drops.

'Oh, I see.'

The Medequip man shows me how to let the air out.

In the evening a nurse arrives to settle Adrian into the new bed. I go out to collect the girls from Rosie's house to deliver them to a party in Mells. I give a couple of boys a lift as well. They are young (naturally), just a bit older than Emily and Fran, but the type of boys who are full of themselves, too confident – probably the best looking in their year at school. The types all the girls go for. They unsettle me in two ways. They make me feel old and grumpy. And I notice Fran is being particularly quiet. Not her usual self. I can imagine why. I would have been the same at her age.

As I drop them off at the party I feel the pull of the kids' excitement. Friday night at a friend's party – and a sleepover. I, in contrast, am down, trapped. Imprisoned. Detached from the outside world. I decide to drive around for a bit, go for petrol, get Adrian a paper and feel much better by the time I get home.

Adrian's sitting up in bed and looking a lot brighter. The diarrhoea seems to have stopped since he took the Imodium. *Why the hell didn't I give it to him before?* Could I have saved all this suffering?

After we've eaten I begin to clear up so the kitchen is clean and tidy for the nurse who, following yesterday's events, is booked to sit with Adrian throughout tonight. I'm so relieved about this. He will be safe with her keeping an eye on him from the kitchen. Meanwhile, I stay in the study with Adrian chatting while we wait for her, but by a quarter to eleven no one has turned up, or even phoned for directions. I ring Lifeline – which is where Lizzie comes from – Dorothy House and Out of Hours. I'm eventually told that no one is booked to come here for the night.

Great.

A very nice doctor then rings me, but I say we will be okay. If I hear any noises tonight I will certainly rush downstairs.

I sit on the lid of the commode next to Adrian's new bed for a bit, making a conscious decision to stay with him for a chat instead of rushing off all the time to do things. Adrian looks ugly. One eye is closed and stuck together, even though I've just bathed it and put the antibiotic eye drops in. He asks for the walking stick and the commode to be moved so he can reach them both in the night.

'But I'm not going to bed yet,' I say. 'I'll come in to see you and make sure you're okay before I go to bed.'

'Well, I'm not to know that,' he says bad-temperedly. Are Adrian and I going to manage to stay friends, after all these years? As adults, we have never fallen out. We've always been friends. We've always got on. For fifty-five years we've been friends.

I sit down on the commode lid again, not to do anything, or spray anything, or ask anything, but just to be there – and to be quiet. With the use of his one good eye, he's doing the crossword and asks for a book to lean on. As I reach for a book from the bookcase I notice the notes Lizzie has left in a folder. I pick up the folder and open it. There's not much in there but one entry says 'family v. supportive'.

'Do you know, when I was lying on the floor last night I kept trying to remember Sharpe's first name,' Adrian says, looking up from his newspaper. 'I kept trying to remember what it was to try to make the time go. I went through lists and lists of men's names in my head. Names beginning with A then B and so on…'

I smile, but somehow I don't get round to asking him whether he did remember it in the end.

I settle him, with the walking stick on the bed and the commode nearby.

'Phone me or bang on the ceiling with your stick if you need me in the night,' I tell him. 'I hope you have a good night.'

'I find it hard to get to sleep,' he says.

I try to reassure him. 'You might find it easier in this bed. It's really comfortable, isn't it?' I've tried it out and it is majorly squishy – it literally swallows you up. This is the bed Adrian should have had from day one.

'Yeah, thanks, Ali,' he says.

Once I'm upstairs I hear him mumbling again, talking to himself perhaps, or maybe on the phone to someone. I'm so tired I try phoning him, rather than going downstairs.

'Hello, Ali,' he says. My name's come up on his phone.

'Are you alright, Adrian? Only I thought I could hear you talking.'

'No, I'm alright. I was just clearing my throat,' he says.

'Okay. Goodnight.'

'Byeee!' he says in his high-pitched, happy voice.

Saturday 1st September 2007

I come down at seven-thirty. A new nurse arrives having driven around for a while, unable to find the house. Joanna is quieter than the other nurses, but gets on with the job of washing Adrian. She sits him up and I can hear them talking.

'I had a good night's sleep,' he tells her. 'Especially after the night before when I spent hours stuck on the floor.'

'Oh, yes. I heard about what happened,' Joanna says.

I come into the study after she's finished. 'Did you go to the loo in the night?' I ask him.

'No!' He snaps the word and I feel as if I shouldn't have asked. It's such a personal question and obviously one I would never have dreamed of asking him before all this happened. Yet at the same time it's such an important part of what's been going on, I feel it's not an entirely unreasonable thing to ask.

'I feel really good after having a wash,' he says. I go back into the kitchen to make up his medication, worrying in case we don't have enough morphine. I'll need to get some more today. Why do I always leave things until the last minute? It's Saturday and I'm not sure we've got enough to last till Monday. I give him a cup of tea, a straw to drink it with, a pro-biotic drink, and a sachet of Dioralyte diluted in water.

'Did you sleep alright?' I ask him.

'Like a log,' he says. The thought passes through my writerly mind that this is a cliché and I almost point this out. However, although this is the sort of thing Peter might laugh at if I said it to him, Adrian might interpret it as criticism. So I bite my tongue and go back into the kitchen to get my own breakfast, leaving Joanna to clean the commode. I put my tea and bowl of cereal on the table and start opening today's post. Most of it is for Adrian.

I'm about to take a mouthful of the cereal when I hesitate. My spoon is in my hand but hasn't yet reached my mouth. In the study I hear Adrian's breathing turn into gasps. About three or four gasps, as if he's short of breath. Joanna is saying his name. There's an urgency in her voice as she repeats his name over and over.

'Adrian? Adrian!' She's still quiet but her voice sounds insistent, cross even.

A few moments pass and as I'm about to get up Joanna comes out of the study. She's standing in the kitchen facing me.

'I think he's gone,' she says.

I put the spoon down, hold my face in my hands. I'm already crying as I stand, leaving my uneaten breakfast and go into the study. Adrian has his head back on the mound of pillows I got from Sainsbury's, with his infected eye still stuck together and the other one wide open, looking smaller and greyer than before. I go back into the kitchen. I'm shaking. Joanna embraces me and I think she's crying too. A stranger who blipped into Adrian's world in the last scene of the final act. A bit player with one line. The last line.

I don't know what to do so I go back into the study, and come out again. By now Peter is downstairs and is filling the kettle.

'He's died,' is all I manage.

'Oh no,' Peter says turning the tap off. He goes into the study and comes back out again. 'No,' he says. 'He's alright. He's just taken a breath.' Peter laughs. 'He can't have *died* – I just saw him take a breath.'

I feel silly now. My tears seem absurd. This is a very embarrassing mistake.

'Oh,' I say and go back into the study.

He is dead, though. The gasping after death is normal, Joanna says.

My friend, my companion, my brother is dead. Admittedly, not beautiful any more, but a man who loved the beautiful things of this world. Things like churches, cathedrals, the pyramids, the sight of horses galloping on a racecourse, a Wimbledon tennis court. The isles of Greece. Women. Music. Films.

A man who was fascinated by history and spent his lunchtimes familiarising himself with each of the Ancient Egyptian rooms in the British Museum. A man of contradictions who embraced smoking at the age of ten, carried an umbrella in the spring and wore a checked woollen scarf in the winter. A man who found a bunch of stones in a hospital forecourt and delighted in what they represented. A man who'd travelled halfway round the world and back. On his own. A single man.

He'd never been to Newcastle he said the other night apropos of nothing in particular. Even a few weeks ago he still wanted to see more things, do more things, visit more places, read more books. Place more bets. Drink more wine.

I go into the study again. He's wearing his Wimbledon T-shirt. Yesterday's *Daily Mirror* is by his bed, open on the crossword page. Some of the squares are filled in with scruffy lettering. *The Innocent Traitor*, bookmarked a quarter of the way in, and his 2007 racing diary are on the table along with three of the tablets he should have taken last night, his mobile, and a dose of Dioralyte. A lottery ticket for tonight is tucked underneath his glasses. His walking stick leans against the commode and his Panama hat is perched on top of the bookcase. I lean over him, hold his still warm body, put my arms around him and lay my head on his chest.

'I loved you so much,' I tell him at last.

NEWS OF ADRIAN'S DEATH

WRITTEN BY MARTIN PHILIPS – JUNE 2014

I was in France when I got Ali's message to say Adrian had died. So he had lived up to his own prediction. It had been a few years earlier, just after his heart bypass, that he first told me he was sure he wouldn't see 60.

I suppose I didn't believe him. Sitting in his local pub, he had been on good form, looking fit and joking about his mortality. 'I've been on these' (he waved his cigarette) 'since I was 10. I've had a bloody good run.' Said with that exaggerated, sing-song intonation which was his hallmark. 'I said to the medics when they gave me [heavy emphasis] *the plan* for recovery – I don't see my two pints of Young's bitter on the daily dose.' Now I wouldn't hear my oldest friend's distinctive voice again: just its echo in my mind when I thought of him. I did that now, in a series of disparate cameos.

The two of us posing for that photo on the scrubby campsite at San Eufemia in Italy's deep south, with Mac and Richard: frozen in time, like the cover shot for an album that never existed. The all-night party in Golders Green where, on an upstairs landing, a technically inadequate would-be musician murdered *Interstellar Overdrive* on a Spanish acoustic guitar: Adrian's wry one-line put down, 'which planet do *you* come from?' While still at primary school, any number of games of football in the rec, coats for goalposts, where we imagined we were players from the Spurs double-winning team. Painting the walls – and ceiling – of his bedsit in Leamington purple, using gloss paint by mistake, on the day he bought *The Low Spark of High Heeled Boys*. Adrian and Lindsay comparing their vitamin supplement regime while each puffing on a cigarette: a collaborative damage limitation seminar. And the night he told me he expected to die young.

The final notice of his death was the full stop at the end of the last paragraph of the narrative he'd predicted. I sat quietly and listened to the echo accompanying memories of our collective back pages. I was to realise later that it was only a partial ending. In the years since, I often glance back at that book. The one where Adrian is forever young.

WRITTEN BY ROBIN INGS – JULY 2014

Adrian was at our 50th reunion at Martin's house in Brittany in the summer of 2006. I knew he'd had a serious heart by-pass operation. 'Make mine a triple' is all he had said about it. He was a very active person, always on the move, but now moved slightly more cautiously. He had not lost any of his sharp observation and wit. We said good-bye at Stansted Airport and went our separate ways.

In the summer of 2007 John called and said he had seen Adrian who was not well, but I did not realise how seriously ill he was. Later that summer Alison mailed to say that Adrian had died.

Adrian, John, Martin myself and other Wickham Common Primary School pupils survived the teaching and discipline provided by the likes of Mrs Osbourne, Mr Woolard and Mr Nielson. We played after-school football, cricket and tennis on Coney Hall Rec, sometimes coached by Adrian's dad. We competed in mad speed biking time trials down Nash Lane on sunny holiday days. Spent hot summer days at the Bromley Lido followed by tennis at the Pickhurst Club in the evenings. This is where Adrian taught us all how to play snooker and billiards, which, of course, he played at school. He entertained us with stories of nut cutlets (St Christopher's School was vegetarian), Sunday escapades to a Wimpy Bar (it was the mid-sixties) in Letchworth and other events that were way beyond our experiences in West Wickham.

Why Adrian, at the age of 12, suddenly left Bromley Grammar School for St Christopher's we never knew. Adrian's father had tried to persuade Martin, John and I not to go to Beckenham Grammar. He came to talk to my parents one evening but we were determined even though, as Adrian's dad pointed out, they did not play football but played rugby at our preferred secondary school. We three went to a different school; maybe Adrian should have come with us. Adrian's father often gave us lifts, played sports with us, indulged in late night card games or charades. He was usually hilarious but occasionally rather scary and I never knew quite how to read him.

Adrian played football like his hero Stan Bowles. Stan was one of the game's greatest mavericks. He played with delicate skills rather than strength in a style not favoured by our primary school football coach, Mr Cole. He regarded this as too much 'fancy Italian' football. I remember at the age of 11 we went for a trial for the Borough of Bromley Primary Schools XI. I played as a tough stopper at center-half with little skill and was chosen to represent the borough and Adrian with all his silky skills on the wing was not. I knew that really he should have been selected instead of me but his style did not quite conform sufficiently to expectations. Adrian would appreciate what Stan Bowles said when asked if he had spent all of his money on gambling, booze and birds. Stan responded: 'Well, at least I didn't waste it!'

School holidays in our teens were not complete without Adrian's return from St Christopher's: with new music, new styles, more stories … He was confident and funny. One summer in Crystal Palace Park in the mid-sixties he shouted at Dick Footner, who was dressed in felt jacket and Bob Dylan cap: 'Hey, Donovan. Sing us a song.' We were chased out of the park by these older boys in stitches of laughter. Adrian was probably, as usual, similarly fashionably dressed but he got his quip in first!

In our late teens and into our twenties we were typical of the kids and young adults from middle-class suburban backgrounds, *born to be mild* and not caring much for what we thought was expected of us. We moved in a pack, listened to lots of music, went to the free concerts, drank barley wine and bitter in Bromley and Beckenham pubs, rolled joints on the album sleeves of Ten Years After, Quicksilver Messenger Service, Traffic, or other of Adrian's favourite bands. Until we all found ourselves gradually involved in our own separated lives in separated places.

These things and many others are what I thought about when I heard Adrian had died. These are real times and places that still exist somewhere in the past.

WRITTEN BY SANDRA INGS – JULY 2014

Adrian was always very special; he was like a breath of fresh air in an ordinary day. Exciting, interesting and motivated, he was a dynamic part before he fell down.

WRITTEN BY PHIL DAVIES – SEPTEMBER 2014

On the morning that I received the sad phone call advising me of Adrian's death my immediate reaction was one of shock and also a curious feeling of surprise that it had actually happened as expected after all. It was as if I had held on to a forlorn thought that Adrian would somehow defy medical opinion and still come through his illness. This feeling lasted a very short time but it did take me back to when, a few weeks earlier, Adrian was actually discussing his very poor medical prognosis with me. I had suggested by way of comfort that the 'doctors might be wrong'.

But Adrian dismissed this as 'ridiculous' and insisted matters had to be faced head on. This stoic and matter of fact attitude seemed to persist with Adrian, certainly in my presence, to the very end. He never seemed to openly give in to any panic or despair that he might have felt. This attitude greatly impressed me because I remembered wondering how I would have behaved under the same circumstances. However, despite Adrian's fortitude and acceptance of things I did, when he died, feel an irrational resentment towards the doctors for being right all the time in their prognosis.

Adrian's death was traumatic and untimely and greatly saddened all his family and friends. For my part, not only did I lose a very good friend, but someone whose company I enjoyed very often. For me he was also an excellent drinking pal. He had a wide range of conversation and an excellent general knowledge of many things with, I may add, some strong opinions to match. It was always a great pleasure putting the world to rights with him over a pint or two. I missed his company very much and still do.

For a while after his death I used to often think of Adrian in terms of the sadness of his passing. Nowadays, with the passage of time, I never do. After all, in life, he was not at all a sad man. I remember him now with pleasure as a good companion and friend. He was well travelled and had a full and interesting, if too short a life. He is also being missed by a loving family and many friends.

WRITTEN BY MAC – SEPTEMBER 2014

Adrian was best man at my wedding, the obvious choice, since we'd spent a lot of time together and shared flats in Muswell Hill and Brighton.

Hearing the news of his death was clearly very sad but it also brought back memories of all the good, fun times we had as friends, the things we did. Pink Floyd's Dark Side of the Moon in quadrophonic sound at Earls Court, David Bowie's last gig at Hammersmith as Ziggy, the trip around the Tate Gallery and its vibrant Rothko, the great escape from that Italian campsite, the endless games of darts, trying to do the Guardian cryptic crossword sipping a beer … the list could go on and on.

How different and boring those earlier years would have been without that friendship with Adrian!

Having escaped London for Bristol we didn't meet up as often as we should have done, but when we did the friendship was still there, his intelligence and humour still fully operational. Of course we miss the guy but at least we still have the memories of all those good times.

WRITTEN BY CAROL TIGRINE – OCTOBER 2014

It was so very sad and final when Jack's partner Willow called to say Adrian had passed away. It was a moment that I had been unable to contemplate happening, even though subconsciously I knew it was coming but I just kept pushing the thought out of my head. When I got the call I was dreading, it was in quite strange circumstances. That weekend I was in Cheltenham visiting my mum and in an upmarket clothes shop, empty except for two middle-aged women running the shop. It was hard not to eavesdrop and their conversation was intriguing. One said: 'Oh, I'd definitely have to leave him if he asked me to do that, I can't imagine anything worse!' and the other woman was agreeing with her. It later became clear the discussion was about the prospect of having to cut someone else's toenails. That immediately took me back to the previous weekend which I'd spent with Adrian at Ali's house when he'd moved in with the family. We'd had a great weekend as he was much happier and feeling stronger than in the previous few weeks. He even insisted on us going to the supermarket to get some shopping for Ali, saying: 'She's been so good to me, I'd like to get her a few things to show her my appreciation.' Before I left him for what turned out to be the final time, I'd given him a foot massage, and then cut his toenails, which seemed like the right thing to do as they needed doing and he was in no fit state to do it himself. And while this memory of Adrian was in my head and the women were still wittering on about toenails, the phone rang and I heard the sad news.

I couldn't describe Adrian better than Ali has already done. He really was a kind and gentle man, charming, funny, clever, an individual, a one-off (and generous). We shared a love of Greece, and holidays are when I seem to miss him the most. I've lots of happy memories of time spent with him abroad as he was a great travelling companion. My favourite memory is when we chanced upon a tiny restaurant on a Greek island with such an eccentric owner that he even had his own write-up in The Guardian, which was pinned on the wall. He never spoke and there were no menus. He just led us to the kitchen and pointed at various dishes in the oven. Then a few incidents started us off giggling, and a chain of events during the evening culminated in our uncontrollable hysterical laughter, which we unsuccessfully tried to stifle. I can still see Adrian sitting opposite me, crying with laughter, shoulders bobbing up and down, almost stuffing a serviette in his mouth to try and stop. We'd both totally lost control. Adrian later said that he couldn't remember having laughed so much and for so long in at least 30 years. That still makes me smile and it's how I like to remember him.

I miss being able to turn to Adrian for advice, and I recently realised that although I'd known my father for 30 years, I'd known Adrian a few years more, so he has been such a significant male presence in my life. I loved him and I'll always miss him as will anyone who knew him well. But there's comfort in knowing he had a great life – he did exactly what he wanted and enjoyed it to the full. Not many folk have the courage to do just that.

Acknowledgements

My thanks go to Crysse Morrison, Frances Liardet and Rosie Jackson – my Friday morning writing buddies. Also thanks to the Marston Mill Bootcampers of 2013 for their help and input. And to Carol Tigrine who edited with her heart and soul.

A lison Clink was born in South London. She went to Bullers Wood School in Chislehurst and read English and European Literature at Essex University. She has a master's degree in Creative Writing from Bath Spa University. More than fifty of her short stories have been published both in the UK and abroad. Her stories have also won prizes and been broadcast on Radio 4. She's had articles published in *The Sunday Telegraph*'s Stella Magazine and the Family section of the *Guardian*. In 2003 she founded the Frome Festival Short Story Competition. Her short plays have been performed in Frome and Bristol.

Alison has been a creative writing tutor for over ten years and currently runs a weekly writing group at Babington House, near Frome.

She has four grown-up children and lives in Somerset with her husband.

www.alisonclink.co.uk